THE R  JR

D1354407

The Rise of New Labour

Party Policies and Voter Choices

Anthony F. Heath
Roger M. Jowell
John K. Curtice

OXFORD
UNIVERSITY PRESS

OXFORD
UNIVERSITY PRESS

Great Clarendon Street, Oxford OX2 6DP

Oxford University Press is a department of the University of Oxford.
It furthers the University's objective of excellence in research, scholarship,
and education by publishing worldwide in

Oxford New York

Auckland Bangkok Buenos Aires Cape Town Chennai
Dar es Salaam Delhi Hong Kong Istanbul Karachi Kolkata
Kuala Lumpur Madrid Melbourne Mexico City Mumbai Nairobi
São Paulo Shanghai Taipei Tokyo Toronto

Oxford is a registered trade mark of Oxford University Press
in the UK and in certain other countries

Published in the United States
by Oxford University Press Inc., New York

British Library Cataloguing in Publication Data

Data available

Library of Congress Cataloging in Publication Data
Heath, A.F. (Anthony Francis)
The rise of New Labour: party policies and voter choices/Anthony F. Heath, Roger M.
Jowell, John K. Curtice.
p. cm.
Includes bibliographical references and index.
1. Labour Party (Great Britain) 2. Elections—Great Britain 3. Great Britain—Politics
and government—1979-1997. 4. Great Britain—Politics and government—1997- I. Jowell,
Roger. II. Curtice, John. III. Title.
JN1129.L32 H374 2001 324.24107—dc21 2001016294
ISBN 0-19-924510-X
ISBN 0-19-924511-8 (pbk)

3 5 7 9 10 8 6 4

Typeset in Times by
Cambrian Typesetters, Frimley, Surrey
Printed in Great Britain
on acid-free paper by
Biddles Ltd, Guildford and King's Lynn

ACKNOWLEDGEMENTS

This book is based on the British Election Surveys (BES) of 1979, 1983, 1987, 1992, and 1997 and the British Election Panel Study 1992–7. We are greatly indebted to the funders of these studies, the investigators, and above all to the respondents themselves.

These BESs have been funded by the Economic and Social Research Council (ESRC), the Sainsbury Family Charitable Trusts, Jesus College, Oxford, and Pergamon Press. The investigators have included Ivor Crewe, Bo Sarlvik, David Robertson, and Pippa Norris in addition to ourselves. We are also grateful to the Data Archive at the University of Essex for providing the data, to Jane Roberts of the Social Studies Computer Research Support Unit at the University of Oxford, and to Ann Mair of the Social Statistics Laboratory, University of Strathclyde.

The work of analysing the data and producing the book has been greatly helped by our colleagues in the Centre for Research into Elections and Social Trends (CREST). CREST is an ESRC-funded research centre linking the National Centre for Social Research, London (formerly SCPR), and the Department of Sociology at the University of Oxford. We are most grateful to our colleagues in CREST: Bob Andersen, Jill Andersen, Catherine Bromley, Geoff Evans, Stephen Fisher, Lindsey Jarvis, Alison Park, Mandy Roberts, and Katarina Thomson.

This is the fourth book that we have produced based on the BES. Like its predecessors, it has taken its toll and no one is more aware of this than our families. Our greatest debt is to Jane Pearce for her continual help and encouragement to complete this task despite all the other hindrances set in our path.

A.F.H.
R.M.J.
J.K.C.

CONTENTS

LIST OF FIGURES

LIST OF TABLES

LIST OF ABBREVIATIONS

BEPS	British Election Panel Study
BES	British Election Survey
BP	British Petroleum
BSA	British Social Attitudes
BSE	bovine spongiform encephalopathy
CND	Campaign for Nuclear Disarmament
CREST	Centre for Research into Elections and Social Trends
EC	European Community
EEC	European Economic Community
EMU	European monetary union
ERM	exchange rate mechanism
EU	European Union
GDP	gross domestic product
NHS	National Health Service
OMOV	one member one vote
RPI	retail price index
SDP	Social Democratic Party
SES	Scottish Election Survey
VAT	value added tax
WES	Welsh Election Survey
WRS	Welsh Referendum Study

1

Introduction

Our central concern in this book is to explore electoral behaviour in Britain in the years from 1979 to 1997. This period covers the eighteen years of Conservative government that began with Margaret Thatcher's first victory over Labour in 1979 and ended in 1997 with New Labour's landslide victory over John Major's Conservatives. This was the longest period of government by a single party in the history of British democracy. It saw major changes in the shape and institutions of British society. And while in a sense it ended with the resounding defeat of the Conservative Party in 1997, it could also be said that Conservative ascendancy over British politics continued since the victorious Labour Party accepted, at least on the economic front, many of the key principles and policies that Margaret Thatcher had espoused.

The political story of the period since 1979 is one of remarkable experiment. The period began with Margaret Thatcher's experiment in radical free market economic and social policy. She felt that the previous twenty years had been ones of muddle and failure that had seen Britain in continuous decline, under both Conservative and Labour governments alike. She blamed this decline on creeping socialism; on excessive intervention by government in the workings of the economy and the labour market; on punitive taxation; on the excessive power of trade unions and 'corporatist' attempts to involve them in planning. She therefore turned her back on the post-war consensus that had used Keynesian economics to try to maintain full employment. In place of collective provision she advocated individual responsibility and individual incentives. In place of Keynesianism she applied monetarist theory in order to attack the 'evil of inflation'. Under her leadership huge swathes of public sector industry were denationalized and public housing was sold off. The miners were defeated and trade union powers eroded. Income tax rates were cut sharply in order to increase incentives. She also tried to replace the system of domestic property rates with the regressive poll tax, but this was not quite so successful. It was hugely unpopular and played a crucial role in her downfall. Margaret Thatcher was voted out of office in 1990 not by the electorate but by her own Conservative MPs who were worried about the likely electoral repercussions of the poll tax (as well as by her abrasive style of leadership and her growing Euroscepticism).

The early 1980s also saw two other almost equally remarkable political experiments. Firstly, on the Labour side, there were many who shared Margaret Thatcher's low opinion of the work of previous Labour governments but who drew the opposite conclusions. The problem with Wilson's and Callaghan's Labour administrations, they believed, was not that they had been too socialist but that they had not been socialist enough. This led to a radical experiment, as bold in its way as Margaret Thatcher's, to persuade the electorate to vote for thoroughgoing socialist economic policies with major programmes of nationalization, government spending, and government intervention in the labour market. They also made commitments to withdraw from Europe and to undertake unilateral nuclear disarmament. The veteran pacifist Michael Foot became leader of the party in place of the moderate Jim Callaghan.

Yet another experiment, not unrelated to Labour's, was the formation of the Social Democratic Party (SDP) by disgruntled Labour MPs in 1981 who wished to resist Labour's move to the left and to 'break the mould' of party politics by establishing a new moderate left-of-centre party. The new party was committed to Europe, to retaining Britain's nuclear weapons, and to moderate economic policies, accepting the role of the free market but adopting a more compassionate approach than Margaret Thatcher's. The SDP fought the 1983 and 1987 general elections in alliance with the long-established Liberal Party.

The SDP experiment was in many respects a precursor of the New Labour experiment. When he became leader of the Labour Party in 1994, Tony Blair decided to make a decisive break from Old Labour's 'statist socialism' and to move back towards the centre of the political spectrum and to the territory that had been occupied by the SDP. He embraced many of the Thatcherite principles that seemed to have been so successful during her eleven years of government but which had been such anathema to socialists at the time. He accepted her commitment to the free market; he accepted the majority of her trade union reforms; he accepted her commitment to low inflation and promised to abide by the Conservatives' taxation and spending plans for the first two years of office.

To symbolize the break from the past Labour was rebranded as 'New Labour' and the term 'socialism' was banished from the leadership's vocabulary. Most strikingly, Tony Blair persuaded the party to repeal Clause IV of its constitution, which had committed the party to the common ownership of the means of production, distribution, and exchange. This clause had become a totem on the left of the party ever since the unsuccessful attempt of a previous Labour modernizer, Hugh Gaitskell, to repeal the clause in 1959 (when the party was at a rather similar point, having just lost its third successive general election). Tony Blair's successful replacement of Clause IV could be seen in some ways as a final victory for Margaret Thatcher over the forces of socialism.

However, while New Labour did make a radical break with the past on the classic socialist issues of nationalization, spending, and government intervention, Tony Blair did not become quite so Thatcherite on the non-economic issues. In particular he retained previous Labour commitments to devolution for Scotland and Wales. These constitutional reforms were strongly opposed by the Conservatives under Margaret Thatcher and her successor, John Major, who both followed a vigorous policy of British nationalism, seeking to maintain the Union internally and vigorously pursuing British national interests externally, especially in the context of Europe. In these respects New Labour was much more similar to the SDP and the Liberal Party than it was to the Conservative Party.

The final experiment was the Referendum Party, which was established by Sir James Goldsmith in 1995 and which was in a sense the heir to the nationalist element of Thacherism. The Referendum Party was a single-issue party devoted to the preservation of British sovereignty in Europe. The aim of the party was to force a referendum on whether or not 'the United Kingdom should be part of a Federal Europe'. It was avowedly Eurosceptic and forced the other parties to propose their own referendums on whether the UK should join the single European currency (a more limited question than the one Sir James Goldsmith wished to put before the electorate).

The aggregate electoral impact of these experiments is well known. Margaret Thatcher's experiment was astonishingly successful, winning handsome majorities in the House of Commons, although she never secured the support of a majority of voters. Her largest share of the vote came in 1979 and thereafter there was gradual decline at the ballot box. She was greatly helped in 1979 by failures in office of the incumbent Labour government (led by Jim Callaghan) and in particular by the 'winter of discontent' when a succession of damaging public sector strikes raised questions about Labour's capacity to govern (and more generally about Britain's governability). Her large majorities in the House of Commons in 1983 and 1987 were not accompanied by landslides at the ballot box. In fact, only Bonar Law in 1922 and Harold Wilson in 1974 have been asked to form majority governments with smaller shares of the vote. It is questionable how far Margaret Thatcher ever had a popular mandate for her transformation of British society.

The Labour experiment in radical socialism was a disastrous failure at the ballot box in 1983 and was even less popular than Jim Callaghan's failing government had been in 1979. Between 1979 and 1983 the Labour Party lost a quarter of its vote and achieved fewer votes per candidate than it had done since the party was formed in 1900. It was their worst result since the establishment of the modern party system and the extension of the franchise to (almost) all adults in 1918. The radical socialists had been given their chance to persuade the electorate to vote for socialism. They were not to be given another chance. Neil Kinnock replaced Michael Foot as leader of the opposition and began the gradual process of modernization that was eventually to culminate in New Labour.

The experiment of the SDP promised much, their combined share of the vote with the Liberals challenging Labour for second place in 1983. That year was the high point for the SDP–Liberal Alliance but as Labour gradually recovered under Neil Kinnock's leadership, the Alliance's share of the vote began to fall. After the 1987 general election, amid some rancour, the majority of the party merged with the Liberals to form what eventually became known as the Liberal Democratic Party. Ultimately, then, the SDP's experiment failed, and it vanished as an independent force. However, it may well have been successful indirectly in that it was an important stimulus behind the New Labour experiment of 1994–7.

The experiment of the Referendum Party was hardly a great success either at the ballot box. It secured only 3 per cent of the vote in the constituencies where it stood, but it could alternatively be described as the strongest ever performance by a British

Table 1.1. Shares of the vote in Great Britain 1979–97 (%)

Year	Conservative	Labour	Liberal	Other
1979	44.9	37.8	14.1	3.2
1983	43.5	28.3	26.0	2.2
1987	43.3	31.5	23.1	2.1
1992	42.8	35.2	18.3	3.8
1997	31.4	44.4	17.2	6.9

Note: Liberal includes SDP in 1983 and 1987 and represents the Liberal Democrats in 1992 and 1997.

Sources: Heath *et al.* (1991); Wood and Wood (1992); Austin (1997).

minor party. Like the SDP, its success may have been more indirect through its influence on Conservative Party policies on Europe.

And the New Labour experiment in 1997 was the most successful experiment of all, at least judged by its seats in the House of Commons, where it secured a landslide majority of 179, the biggest in the post-war period. Its appeal at the ballot box was not quite so impressive, however. As with Margaret Thatcher's landslide in 1983, the party's share of the vote was not unusually high in 1997. The 44.4 per cent of the vote that New Labour won in 1997 was rather similar to the share that Old Labour had won in 1964 under Harold Wilson and distinctly lower than the shares that losing Labour parties had obtained in the 1950s.

However, just as Margaret Thatcher had been helped in 1979 by Labour's failures in office, so in 1997 New Labour was greatly helped by the Conservatives' failure to govern. John Major's Conservatives had unexpectedly won the 1992 general election, possibly as a result of some astute pre-election tax cuts. But the tax cutting had to be reversed, and even more crucially in the autumn of 1992 sterling was driven ignominiously out of the European exchange rate mechanism. The Conservative government immediately lost, and never recovered, its reputation for sound economic management. It is hard to resist the conclusion that Labour would almost certainly have won anyway even without New Labour. Table 1.1 reports the parties' share of the vote over this period.

The common theme behind these different experiments is their focus on policies: free market policies from Margaret Thatcher and Tony Blair, socialist ones from Michael Foot's Labour Party, Europhile ones from the SDP, and Eurosceptic ones from the Referendum Party. All the parties believed that electoral success depended on the popularity of one's policies and that conversely electoral failure discredited the policies that had been espoused. In a sense this is the normative theory underpinning representative democracy: the election implements the popular will and gives the governing party a mandate to pursue the policies espoused in its manifesto. It is also a fashionable empirical theory of how voters decide. The 'rational choice' theory of electoral behaviour holds that voters are analogous to consumers in the marketplace while parties play roles analogous to firms. The consumer/voter chooses the products/policies that he or she likes best; the firm/party that provides the most attractive products/policies thus increases its market share at the expense of its rivals. The free market in votes thus ensures that unpopular policies are voted out and popular ones voted in.

Margaret Thatcher certainly believed that her electoral success was due to the popularity of her radical free market policies with the voters. 'In education, housing and health the common themes of my policies were the extension of choice ... This was the application of a philosophy not just an administrative programme ... this approach was successful: it was also popular. Indeed, if it had not been the Conservative Party would have lost the three general elections it fought under my leadership, not won them' (Thatcher 1993: 618).

In the standard rational choice theory of political behaviour, voters' preferences are taken as 'given'. That is, the theory assumes that voters' policy preferences are unaffected by the actions of the political parties and are to be explained by outside, non-political factors. If, through advertising for example, firms could mould consumer preferences so that consumers came to prefer the particular products that powerful firms wished to supply, the moral justification for the free market would be undermined. In the 1970s some radical critiques of the free market argued that advertising did in fact play this role and led to the creation of 'false wants'.

Old Labour almost certainly accepted the radical critique of the free market. They also probably believed that parties too could shape voters' preferences. We doubt if Old Labour spent much time consulting opinion polls on the popularity of nationalization (see, for example, Butler and Kavanagh 1983: 140). They would probably have argued that, by providing an intellectual framework and vision which enabled the disadvantaged to make sense of their plight, it should be possible to educate them to see the necessity of socialist remedies. This is a strand of thinking that goes back to Marx and his emphasis on the role of political organization in transforming the working class into a politically conscious formation.

While she would have had little time for the Marxist analyses, Margaret Thatcher's implicit model of the electorate had some similarities with Old Labour's. Her policy experiments were based not on close consideration of the electorate's preferences (she would certainly never have introduced the poll tax if she had paid attention to the opinion polls) but on her own diagnosis of where previous governments had gone wrong. She also seems to have believed that the electorate could be persuaded to embrace her vision and that it could be educated into seeing the good sense of her policies. 'It is up to us to give intellectual content and political direction to these new dissatisfactions with socialism in practice, with its material and moral failures, to convert disillusion into understanding' (quoted in Campbell 2000: 384).

Despite their profound differences, then, Margaret Thatcher and Old Labour under Michael Foot shared a model of the electors as people who could be led or educated into accepting their own party's vision of society. If they had not shared such a model, it is rather unlikely that they would both have taken up such extreme positions on the political spectrum. The logic of the rational choice model is that parties will be forced towards the centre of the spectrum where the median voter lies, and a rational party leader will foresee this and position his or her party closer to the centre than rival parties. To resist such a move suggests that parties do not accept the premises of the rational choice model.

New Labour, on the other hand, appeared to be in no doubt that the standard rational choice account was correct and that parties must adapt to the voters, rather than persuading the voters to adapt to the party. Both under Neil Kinnock and under Tony Blair, the Labour leadership's policy changes seem to have been motivated in part by these electoral calculations. In passing, however, we might note that one element of closet Marxism seemed to remain in New Labour thinking—the concern with the tabloid press. Old Labour believed that one explanation for their electoral failure was the hostility of the Conservative tabloids; in the run-up to the 1997 election New Labour was equally concerned about the opinions of the tabloids and appeared to believe that hostile newspapers might influence voters' political preferences.

In general, however, New Labour seems to have accepted the standard account that voters' preferences are determined by non-political processes and in particular by external processes of social change. In this respect the standard rational choice theory of the electoral decision has to be supplemented by and set within a broader sociological account of the formation of preferences. Sociologists have repeatedly shown that political preferences are not randomly distributed throughout the electorate: as is well known, the working class, council tenants, trade union members, and ethnic minorities tend to prefer more egalitarian and left-wing policies, while the middle classes, entrepreneurs, and managers tend to favour free market, laissez-faire policies. These preferences can in turn be related to the various groups' economic interests deriving from their positions within the structure of British society (Heath *et al.* 1985).

These are general tendencies (which can be found in most other industrial or post-industrial societies) rather than uniformities, and there is considerable variation within each group. One of the factors that is believed to lie behind Margaret Thatcher's electoral success is that she rightly saw that many members of the working class wanted to 'get ahead' and had aspirations for upward social and economic mobility. She believed that these groups had a considerable potential to support the Conservative Party. For example, her policy of selling council houses to their sitting tenants was designed to appeal to these aspiring members of the working class. In a sense this was a piece of right-wing social engineering designed to undermine Labour's social base and promote groups with an interest in Conservative policies.

It was also widely recognized that autonomous processes of social change were tending to reduce the numbers of voters who favoured egalitarian and interventionist policies. The working class was gradually shrinking in size while the salaried middle classes were expanding (Heath and McDonald 1987). This sociological account has been most evident in the thinking behind New Labour. In an influential Fabian pamphlet entitled *Southern Discomfort* Giles Radice argued

The Labour Party has itself recognized that social change is a crucial factor in Labour's decline. A report produced for the Shadow Cabinet and the NEC after the 1987 election warned that, while Labour's traditional support in manufacturing industry, in trade unions, among manual workers and on council estates was being eroded, the Conservative "core" amongst white-collar workers, those not in unions, and home owners, was expanding. One estimate of the 'natural' level of support in 1987 (that is to say the level of support that might be expected from underlying trends) was about 39 per cent for the Tories and only about 35 per cent for Labour. During the nineties, these underlying social and economic trends are likely to continue to work to the advantage of the Tories. (Radice 1992: 3–4)

In essence, then, the shrinking size of the working class had diminished the size of the potential pool of voters with left-wing policy preferences. Tony Blair himself put it this way:

I can vividly recall the exact moment that I knew the last [1992] election was lost. I was canvassing in the Midlands, on an ordinary, suburban estate. I met a man polishing his Ford Sierra. He was a self-employed electrician. His dad always voted Labour, he said. He used to vote Labour, too. But he'd bought his own house now. He'd set up his own business. He was doing quite nicely. 'So I've become a Tory,' he said . . . that man polishing his car was clear. His instincts were to get on in life. And he thought our instincts were to stop him. (quoted in Fielding 1997: 25; see also Blair 1994)

New Labour's experiment was based on the theory that social change had undermined the possibility of a socialist party winning power through the ballot box. Social change meant that Labour had to broaden its appeal to incorporate the aspirations of the more affluent sections of the working and middle classes. In Blair's terms, the party had to appeal to 'middle income, middle Britain'. The same sociological account had also been espoused, albeit more quietly, by Tony Blair's predecessor as leader of the Labour Party, Neil Kinnock. After Labour's defeat at the 1987 general election Neil Kinnock instituted the policy review precisely in order to get rid of Labour's more left-wing policy commitments and to broaden the party's appeal.

While this sociological account became the orthodoxy among British politicians, there were also dissenting analyses. Most notably Will Hutton argued that processes of economic change might themselves be increasing the potential support for radical initiatives. The main thrust of his argument was that increased competition, largely arising from globalization but also in part driven by some of the very processes of deregulation that Margaret Thatcher herself had promoted, were leading to a spread of insecurity which was beginning to infect not only the working class, who had long been exposed to the risks of redundancy and unemployment, but also the previously secure middle classes.

A second element in Hutton's account was the growth of social and economic inequality that had also accompanied the affluence of the Thatcher years. Hutton's argument was that even the beneficiaries of Thatcherism might become concerned at the growing inequality they saw around them and the growing risks of crime and disorder that threatened their own affluent lifestyles. In these ways the deregulation and tax-cutting of the Thatcher years could be argued to have had unintended consequences that in various ways tended to undermine the Thatcherite project. Perhaps Thatcherism contained the seeds of its own destruction. At any rate, the growing sense of insecurity and growing concern about *la fracture sociale*, as the French termed it, were often seen as factors that contributed to the disillusionment with Conservative policies under John Major and to the Conservative defeat in 1997.

The central aims of this book are to look at the evidence on these electoral experiments, to assess the reasons for their electoral success and failure, and more generally to explore their implications for the underlying theories of electoral behaviour. Was Margaret Thatcher right to suppose that her policies were popular? Did 'harsh electoral reality' mean that Kinnock and Blair were forced to the centre of the political spectrum? What can we learn from these five experiments about the rival models of electoral decision-making and party competition?

To answer these questions we draw on the series of British Election Surveys (BESs) that have been undertaken immediately after every election since 1964. These surveys are based on representative samples of the British electorate, drawn according to scientific principles of random probability sampling. They provide the most authoritative basis available for investigating the policy preferences and voting choices of the British voter.

We also draw on the 1992–7 British Election Panel Study (BEPS). This study carried out annual reinterviews with respondents who had originally been interviewed as part of the 1992 BES and followed them up until the 1997 general election. This panel study is particularly valuable for our current purposes since it contained a round of interviews in 1994, just before Tony Blair became leader of the Labour Party. We can thus obtain a more direct measure of the impact of New Labour. (For details of the BES series and of the 1992–7 BEPS, see the Appendix to this volume.)

We begin in Chapter 2 with social change, and we compare the rival interpretations of Giles Radice and Will Hutton. We ask how far New Labour was constrained by social change to abandon its class appeal or whether Hutton was right to suggest that, as a result of the growth of insecurity, there was still considerable potential support for radical, egalitarian policies in the 1990s.

In Chapters 3 and 4 we explore the electorate's perceptions of and response to Thatcherism. Chapter 3 covers economic policies such as privatization, the control of inflation, the struggle with the unions, and the vexed question of the electorate's attitudes towards taxation and public expenditure. Would the electorate really be willing to pay higher taxes in order to improve public services? More generally, does Margaret Thatcher's electoral success mean that her policies must have been popular too?

Chapter 4 then covers the principal non-economic policies of devolution, defence, and Europe. Why have these issues proved so divisive within British political parties? What lessons are to be drawn from the success, or otherwise, of the successive experiments of the Labour, Conservative, and Referendum Parties with Euroscepticism?

Chapter 5 focuses on the Old Labour and SDP experiments of 1983. How far was Labour's debacle in 1983 due to its experiment with radical socialism and pacifism, and how far was it simply a result of incompetence and division? More generally, what is the role of policy changes in explaining a party's electoral success or failure?

Chapters 6 and 7 look at the rise of New Labour, beginning with Neil Kinnock's gradual modernization of the party between 1982 and 1992 and then at Tony Blair's more dramatic and symbolic changes after his election as leader in 1994. Chapter 6 focuses on New Labour's ideological realignment and the squeeze on the Liberal Democrats. How much difference did Blair's ideological changes actually make? How different would the electoral outcomes have been if John Smith had remained leader of the party?

Chapter 7 then focuses on the changing social bases of support for the parties. Did the various policy experiments carried out by the Conservatives, Old and New Labour, and the SDP lead to changes in the propensity of different social groups to support them? Was there a pattern of general dealignment, with all social groups converging in their political choices, or were there specific realignments reflecting the nature of the specific political experiments?

Chapter 8 turns from voting to non-voting. It explores whether New Labour's move towards the centre ground and its courting of the middle classes alienated its traditional supporters in the working class. Is there, as Przeworski and Sprague (1986) have suggested, a trade-off—formerly socialist parties gaining votes from the middle class as they abandon socialism but discouraging their traditional working-class supporters from turning out?

Chapter 9 then reflects on the implications of our research for theories of voting behaviour. What kind of model of the elector do our findings support? Is there a general framework within which we can place our results and which can make sense of why some experiments succeeded while others failed?

2

Social Change and the Future of the Left

A key element that lay behind Labour's modernization was a sociological analysis of the changing size and character of the working class and of the implications of these changes for Labour's long-term electoral prospects. Throughout the advanced Western democracies the post-war period has seen a decline in the size of the working class. One of the few regularities of political behaviour is that the left tends to be stronger in the working class, and the declining size of the working class implies that it will become more and more difficult for a traditional left-of-centre party to win a majority in Parliament. To be sure, even when the working class was a majority of the electorate, the Labour Party still found it difficult to win, and a third of workers regularly supported the Conservatives even in the 1950s (spawning a huge literature). Working-class support on its own was never enough for a Labour victory, but as the working class became smaller, the prospects of Labour victory appeared to become bleaker.

The decline in the size of the working class has been a long-standing trend, covering almost the whole of the post-war period although accelerating in the 1960s. However, until 1979 the political effects were perhaps masked by the increase in trade union membership and the growth of council housing (see Heath *et al.* 1991, ch. 13). Council tenancy and union membership are both of course associated with Labour voting, and both increased in the 1960s and 1970s—partly because they were encouraged by Labour governments. The growth of public sector employment also stimulated the spread of white-collar unionism, with increasing unionization among teachers, health service workers, and white-collar employees generally. The net impact of social change on Labour fortunes until 1979 was probably thus rather modest. However, Margaret Thatcher's first victory in 1979 marked a watershed. The growth in council housing and union membership was sharply reversed, partly as a consequence of the policies of her administrations and partly reflecting wider social processes.

In an article in the *Political Quarterly* immediately after the 1987 election we argued that Labour's 'core' supporters, consisting of working-class people who were either union members or council tenants (or both), had shrunk to only 23 per cent of the electorate (Heath and McDonald 1987). We calculated that social change, in the period between 1964 and 1986, had probably cost the Labour Party 5 percentage points in their share of the vote, reducing their 'natural' level from 40 per cent to 35 per cent, while the Conservatives had benefited by four points, up from 35 per cent to 39 per cent. The alliance between the SDP and the Liberals was the other net beneficiary, since their support was also somewhat stronger in the expanding groups of the highly educated middle classes. We saw every reason to suppose that these trends, and hence the fall in Labour's natural level of support, would continue for the foreseeable future. We explored the possible responses that the Labour Party might make, although we emphasized that social change should not be made the scapegoat for political failures such as weak and divided leadership. Much of our analysis was apparently accepted by the Labour Party itself and formed the basis of a report to the Shadow Cabinet.

A second element in the New Labour analysis was the argument that the working class not only had shrunk but had also changed in character. It was widely believed that class boundaries had blurred, that the more affluent members of the working class, particularly home-owners in the south-east, were converging with the lower middle class in their aspirations and lifestyles and, crucially, were becoming detached from the Labour Party. On this view, core Labour support was increasingly limited to the more disadvantaged sectors of the working class, those in less skilled jobs, and in the declining stock of council housing. In a Fabian pamphlet David Lipsey argued:

So far as Western advanced capitalist societies are concerned . . . the '10 : 70 : 20' model seems systematically universal. The political significance of this change cannot be overstated. It transforms the character of Labour's natural vote. Labour can be reasonably sure of winning most of the bottom 20 per cent, though this is the segment of the population least likely actually to vote. It will only win a few votes at the top. It thus has to appeal to the broad mass in the middle. (Lipsey 1992: 7–8)

Reformist Labour writers such as Giles Radice took the view that this 'broad mass in the middle' had to be the key target for Labour recruitment. But crucially they also argued that the aspirations and concerns of this broad mass in the middle were in important respects different from those of the bottom 20 per cent who constituted Labour's core supporters. They were seen as voters with aspirations for social mobility for themselves and their children; they were believed to be individualistic and materialistic, lacking the collective solidarity of the now vanished traditional working-class communities: 'The bottom line is "how is this going to affect me and my family?" ' (Radice and Pollard 1993: 14). These aspiring voters, Radice argued, did not consider themselves to be working-class, and hence 'Labour cannot afford a class approach' (Radice 1992: 15). 'They felt that Labour—seen as a class-based party—had nothing to offer upwardly mobile families such as their own' (Radice and Pollard 1993: 1).

Even more important, they do not believe that [Labour] understands, respects or rewards those who want to 'get on'. Far from encouraging talent and promoting opportunity, Labour is seen as the party that is most likely to 'take things away'. From the perspective of the aspirant voters, voting Labour is simply not 'in their interests'. The message of the survey is that if Labour is serious about assembling a winning majority, it has to take into account the aspirations and interests of these crucial groups of potential 'swing' voters. It cannot afford to rely simply on its 'core' voters because there are not enough of them. (Radice 1992: 13)

Blair himself seems to have accepted this analysis. 'The reason Labour lost in 1992' he wrote, 'as for the previous three elections, is not complex, it is simple: society had changed and we did not change sufficiently with it' (Blair 1992; quoted in Sopel 1995).

This line of argument reflected many previous commentaries on the Conservatives' electoral successes in the 1980s. It was held that the Conservatives' brand of tax cuts and incentives had successfully appealed to the aspiring skilled workers, especially in the south-east of England—so-called 'Essex man'. And it was certainly true that, outside London, Labour had lost virtually all its seats in the south-east including many in apparently working-class constituencies. It also had a lot in common with an even earlier debate about affluent workers. After Labour's third election defeat in a row in 1959, Abrams, Rose, and Hinden argued that 'the old working class ethos is being eroded by prosperity and the increasing fluidity of our society. People now know that they can improve their lot by their own efforts. And as they succeed, they change their values and cease to identify themselves with the class from which they sprang' (1960: 106). In many ways the current debates about social change and the Labour Party are a reprise of the debates of the late 1950s.

A rival line of argument, however, has been put forward by Will Hutton. In place of Lipsey's 10 : 70 : 20 society, Hutton argued that there is now a 30/30/40 society. And crucially he believed that the majority of this society would favour progressive social policies. In Hutton's analysis the first 30 per cent are the disadvantaged—the unemployed, discouraged workers, and people caught in the poverty trap. This has a lot in common with some notions of the underclass and with Lipsey's account of the bottom 20 per cent, although Hutton draws the lines rather more broadly. The second 30 per cent are the marginalized and the insecure—employees, particularly part-timers, who lack legal protection; people who have been forced into self-employment; workers on temporary contracts; and full-timers in the peripheral labour market. The third category is that of the privileged—full-time workers and self-employed who have reasonable security—who make up 40 per cent of the labour force (Hutton 1995: 105–9).

Moreover, in contrast to the New Labour analysis, Hutton believed that the groups of the disadvantaged, marginal, and insecure had grown substantially under Thatcherism. The ranks of the disadvantaged had been growing as a result of the unemployment of the Thatcher years, while the ranks of the marginal and insecure had grown as a result of the removal of some legal measures of employment protection, the increasing pursuit by powerful corporations of a flexible labour force, with increased contracting out, part-time work, and the like, and also as a result of the increased competitive pressures arising from globalization.

Hutton went on to argue that these changes had in fact increased the potential support for radical, left-of-centre policies in Britain.

Within the 30/30/40 society, there is a comfortable majority that would benefit from a less unfair, less insecure and more equitable society who might be prepared to enter a new social compact. Within the ranks of the marginalised and insecure, who together comprise nearly

60 per cent of the population, the majority for change is overwhelming, and it is extending into the privileged 40 per cent, alarmed by the society they see around them. (Hutton 1995: 324).

In this chapter we first document the social changes that took place over the eighteen years of Conservative government. We then ask about the political implications of these changes and attempt to adjudicate between these two alternative views of the contemporary potential for radical policies.

The Decline of Labour's Social Base

Recent data confirm the story that we had told in 1987 in our analysis of social change and the future of the left. As we had expected, the working class has continued to decline in size in recent years. Table 2.1 shows the decline in the size of the working class over the post-war period.

At the time of Labour's last historic landslide in 1945 the working class had made up two-thirds of the labour force, although even then Labour secured slightly less than a majority of the vote. In 1979 the working class, broadly defined, still made up half the labour force, although by this time Labour support had fallen to 39 per cent. By the 1990s the working class had fallen to less than

Table 2.1. The decline of the working class and of Labour voting, 1945–1997

Year	Labour share of GB vote (%)	Percentage of labour force who are working class	
		BES	Census
1945	48.8		
1950	46.8		
1951	49.4		64.9
1955	47.3		
1959	44.6		
1961			60.6
1964	44.8	58.2	
1966	48.9		
1970	43.9	56.5	
1971			55.0
1974	38.0	51.1	
1979	37.8	49.0	
1981			49.6
1983	28.3	45.1	
1987	31.5	40.6	
1991			38.4
1992	35.2	36.9	
1997	44.4	34.1	

Notes: The labour force is defined as persons who are economically active (incl. the unemployed who are looking for work). The working class includes manual foremen and supervisors but excludes own-account workers.

Sources: Column 1, Heath *et al.* (1991), updated; column 2, *BES 1964–97*; column 3, Heath and McDonald (1987), updated.

Table 2.2. The decline of council housing, 1979–1997

| Year | Owner-occupied | Rented privately | (% of dwellings) | | All dwellings (000s) |
			Rented from housing associations	Rented from local authorities	
1979	55.3	13.1	—	31.5	20,826
1983	59.9	9.2	2.3	28.6	21,250
1987	62.7	9.6	2.6	25.1	22,293
1992	66.3	9.8	3.3	20.5	23,314
1997	67.2	10.6	4.9	17.0	24,216

Sources: Department of the Environment (1978, 1998, 1999).

two-fifths of the labour force, although Labour's share of the vote had recovered somewhat.

In the period until 1979 the decline of the working class had been compensated from Labour's point of view by a growth in council housing, council tenants being traditionally one of Labour's best sources of electoral support. The first part of the post-war period had seen the gradual decline of private renting and the gradual increase, under both Labour and Conservative governments, of local authority housing as well as of owner occupation. However, the trend towards social housing went into sharp reverse after the Conservative victory in 1979, as can be seen in Table 2.2.

The Conservative government's increased control of local authority expenditure meant that very little new council housing was undertaken after 1979, but most importantly the Conservatives' highly popular 'right to buy' programme encouraged a massive sale of council housing to tenants. Over the period from 1979 to 1997 about 2 million homes were sold to their tenants (Murie 1997). This programme peaked in 1982, when sales to sitting tenants exceeded 200,000. By the 1990s, however, the programme had tailed off as there were relatively few local authority tenants left who were in a position to buy or who were renting accommodation that they would wish to buy.

One consequence of this programme was a phenomenon that has been termed 'residualization'. The kinds of tenant who remained in local authority housing in the 1990s were rather different from those in the 1970s or earlier. Fewer of them were in full-time employment on average earnings or above, and many more of them were either state pensioners or dependent on other state benefits (Forrest and Murie 1984; Heath *et al.* 1991). (We shall need to bear this in mind when in later chapters we look at trends over time in the attitudes and voting behaviour of this evolving group.)

On the union side, the trends paralleled those for council housing. Membership had been rising under Labour in the 1970s but went into sharp decline after 1979. This was partly a consequence of the Conservatives' repeal of

Table 2.3. The decline of union membership, 1979–1997

Year	Percentage of the labour force who were trade union members	Union membership (millions)
1979	52.7	13.3
1983	47.3	11.2
1987	41.4	10.5
1992	29.5	9.0
1997	27.3	7.8

Source: *Labour Market Trends* (London: Office of National Statistics, 2000).

the previous Labour government's 'closed shop' legislation. It was also in part a consequence of industrial restructuring, again encouraged by the Conservative administrations. Heavy industries, which had had the highest densities of union membership, were sharply reduced in scale and manpower, partly as a result of the withdrawal of subsidies, partly as public sector corporations were privatized, and partly under the pressures of international competition. In contrast the expanding, higher-tech industries in the south-east were less unionized, and workers who moved to them rarely rejoined unions at the new workplaces (Gallie 1998: 172–3).

These changes had of course affected the working class. Even though it was shrinking, the proportion of council tenants was shrinking even faster. Thus, whereas 44 per cent of the working class had been council tenants in 1979, this had shrunk by 1997 to 24 per cent. The percentage of the working class who were trade union members had shrunk over the same period from 38 to 21 per cent. But even more remarkably, the proportion of the working class who were both council tenants and trade union members had almost reached vanishing-point—down from 18 to 3 per cent. This partly reflected the residualization of council housing: as council housing had become more and more of a safety net for the most disadvantaged members of society (especially the unemployed, pensioners, and single parents dependent on state benefits), who could not compete in the private market for housing, very few of the remaining tenants were therefore trade union members. Broadly speaking most trade union members were in work, and hence did have some financial power to compete in the market. Often they would be the ones who had taken advantage of the 'right to buy' programme of council house sales.

Following our *Political Quarterly* analysis of social change and the future of the left, Table 2.4 gives a summary sketch of the changes in the social composition of the electorate over the eighteen years of Conservative government. We begin with the petite bourgeoisie—employers, farmers, and self-employed workers. The great majority of the petite bourgeoisie, even back in 1979, were home-owners, and virtually none of them was a trade union member. It is also a relatively small formation and hence it does not make sense to subdivide it further. As we have shown in our earlier work, the petite bourgeoisie is the most Thatcherite of all groups, and of

Table 2.4. The social composition of the electorate, 1979–1997

Percentage who were	1979	1997	Change
Petit bourgeois	8.3	10.0	+1.7
Salariat			
Non-union	17.4	26.6	+9.2
Union members	7.1	5.8	−1.3
Routine non-manual	14.2	17.7	+3.5
Working -class			
Non-union, home-owners	12.0	16.5	+4.5
Non-union, council tenants	12.7	7.0	−5.7
Union members	19.5	7.9	−11.6
Other working-class	6.0	3.7	−2.3
Unemployed	2.8	4.8	+2.0
N	1726	2390	

Note: For details of the construction of these variables, see App. 2.1.

Sources: *BES 1979* and *1997*.

course it is the one from which Margaret Thatcher herself came (Heath *et al.* 1985). However, in absolute terms it has shown little growth over the period since 1979.

We then come to the largest single group: members of the salariat who did not belong to trade unions. By the salariat we refer to salaried professionals, managers, and administrators who hold secure and economically advantaged positions. This group is also strongly Conservative, but, unlike the petite bourgeoisie, it has expanded very substantially over the course of the Thatcher years, up from 17 per cent in 1979 to nearly 27 per cent in 1997.

We next distinguish the unionized members of the salariat. This group of salaried trade unionists is an important one theoretically. It tends to be more radical than our first two groups, and is the home of what is often described as the 'New Left' (in contrast to the Old Left of the working class proper). This group, or ones with which it overlaps substantially such as salaried public sector employees, is sometimes thought of as a 'new middle class', and it is certainly less inclined to vote Conservative than is the 'old middle class'. (For a more detailed discussion of political divisions within the middle class, see Heath and Savage 1995.) However, as Table 2.4 shows, this is not a group that had been growing in size since Margaret Thatcher came to power.

There is next the routine non-manual class, which is in many respects intermediate between the salariat and the working class. We then turn to the working class. Here our first main group consists of the non-union home-owners. Even in 1979 this was quite a large group, and it would probably have contained many of the aspiring, upwardly mobile workers that Radice described, although we would not wish to exaggerate the links between aspirations and home ownership. In their voting patterns this group is more or less equally balanced between Conservative and Labour, and it is easy to see why Labour reformists would believe this group to contain the crucial 'swing voters' on whom election outcomes are believed to depend. It had, moreover, been growing in size quite substantially, up from 12 per cent in 1979 to nearly 17 per cent in 1997.

We then have two large groups of 'core' Labour supporters where there has typically been a healthy Labour lead over the Conservatives. These are the working-class union members and the working-class council tenants. In our 1987 *Political Quarterly* article we described these two groups as the 'integrated working class'—people who were integrated into the labour movement through trades unions or into working-class communities via council housing estates. In contrast, the non-union owner-occupiers can be thought of as less integrated members of the working class who are more remote from traditional sources of working-class collectivism and solidarity.

However, the integrated working class has been in serious decline, with working-class union members down by nearly 12 percentage points and (non-union) council tenants down by nearly 6 points. The only Labour-inclined group to be growing in size was the unemployed, up by 3 percentage points. Quite clearly, then, the eighteen years of Conservative rule had seen a transformation in the size and composition of the working class. Some of this was due to processes that were occurring throughout the advanced post-industrial societies of western Europe, but these processes had also been actively encouraged by Conservative governments. By 1997 the electoral landscape faced by the Labour Party bore little resemblance to that when Labour had last been in power: in 1979 the social core of the Labour Party amounted to roughly 35 per cent of the electorate and was rather larger than the Conservative core (26 per cent). In 1997 the Conservative core had grown to 37 per cent while the Labour core had shrunk to 20 per cent.

These changes were clearly bad news for Labour, and they appeared to justify Labour's concern in 1987 with the implications of social change. The electoral implications of these changes can perhaps be exaggerated, however. In our previous work we argued that shifts from council tenancy to owner occupation do not necessarily lead to immediate changes in values or political preferences (Heath *et al.* 1991; Norris 1990). People who bought their own council houses tended to be somewhat more inclined to the Conservatives before they bought than were the other council tenants, and panel studies have failed to show any short-term conversion to the Tories on the part of house purchasers. Similarly, upwardly mobile voters from the working class tend to come from more Conservative backgrounds than the immobile members of the working class. Social change does not therefore necessarily have immediate electoral consequences. In the longer run, however, voters will tend to move away from the political orientations of their origins and towards those of their destinations, although retaining some imprint from their class of origin.[1] As we argued in

---

[1] Studies of the impact of social mobility show that the political preferences of socially mobile people tend to be in between those of their class of origin and their class of destination. This does, however, depend on the age of the respondent. In general, younger mobile respondents tend to be closer to the political preferences of their class of origin while older mobile respondents are closer to those of their class of destination. Assimilation to the political orientations of one's class of destination thus seems to be a gradual and long-term process. See Graaf *et al.* (1994).

our *Political Quarterly* paper, social change should not be made the scapegoat for political failures, but the long-term strategy of any party, and especially a left-of-centre party, must clearly take on board the changes exhibited in Table 2.4.[2]

Room for Class Politics?

The Labour modernizers were clearly correct, therefore, to address the electoral problems arising from the shrinkage of its social base. As Radice and Pollard argued, Labour clearly had to appeal to the broad mass in the middle.

If Labour is to win more seats in the South and so gain power at the next election, then it must improve its performance among the white collar and skilled manual groups . . . These voters now comprise more than half the electorate . . . Above all, they are the crucial swing voters whose behaviour decides elections . . . Those who argue that the party can afford to ignore these crucial 'middle' groups where Labour has been underperforming and should instead concentrate on maximizing its support among its 'core' voters forget that the [latter] now amount to less than a third of the electorate'. (Radice and Pollard 1993: 3)

However, the precise character of this broad mass in the middle is more contentious. A key element of the New Labour analysis was that the aspiring working class no longer thought of themselves in class terms and that a class appeal to them would therefore be ineffective. This led to the conclusion that one should draw the boundaries rather differently—not between middle class and working class but between the disadvantaged minority and the broad mass of middle-income Britain that made up the great majority of voters. Social change, it was argued, had changed the meaning of social class to the voters. New Labour, like John Major, believed that Britain was becoming a classless society.

We do not in fact disagree with Radice that a class appeal, couched simply in terms of class *per se* rather than in terms of policies such as redistribution or control of unemployment, would be silly for the contemporary Labour Party. The evidence from the BES shows that most voters disapprove of a sectional party that looks after the interests of one social class alone—even if that class happens to be one's own. People like to believe (or like to report to interviewers) that the party they vote for is good for all sections of society. However, this has been true for a long time, and certainly goes back to 1974, when the relevant question was first asked in the BES. And it holds true for the disadvantaged 20 per cent just as it does for the rest of society.

Where we are less inclined to agree with the New Labour analysis is that social change has led to a major blurring of class boundaries and that the working class no

---

[2] In our previous estimates of the impact of social change, as in Heath and McDonald (1987) or Heath *et al.* (1991), we assumed that the conditional probabilities of supporting a given party remained constant. This in effect assumes that the mix of mobile and immobile respondents within a given social category has remained constant. Our estimates of the political effect of social change should therefore be revised downward slightly if the proportion of mobile respondents has increased.

longer think of themselves in class terms. To explore this we can look at the BES evidence on people's subjective class identities. The surveys have regularly asked the question

Do you ever think of yourself as belonging to any particular class?

IF YES: Which class is that? (*BES 1997*, question 587)

IF NO: Most people say they belong either to the middle class or the working class. If you had to make a choice, would you call yourself middle class or working class? (*BES 1997*, question 589)

The prompt 'Most people say they belong either to the middle class or the working class' tends to push respondents into identifying with one class or the other, but we can use the first, unprompted question to see who voluntarily adopts a class perspective.

Overall, Table 2.5 shows that in 1997 just over half the electorate voluntarily assigned themselves to the middle or working class. It is arguable whether these proportions support the 'classless society' thesis or not, but what is also clear is that all sections within the working class (as defined on the basis of our 'objective' measures) were more likely to describe themselves as working-class than as middle-class.

On the other hand, Table 2.5 does show some major differences between the various social categories in their propensity to think of themselves in working-class or middle-class terms. Among those who did volunteer a class identity there were fairly substantial differences in the ratio of middle-class to working-class self-assignments, working-class identities as expected becoming more common as we move down the table. The key points are that:

Table 2.5. Class awareness among different social groups, 1997

Social group	Percentage who describe themselves as			
	Middle-class	Working-class	Neither	N
Petit bourgeois	16	34	50	240
Salariat				
Non-union	32	18	50	636
Union members	29	24	49	139
Routine non-manual	20	25	54	424
Working-class				
Non-union, home-owners	16	40	44	394
Non-union, council tenants	7	51	42	166
Union members	8	56	36	187
Other working class	7	46	47	87
Unemployed	7	36	58	115
All	20	31	49	2,389

Source: BES 1997.

- the salariat were the only group that was more likely to volunteer a middle-than a working-class self-description, with the non-unionized members being much more likely than the unionized to adopt a middle-class identity;
- the salaried union members split fairly evenly between the middle-class and working-class identities;
- the working-class home-owners divided in the ratio of 1 : 2.5 between the two identities; that is, they were over twice as likely to give a working-class as a middle-class identity;
- the two core Labour groups were the most likely to volunteer a working-class identity, both of them showing a ratio of 1 : 7.

The home-owning manual workers do, then, fall roughly in the middle between Labour's core of working-class union members and council tenants on the one hand and the Conservatives' core of the non-union salariat on the other. In this sense, then, the New Labour analysis is again correct: the aspiring working class (whom we are equating for the sake of argument with the working-class home-owners) clearly do differ in their subjective identities from Labour's traditional core groups in the council estates and trades unions.

More surprisingly, however, it turns out that there is nothing especially new about this. Analysis of earlier BESs shows almost exactly the same pattern: for example, the comparable ratios in 1974 were approximately 3 : 1 in the Conservative core, 2 : 1 among the salaried trade unionists, 1 : 2 among working-class home-owners, 1 : 6 among council tenants and 1 : 7 among working-class trade union members. (For full details see Table A2.2.) New Labour had perhaps simply caught up with something that had long been true in Britain. In this respect Blair would be wrong to say that 'society has changed and we have failed to change with it'. It would be more accurate to say that 'society has never conformed with Labour assumptions, but we have failed to realize that until now'.

Increasing Disadvantage and Insecurity?

Still, even if the Labour leadership had been slow in appreciating the nature of the working class in post-war Britain, the bulk of our evidence so far generally supports the New Labour analysis. Does this leave any room for the alternative view, put forward notably by Will Hutton, that the growth of insecurity had actually expanded the potential for left-of-centre policies? As Hutton argued, the Thatcher period was not just a period in which Britain became a more middle-class nation of home-owners; it was also a period characterized by growing social inequality, by increased unemployment, and, even among the employed, by a greater sense of job insecurity. In other words, while average levels of affluence were rising, the spread around that average was also becoming greater.

As we noted earlier, Hutton argued that there was now a 30/30/40 society. The first 30 per cent were the *disadvantaged*—the unemployed, the discouraged workers who were no longer looking for work, women married to unemployed men, together with people on government unemployment schemes. The second 30 per cent were the *marginalized* and the *insecure*—some but not all part-timers, people who had been forced into self-employment, temporary workers, full-timers on low pay and with little employment protection. Hutton's last category was that of the *privileged*—full-time workers and self-employed who had held their jobs for two years, or part-timers who had held their jobs for more than five years (Hutton 1995: 105–9).

In this way Hutton rightly drew attention to a number of countervailing trends that cut across, or perhaps indeed were a product of, the affluence of the Thatcher years. He was clearly correct to argue that there had been a growth in the numbers of the disadvantaged: the growth of unemployment during the Thatcher years is unarguable. But it is the second of Hutton's groups, the marginalized and the insecure, that is perhaps of key political significance. It is here that Hutton's and Radice's analyses are at greatest odds. Where Radice saw a growing number of aspiring workers anxious to leave the council estates and get on in life, Hutton saw a growing number of insecure workers who were increasingly vulnerable to ruthless corporations: 'This is not the world of full-time jobs with employment protection and benefits such as pensions and paid holidays. Instead people in this category work at jobs that are insecure, poorly protected and carry few benefits.' Of course, both views could have been true at different times—Radice's during the long boom of the 1980s and Hutton's during the recession of the 1990s. Or both may have been true simultaneously, aspiring upwardly mobile workers facing poorer employment conditions as employment protection was gradually withdrawn. Table 2.6 shows trends over the Conservative years in some key indicators of disadvantage and marginality.

As the table shows, after Margaret Thatcher came into office in 1979 there were clear increases in the proportions of the unemployed, temporary workers, part-time workers, self-employed, and people on low income. Unfortunately these data do

Table 2.6. Trends in economic disadvantage, 1979–1997

Year	Percentage of the labour force				
	Unemployed, ILO definition	Part-timers as percentage of all female employees	Self-employed	Temporary workers	Individuals with less than half average income
1979	4.9	39.6	7.3	—	8
1983	11.7	41.5	9.9	5.3	9
1987	10.7	42.8	12.1	5.6	15
1992	9.9	44.9	12.8	5.9	20
1997	8.2	46.8	12.5	7.7	18

Notes: The ILO definition defines someone as unemployed if they are out of work, have been looking for work in the last two weeks, and are available to take work up within two weeks. It is typically measured from survey data and it is now widely regarded as preferable to the 'claimant counts' derived from official sources.

Sources: *Labour Market Trends, 2000;* income: Hills (1998, fig. 3), which includes pensioners.

not tap precisely the same concepts that Hutton himself had in mind. For example, it is hard to know from official figures how much of the growth in self-employment was 'forced' and how much was 'voluntary'. Similarly, as Hutton recognized, not all part-timers can be regarded as insecure: Gallie's work suggests that about half of part-timers were covered by employment protection, compared with three-quarters of full-timers. There is also the more fundamental point that lack of legal employment protection may not translate into *de facto* insecurity: Gallie and his colleagues in fact found that there was no difference between full- and part-timers in their subjective assessments of their risks of unemployment or of their actual probabilities of becoming unemployed (although in other respects part-timers are indeed seriously disadvantaged particularly with respect to their hourly rates of pay and their access to fringe benefits) (Gallie 1998: 163–4).

There can be little doubt, however, that Hutton was broadly correct in his account of the trends under Thatcherism. The central point is that increasing affluence on average was accompanied by a growing polarization around that average. As Hutton argues: 'The polarisation of the advantaged and the disadvantaged has done little to check average earnings growth or lower the real wages' (1995: 108).

From the electoral point of view, on the other hand, it is the size of Hutton's three groups rather than the trends that is perhaps more significant. As Hutton himself recognized, while his first group of the disadvantaged had undoubtedly been growing and was also quite likely to support Labour, it was not on its own anything like a sufficient social base for a party such as Labour which aspired to win an overall majority.[3] Indeed, this was one of the groups that New Labour was perhaps rather anxious to dissociate itself from.

The key group for electoral research, therefore, is Hutton's second group of the marginalized and insecure. Has the spread of insecurity infected the expanding groups of middle Britain, Radice's crucial swing voters? For electoral purposes we also need to move beyond Hutton's concerns with the composition of the labour force to that of the electorate as a whole. We thus need to include the large numbers of pensioners. Among pensioners we expect to find that there is a major difference between people on occupational pensions, who will tend both to have higher pensions and to have ones that are likely to keep pace with inflation, and people on the basic state pension. People with occupational pensions, then, should probably be

---

[3] As Table 2.7 shows, unemployment on its own clearly does not include 30% of the labour force. In addition to the unemployed, however, Hutton quite reasonably includes all men of working age who are not actually in work (apart from those in full-time education); this will include men who are sick and permanently disabled and no longer looking for work, as well as those who have taken early retirement plus a small proportion who are looking after the home. Many of these men can be regarded as 'discouraged workers' and their numbers seem to have been increasing too. Hutton also includes all unemployed women together with 'women married to economically inactive men who are unable to take work because the loss of their husband's income support would more than offset any wage they might earn' (1995: 206). 'Altogether some 28% of the adult working population are either unemployed or economically inactive' (1995: 106). Of course, this will be a rather smaller proportion of the electorate. It is also likely that the disadvantaged have rather lower propensities to turn out and vote, thus reducing further their electoral weight.

assigned to the ranks of the privileged while people on state pensions should be assigned to the marginal and insecure (or even perhaps to the disadvantaged).

The major problem that we have, however, is in identifying insecure and marginal workers. The BESs do not include the kind of criteria that Hutton used[4] (e.g. whether people are covered by employment protection), but in any event it is likely to be people's own assessments of their insecurity rather than the formal legal situation that influences their electoral behaviour. Fortunately, in the 1997 survey we did include a number of questions designed to measure people's own subjective perceptions of their insecurity. We used different questions depending upon whether the respondents were employees, self-employed, unemployed, or retired. The questions were:

These days some people have to leave their job, without having a choice in the matter. How about you? Please say how confident you are that you will be able to stay in your current job over the next year if you want to do so. (*BES 1997*, question 776)

These days, some businesses make losses or have to close down. Please say how confident you are that you will make enough profit to stay in business over the next year. (*BES 1997*, question 778)

These days, some retired people do not have enough income to provide for themselves. Please say how confident you are that you will be able to provide for yourself as you grow older. (*BES 1997*, question 780)

These days, some unemployed people are unable to find suitable jobs. Please say how confident you are that you will find a suitable job within the next three months or so. (*BES 1997*, question 779)

There were four response codes: 'very confident', 'fairly confident', 'not very confident', and 'not at all confident'. Because of the small numbers involved, we combine the last two categories.

Table 2.7 shows the answers that our respondents gave to these questions and therefore allows us to gauge how much subjective confidence our respondents felt in 1997. There is a very clear gradient as we move from employees to the unemployed; over 50 per cent of full-time employees felt very confident that they would be able to keep their current jobs, while only 9 per cent of the unemployed felt very confident that they would find a suitable job in the next three months. (Of course the questions change as we move down the table, so we are comparing functional equivalents not exact equivalents.)

Confirming Gallie's work, we find little difference between the full-time and part-time employees in their levels of confidence, and we also find that income level makes rather little difference. In both cases, the difference is in the direction

---

[4] Hutton himself distinguishes four main components of this group: first, part-timers, especially those who work less than sixteen hours a week since they have no right to appeal against unfair dismissal and so on. Secondly, the self-employed, especially those in contracted-out work where firms have exploited their new power to avoid all social overheads, forcing employees to take out individual contracts. Thirdly, people in full-time work who are on low pay or who lack employment protection (e.g. because they had had less than two years with their employer). And, fourthly, temporary workers.

Table 2.7. Confidence of employees, self-employed, pensioners, and the unemployed, 1997

Economic position	Percentage who felt			
	Very confident	Fairly confident	Not very confident	N
Full-time employee	53	37	10	1,003
Part-time employee	52	37	12	207
Top quartile of income	55	36	10	305
Second quartile	56	35	9	277
Third quartile	51	40	9	286
Lowest quartile of income	51	34	15	262
Self-employed	40	47	13	218
Occupational pensioner	38	59	4	175
State pensioner	21	53	26	264
Unemployed	9	31	60	77
All	43	42	15	1,944

Notes: The figures in the table for employees relate to question 776; for the self-employed they relate to question 778; for the pensioners to question 780; and for the unemployed to question 779.

Source: BES 1997.

predicted by Hutton, but the magnitude of the differences is not such as to suggest that part-time working in itself is an important source of subjective job insecurity. Similarly, there is little difference between people on high and low income in their feelings of insecurity.[5] On the other hand, there are some quite large differences between people on state and occupational pensions: we find that state pensioners are considerably less confident than are people with occupational pensions that they will be able to provide for themselves as they grow older.

However, the most striking feature of the table is that, with the notable exception of the unemployed, the great majority of all groups felt either very or fairly confident about their security. If we combine answers to our four questions on insecurity (recognizing that they are functional equivalents), we can see that overall 43 per cent felt very confident, 42 per cent fairly confident, and only 15 per cent were not confident. (We should remember that there will also be some people, such as the permanently sick and disabled, who were not asked any of four questions, and these would probably swell the ranks of the insecure.)

Whether we regard these figures as supporting or refuting Hutton's account is not entirely clear. It depends on how we treat people who say they feel 'fairly confident'. If we regard them as falling into Hutton's category of the 'marginalized and insecure', then we do get a picture that is not too different from that of his 30/30/40 society. On the other hand, we could also plausibly treat them as falling into Lipsey's 'broad mass in the middle'. The crucial question for settling this dispute is

[5] It should be noted, however, that our income variable refers to household income and will not therefore have a straightforward relationship with the respondent's own pay level. It may also be the case that people on lower income suffer from forms of insecurity other than job insecurity.

how these feelings of insecurity translate into support for radical politics. It is to this that we now turn.

Room for Socialism?

What, then, are the political implications of these patterns of security and insecurity? What do they suggest about the potential electoral base for socialist, or at least for left-of-centre, policies? In particular what can we say about the 'broad mass in the middle'—the supposedly key swing voters. Do these represent, as the New Labour analysis suggests, aspiring materialists who feel that class politics has nothing to say to them. Or are they, as Hutton suggests, marginalized and insecure with an overwhelming majority for change?

One simple measure of the potential for radical left-of-centre politics, and one that is central to most definitions of socialism, is support for the redistribution of income and wealth. This was the heart of the Old Labour conception of socialism as exemplified by Tony Crosland's *The Future of Socialism* (1956). We might expect self-interested and aspiring workers to be unwilling to assent to redistributive policies that might well not benefit themselves in the long run. To measure this we can use a question that has been regularly included in the BES and that asks respondents whether they agree that 'Income and wealth should be redistributed towards ordinary working people' (*BES 1997*, question 455). Conversely, we might expect the marginalized and insecure to want to see a greater role for government intervention in the labour market to protect workers' positions. To tap this aspect we can use a question which asks respondents whether they agree that 'It is the government's responsibility to provide a job for everyone who wants one' (*BES 1997*, question 204a).

In Table 2.8 we divide our respondents according to their levels of subjective insecurity. Since we had four functionally equivalent questions for employees, the self-employed, the retired, and the unemployed respectively, we preserve these distinctions in the table. Several points stand out from the table. First, the unemployed are consistently the most left-wing group, with a very large majority supporting redistribution and full employment policies. Their level of subjective insecurity makes little difference to their support for these policies (and, because of the small numbers of respondents in these categories, is not in fact statistically significant).

Secondly, the self-employed are as a whole the group least likely to support redistribution or full employment. The very confident entrepreneurs do appear to be the least supportive of redistribution and full employment, but again the differences in support are not statistically significant (again reflecting the small numbers of respondents involved).

The other two groups of the employees and the retired fall somewhere in between. There also prove to be some statistically significant differences according to their levels of subjective insecurity. In particular, employees who were not very confident about keeping their jobs were more or less as left-wing as the unemployed

Table 2.8. Support for left-of-centre politics among the secure and insecure, 1997

Group	Percentage agreeing		N
	Income and wealth should be redistributed	Government's responsibility to provide jobs	
Employees			
Very confident	62	56	563
Fairly confident	57	60	400
Not very confident	76	69	116
Self-employed			
Very confident	35	42	88
Fairly confident	50	52	92
Not very confident	43	52	26
Retired			
Very confident	47	49	120
Fairly confident	54	62	247
Not very confident	63	71	72
Unemployed			
Very confident	—	—	9
Fairly confident	68	88	31
Not very confident	73	76	59

Notes: Agree and strongly agree combined.

Source: *BES 1997*.

in their political attitudes. This makes good theoretical and practical sense since these people are likely to constitute the pool from which the unemployed themselves are drawn. However, there are relatively few people who were not very confident about keeping their jobs—roughly 10 per cent of all employees. Among the much larger numbers who felt very or fairly secure, support for left-wing policies was markedly lower.

Subjective insecurity thus has at best a modest association with support for left-wing goals; attitudes towards redistribution can be predicted much more accurately from one's social group than from one's sense of personal security. (For technical details, see Table A2.2.). This is hardly a ringing endorsement of Hutton's thesis. It follows that the growth in insecurity is unlikely to have had any major implications for increase in radicalism. For example, the gap between the very confident employees and the employees who felt little confidence comes only to 14 percentage points. But since this latter group amounts to about 5 per cent of the electorate as a whole, the effect of their growth can at best have been an increase of 0.7 per cent (i.e. 0.14×5 per cent) in the overall level of support for redistribution. Small differences that affect small groups are not going to have a major impact on support for socialism.

On the other hand, the overall levels of support for redistribution do accord much more closely with Hutton's argument. Overall, 60 per cent of respondents agreed that income ought to be redistributed, while 59 per cent agreed that it was government's responsibility to provide jobs. It must be admitted that the precise nature of

Table 2.9. Support for redistribution, 1974–1997

Year	Percentage agreeing income and wealth should be redistributed	N
1974	54	2,289
1979	52	1,857
1983	48	3,931
1987	50	3,809
1992	47	2,840
1997	60	2,127

Note: The 1974 figures are from the Oct. survey. Minor wording changes in 1983 and 1987 may affect the trends.

Sources: *BES 1974–97*.

the question wording can have a marked effect on responses, and we should not place too much weight on the absolute figures. However, alternative question wordings all suggest that a majority of the electorate place themselves to the left of centre on this central issue of redistribution.[6]

Equally crucially we need to look at trends over time in levels of support for redistribution and government intervention. The central thrust of Hutton's argument was that the ranks of the insecure had been growing—hence increasing the number of people with a direct interest in left-of-centre policies—and, furthermore, that growing inequality was a source of worry to the more comfortable sections of society, giving them perhaps a growing indirect interest in redistributive policies. While we are sceptical about the overall impact of the first part of Hutton's argument, the second part is independent of the first and perhaps raises the more fundamental challenge to the New Labour analyses. Radice and New Labour tended to believe that voters were essentially concerned solely with their own short-term material interests and hence would not vote for redistributive policies. Hutton took the view that privileged voters might feel that rising unemployment and social inequality, with the associated increases in crime and risk of social disorder might make it in their long-term interests to support some degree of redistribution. Table 2.9 looks at the trends in support for redistribution.

The table suggests that there was a general trend to the right from 1974 to 1992. This is in line with the general social changes, such as the expansion of the middle classes, described earlier in this chapter, and thus tends to support the New Labour

[6] In the 1997 BES we included a number of other questions that ask about the respondent's attitudes towards redistribution. We have one question, asked in the self-completion supplement, that reversed the question direction from that used above and asked respondents whether they agreed that 'ordinary working people' receive their fair share of the nation's wealth (*BES 1997*, question 203a). 48.1% disagreed with this statement and a further 12.75% disagreed strongly. We also asked respondents to place themselves on an eleven-point scale the two poles of which were 'some people feel that government should make much greater efforts to make people's incomes more equal' and 'other people feel that government should be much less concerned about how equal people's incomes are' (*BES 1997*, question 386). 66% of respondents placed themselves to the left of the centre on this scale.

analysis. However, there was a remarkable reversal in 1997 with support for redistribution rising to its highest level in our period. The timing of this rather abrupt change suggests that it cannot be attributed solely to the increase in insecurity and inequality that Hutton describes, since the increase in inequality substantially preceded this swing to the left. Rather, we suspect that the electorate may have become disillusioned with the Thatcherite project and hence tended to reject some of the principle articles of Thatcherite thinking. In other words we should not treat social values as wholly autonomous from the political process. We turn to this in the following chapters.

Conclusions

The data we have reviewed suggest that both Radice's and Hutton's theses have some solid basis, but both are at best partial and one-sided views of social change. They focus on different aspects of reality—what we might call the two faces of Thatcherism—but they both overstate their cases.

On the one hand, Radice was right to argue that Labour's core had indeed declined in size during the Conservatives' eighteen years of government, and he was surely right to say that the broad mass in the middle must be Labour's target group. The New Labour analysis was also right to point out that the aspiring working class (whom we have equated with those who owned or were buying their homes) were less likely than Labour's traditional core in the unions and council estates to think of themselves in class terms. And the New Labour analysis was also right to reject a purely class appeal. However, in these respects New Labour was simply catching up with social patterns that had held true for a long time. The working class has never been homogeneous in its identities, aspirations, or voting behaviour (as the large and aged literature on working-class Conservatism testifies). What has changed is the size of the different fractions, not their existence.

On the other hand, Hutton was right to draw attention to growing inequality and insecurity. However, we doubt if a sense of personal insecurity had really infected the broad mass of middle-income Britain, rendering them marginal and insecure and thereby leading them to support radical policies. Our evidence suggested that most people felt either very confident or fairly confident about their prospects and that there was little difference between these two groups in their attitudes towards left-wing policies. The group that was distinctive in their attitudes was the relatively small number who did not feel confident about the future, among whom the unemployed, state pensioners, and no doubt other people dependent on state benefits would form a large proportion. No one denies the existence of this group, but it does not on its own provide a major challenge to the New Labour analysis. Widespread feelings of insecurity among the aspiring members of the working class would have provided a more serious challenge to Radice's or Lipsey's analysis, but we could find little evidence that such feelings were widespread.

On the other hand, Hutton was right to draw attention to the widespread, and in the 1990s growing, support for redistribution. It does seem to be clear from the BES evidence that support for redistribution had grown by the time of the 1997 general election and that a majority of the electorate espoused egalitarian views. We cannot be sure why there was this increase, but it is fairly clear that individuals' own sense of job insecurity cannot have played a very large role. Hutton's argument that the secure and privileged were themselves alarmed at the growing inequality they saw around them may have some truth. Alternatively, the disillusion with the Conservative government in office that occurred after 1992 may have led to a wider disillusion with the Conservative project. In 1979 Labour failures in office were associated with a swing to the right on major economic issues. In 1997 Conservative failures in office may have contributed to a swing back towards the left. We can think of this as a kind of 'forked tail' effect, in contrast to the 'halo effect' that seemed to surround the Labour Party in 1997.

Whatever the explanation, it is also evident that support for radical values cannot be read off mechanically from social change. In a sense this provides the more profound challenge to the New Labour analysis. The series of BESs have shown that attitudes and values can occasionally change quite abruptly and are not simply the inevitable consequences of structural changes in the social class, trade union, or housing profile of society, all of which tend to change in a slow and gradual fashion. This in turn suggests that values may not be wholly exogenous to the political process. Social change may not constrain the parties quite as much as New Labour supposed.

Appendix 2.1. The Construction of the Measure of Social Group

To construct our profile of social groups we begin by assigning respondents to social classes, using the seven-category Goldthorpe classification (Goldthorpe 1987). Following the procedure we have used in previous election studies (see Heath *et al.* 1985, 1991), we assign economically active and retired respondents to classes on the basis of their current or last main occupation. Economically inactive respondents are assigned to classes on the basis of their partner's occupation (provided their partner is economically active or retired). We then recode the seven classes into four broader groupings: the petite bourgeoisie (Goldthorpe class IV), the salariat (Goldthorpe classes I and II), the routine non-manual class (Goldthorpe class III), and the working class (Goldthorpe classes V, VI, and VII). This yields essentially the same class schema that we have used in our previous publications, with the one exception that we now merge the manual foremen and technicians (Goldthorpe's class V) into the working class.

The salariat is then divided according to whether the respondent is a union member or not, while the working class is subdivided into non-union home-owners, union members (including union members who owned their own homes), and non-union council tenants. Union membership thus overrules housing tenure.

Finally, we assign the unemployed, whatever their class, tenure, or union position, to a separate category. Unemployment thus overrules class, housing tenure, and union member-ship. In assigning respondents to the unemployed category we follow the same procedure as with class membership: economically active respondents are assigned on the basis of whether or not they themselves are unemployed, whereas inactive respondents are assigned on the basis of their partner's employment situation. (We should note that unemployment and retirement are mutually exclusive categories.)

A considerable proportion of respondents (about 10 per cent in most of the BESs) could not be assigned to a social class or to the unemployed and were excluded from the analysis. This runs the risk of selection bias, but in practice the attitudes and voting behaviour of these excluded respondents proves to be very close to the overall distribution.

Table A2.1. Class awareness among different social groups, 1974

Social group	Percentage who describe themselves as			
	Middle-class	Working-class	Neither	N
Petit bourgeois	12	15	73	132
Salariat				
Non-union	28	10	62	282
Union members	30	17	53	118
Routine non-manual	21	22	57	330
Working-class				
Non-union, home-owners	11	27	64	191
Non-union, council tenants	6	37	57	217
Union members	6	42	52	375
Other working-class	12	32	56	114
Unemployed	12	37	51	41
All	15	27	58	1,800

Source: BES Oct. 1974.

Table A2.2. Goodness of fit of ordinal logistic models of attitudes towards redistribution, 1987

Model	Change in −2 log likelihood	Degrees of freedom
Social group model	175.3	8
Security model	38.7	3
Both social group and security model	189.5	11

Source: BES 1987.

3

The Electoral Success of Thatcherism

The institutional success of Thatcherism cannot be doubted. British politics will not be the same again. Quite simply no Labour government could hope to return into public ownership the huge swathes of industry that were privatized between 1979 and 1997. Previous swings of the electoral pendulum had seen, for example, steel nationalized in 1949, denationalized in 1953, renationalized in 1967 and denationalized again in 1988. But despite its hostility to the rail privatizations of 1995–6, Labour has made no attempt to renationalize them now it is in office. The cost would be just too great.

In addition to this institutional legacy, the New Labour modernizers appear to have assumed that Margaret Thatcher also left behind a political legacy that constrains the options open to her successors. Her electoral successes (and the fall of communism in 1989) have effectively led to the triumph of free market ideology: a return to the interventionist strategies pursued by Old Labour are not, the modernizers argue, practically possible or electorally viable. It is widely believed, probably rightly, that the electorate would punish any return to the high tax, high inflation, or high strike regime that is associated in people's minds with the Labour governments of the 1960s and 1970s. That indeed seems to have been the thinking behind a great deal of New Labour policy-making, leading to the commitments to stay within Conservative tax and spending plans (for the first two years of a new Parliament), to maintain most of the Conservatives' trade union legislation, and to leave the privatized industries in private ownership.

When Margaret Thatcher won her first victory in 1979, the evidence suggested rather strongly that the electorate had indeed rejected the corporatist, interventionist strategy of the previous Labour government and that there was a marked swing to the right, particularly on issues like nationalization and wage controls (Särlvik and Crewe 1983). Labour failures in office thus seem to have led to a rejection by large sections of the electorate of an interventionist approach to economic problems. However, the subsequent conversion of the electorate to a Thatcherite view of the world has been questioned by much academic research. Ivor Crewe, for example, has cogently shown that Margaret Thatcher's crusade to change social values failed:

Not since Gladstone has Britain been led by such an opinionated and evangelical Prime Minister as Mrs Thatcher. But there is precious little evidence that she has succeeded. Her missionary preaching has fallen on deaf ears. Let me now pepper you with polling evidence that the public has not been converted to economic Thatcherism—not to its priorities, nor to its economic reasoning, nor to its social values. (Crewe 1988: 35)

On this account Tony Blair and New Labour did not need to feel constrained electorally by the ideological legacy of Thatcherism: the electorate had not become Thatcherite, and therefore there was no electoral need for the Labour Party to adopt so many Thatcherite principles. In this chapter we update Ivor Crewe's work and we ask which, if any, of the key elements of the Thatcherite programme were accepted by the electorate. Were there any areas where the electorate was converted to a Thatcherite view of society, and how constrained are subsequent governments by the ideological legacy of Thatcherism?

But first what do we mean by Thatcherism? Margaret Thatcher herself summed up her approach as 'freedom and free markets, limited government and a strong national defence' (Thatcher 1993: 15). We deal with national defence and related issues in the next chapter and concentrate here on the economic aspects of Thatcherism. There were four crucial aspects of Margaret Thatcher's economic reform programme: the defeat of inflation, the curbing of union power, the privatization of industry (and the introduction of an element of market competition into public services such as health and education that remained in the public sector), and the control of public spending in order to allow cuts in direct taxation (Minford 1988).

While this reform programme has been dignified with the term Thatcherism, the broad outlines were really no more than a traditional laissez-faire or free market programme emphasizing the virtues of competition, individual incentives, and private ownership rather than state regulation, collective provision, and public ownership (Skidelsky 1988).[1] The socialist/laissez-faire or, as it is often termed, the left–right dimension has been the principal ideological terrain over which Conservative and Labour governments have fought throughout the post-war period in Britain (Budge 1999). It consists of a number of interrelated contrasts such as nationalization versus privatization of industry, government intervention and regulation of the economy versus the free market, collective responsibility and provision versus individual responsibility for welfare. Historically the attitudes of both parties and voters on these choices tend to go together and to form reasonably coherent packages, and hence can be thought of as comprising rival ideologies. Voters' positions on this ideological dimension have historically been one of the main predictors of the way they would vote (Heath *et al.* 1991; Sanders 1999). And in general working-class voters, particularly those in Labour's core groupings, have tended to take more left-wing views on the various elements of this programme, while those in the salariat and the petite bourgeoisie have tended to favour the laissez-faire options.

---

[1] Indeed Frank Hahn has suggested that 'Thatcherism as represented by Mrs. Thatcher herself is intellectually without interest. It consists of homilies on the virtues of hard work and ambition and on providing the carrot and the stick' (Hahn 1988: 123).

Table 3.1. Socialist/laissez-faire views among different social groups, 1987

Social group	Percentage who favour			
	Privatization	Stricter trade union laws	Greater spending	N
Petit bourgeois	46	67	35	290
Salariat				
Non-union	44	57	43	752
Union members	30	41	60	210
Routine non-manual	31	57	47	661
Working-class				
Non-union, home-owners	26	51	49	493
Non-union, council tenants	16	49	45	309
Union members	22	33	52	400
Other working-class	33	49	39	83
Unemployed	19	39	57	255
All	30	51	47	3,464

Notes: Since there are slightly different levels of missing data with these three questions, the final column of the table reports min. N.

Source. *BES 1987*.

As Table 3.1 shows, in 1987, at the high point of Thatcherism, there were substantial class differences in attitudes towards privatization, trade union legislation, and tax cuts.[2] Hence the primacy of class as the social basis of party competition, and the primacy of the socialist/laissez-faire dimension as the ideological basis of party competition, have tended to reinforce one another.

As Budge has shown in his analysis of party manifestos, the Conservative and Labour Parties were relatively far apart on this left–right dimension at the time of the 1945 election (although they may well have been even further apart before the war). The gap then narrowed in the 1950s and 1960s as both main parties accepted a Keynesian, interventionist approach to the economy and endorsed Beveridge's outline for the welfare state with universal public services financed through taxation. However, with the increasing development of a global economy, Keynesian strategies to maintain full employment within a single country appeared to become less viable, and the cost of universal welfare provision appeared to threaten the public finances. Indeed, in office even Labour governments were forced to retreat from

[2] On nationalization we used question 36a: 'Just to make sure of your views, are you generally in favour of . . .More nationalization of companies by government, More privatization of companies by government, Or should things be left as they are now?' On trade union legislation we used question 37a: 'Do you think the government should or should not do the following, or doesn't it matter either way? . . . introduce stricter laws to regulate the activities of trade unions?' We combine the response codes 'definitely should' and 'probably should'.On government spending we used question 31: 'Just to clarify your views, suppose the government had to choose between the three options on this card. Which do you think it should choose? Reduce taxes and spend less on health, education and social benefits, keep taxes and spending on these services at the same level as now, increase taxes and spend more on health, education and social benefits.'

their left-wing manifesto commitments, most notably in 1976, when a financial crisis forced the government to call in the International Monetary Fund for assistance, to cut public expenditure, and to instigate deflationary measures.

Once she became leader of the Conservative Party, Margaret Thatcher broke from the post-war consensus on a mixed economy and collective provision and moved the party decisively to the right. In place of the mixed economy, full employment achieved through Keynesian demand management, and high levels of public spending and taxation, she promised privatization of industry, the control of inflation (to be achieved through a monetarist economic policy), and reduction in public expenditure. In this sense her governments simply took up a more extreme position on the socialist/laissez-faire (or left–right) dimension than her recent Conservative predecessors had done.[3] More novel was her government's switch from Keynesian to monetarist economic theory, which had recently become fashionable in right-wing American circles, although in many respects Margaret Thatcher's own emphasis on 'sound money' was little different from pre-war Conservative thinking.

Monetarism quietly disappeared in the later Conservative administrations, but belief in the control of inflation, privatization, tax cuts, and the control of spending on public services continued unabated throughout Margaret Thatcher's years in office. They also remained the guiding principles of John Major's administrations, which succeeded hers. Margaret Thatcher was toppled in the autumn of 1990 not by the electorate but by Conservative MPs. The main reasons for her downfall were probably her overbearing style of leadership, the emerging divisions within the party over Europe, and the disaster of the poll tax (Gibson 1990). She indicated that her chosen successor would be John Major, and he duly defeated his main challengers, Michael Heseltine and Douglas Hurd. The parliamentary party thus in effect voted for a continuation of Thatcherite policies but without the abrasive leadership of Margaret Thatcher herself.

As Budge (1999) shows, the policy positions of the Major administrations were indeed largely continuations of his predecessor's (although there were divisions within the party between the 'consolidators' and the 'radicals' who wanted to continue further down the Thatcherite road). In particular, privatization was continued, as was the policy of cutting taxes and squeezing public expenditure, although tax cuts now had more the appearance of a device to win elections by appealing to voters' self-interest rather than the principled implementation of an overall vision of society. The general thrust of John Major's policies on inflation, taxation, and privatization were thus largely in the mould of Margaret Thatcher's. In none of these areas was there a substantial departure from Thatcherite policy, and, as we shall see later in this chapter, the electorate perceived little difference between the Thatcher and Major administrations in these areas of policy.

---

[3] It should be remembered that Edward Heath had embarked on a very similar programme when he won the 1970 election. As Margaret Thatcher herself wrote: 'When we went into opposition after the 1964 and 1966 defeats, I joined with Ted Heath in rethinking of party policy which seemed to foreshadow much of what we later came to call Thatcherism. "Selsdon Man" won the 1970 election on a radical Conservative manifesto' (Thatcher 1993: 13).

In this chapter, then, we focus on the principal aspects of the Thatcherite economic reform programme. To what extent were the different aspects accepted by the electorate?

Inflation and Unemployment

As Minford (1988) has suggested, the main priority for the first Thatcher administration was the control of the 'evil' of inflation. In a famous speech in 1979 Margaret Thatcher said that 'The evil of inflation is still with us. We are a long way from restoring honest money . . . We should not underestimate the enormity of the task which lies ahead. But little can be achieved without sound money. It is the bedrock of sound government' (quoted in Thatcher 1993: 36). The OPEC oil shock of 1973–4 had been largely responsible for a worldwide rise in inflation, and inflation in the UK had reached 24 per cent early in 1975. The Labour government had had some success in reducing the rate, albeit at the cost of rising unemployment (leading to the famous Tory election poster 'Labour's not working'). At the time of the 1979 election inflation was still running at about 9 per cent and government expenditure was far outstripping revenue. Guided by monetary theory, the Thatcher government raised first interest rates and then taxes in an effort to bring the money supply under control. As Figure 3.1 shows, these policies initially led to an increase in inflation back to the levels it had seen under Labour, but the tactics eventually worked and inflation was brought more or less under control, falling to about 5 per cent by the time of the 1983 election. (But, as Margaret Thatcher herself would have

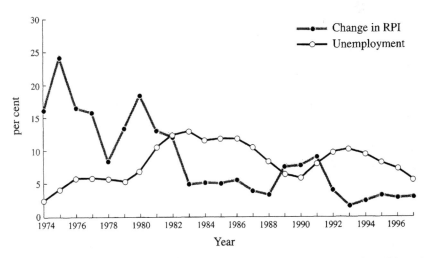

Fig. 3.1. Inflation and unemployment, 1974–1997. RPI is the retail price index (all items). Unemployment is measured according to the ILO (International Labour Office) definition.
Source: Economic Trends (London: HMSO, 1999)

pointed out, the battle against inflation is never lost and the rate of inflation rose once more during the 'Lawson boom' of the late 1980s.)

However, the control of inflation came at a high price in unemployment, which increased rapidly in 1979–80 and remained above its 1979 level throughout almost the whole of the Conservatives' period in office. To be fair, it should be said that unemployment had already been rising under Labour, and also rose in other industrial countries. It would probably have risen anyway even if Labour had remained in power. What the Conservatives' policies probably did was to lead to a larger and faster increase in unemployment than would otherwise have happened.

The electorate, while initially approving the priority given to the control of inflation, rapidly switched to worrying about the new problem of unemployment. This is evident from a question that Gallup has regularly asked: 'Which do you think the government should give greater attention to—trying to curb inflation or trying to reduce unemployment?' As we can see from Table 3.2, initially when inflation was indeed relatively high and unemployment relatively low, the electorate gave greater priority to the battle against inflation, with a clear majority in favour of curbing inflation. But as soon as the battle against inflation appeared won and unemployment began to rise, the electorate focused on unemployment. This is surely not unreasonable: after all, the Gallup question asked about the trade-off and the electorate simply, and appropriately, responded to the different economic situation in which it found itself from 1980 onwards.

Successive Conservative governments, however, did not appear to be as flexible as the electorate. Whether they were working on the basis of erroneous economic theory, or whether they simply did not give unemployment the changed priority that the electorate gave it, we cannot say. But it seems that from 1983 onwards the electorate were out of sympathy with what they perceived to be the Conservatives' priorities. This is confirmed by a series of questions asked in the BESs from 1983 onwards. In the case of unemployment and inflation the respondents were presented with two contrasting statements: 'Getting people back to work should be the

Table 3.2. Attitudes towards inflation and unemployment, 1976–1996

Date	Percentage thinking the government should give greater attention to		
	Curbing inflation	Reducing unemployment	Don't know
Oct. 1976	54	36	10
June 1980	52	42	7
Nov. 1980	30	62	8
May 1983	22	69	9
May 1986	13	81	6
Mar. 1992	21	75	4
Nov. 1992	14	81	5
Mar. 1996	21	71	7

Sources: Crewe (1988: 36); Gallup (1992–6).

Table 3.3. Positions relative to the Conservatives on unemployment and inflation, 1979–1997

Year	Percentage who were			
	Left of Conservatives	Same as Conservatives	Right of Conservatives	Net balance
1979 (inflation)	34	35	31	−3
1979 (unemployment)	46	40	14	−32
1983	70	21	9	−61
1987	65	24	11	−54
1992	66	22	12	−54
1997	65	20	15	−50

Notes: In the 1979 *BES* separate questions were asked about positions on inflation and on unemployment. In other years these were combined in a double-sided question.

Sources: *BES 1979*, min. N = 1,560; *1983*, N = 3,743; *1987*, N = 3,742; *1992*, N = 1,359 (half-sample); *1997*, N = 2,600.

government's top priority'; 'Keeping prices down should be the government's top priority' (*BES 1983*, question 28a).

Respondents were asked to place themselves and the parties on scales running from one statement to the other.[4] From their responses we can determine how many of our respondents placed themselves to the left of the Conservatives, how many to the right, and how many shared the Conservative priorities. (Somewhat analogous questions, but asking about inflation and unemployment separately, were also asked in the 1979 BES.[5])

Table 3.3 shows that, from 1983 onwards, about two-thirds of the electorate placed themselves to the left of the Conservatives, that is they gave greater priority to the control of unemployment than they believed the government at that time did. Only a tenth or so of the electorate placed themselves to the right of the Conservatives. The net balance, that is the percentage lying to the Conservatives' right less the percentage lying to their left, was −61 points in 1983 and, while dropping slightly, remained at a very high level even under John Major in 1992 and 1997.

This contrasts with the position in 1979, when the electorate seemed to be

[4] 7-point scales were used in 1979, 21-point scale in 1983, and 11-point scales subsequently. 'Don't knows' and 'not answereds' are excluded throughout. The 11-point scales were asked only of a half-sample in 1992.

[5] The 1979 survey asked two separate questions, one on unemployment and one on inflation. On unemployment (1979, question 25) respondents were asked whether they agreed that 'the best way to tackle unemployment is to allow private companies to keep more of their profits to create jobs'(the Conservative view) or that 'it is mainly up to the government to tackle unemployment by using tax money to create jobs' (the Labour view). On inflation respondents were asked (1979, question 66) whether 'The government should set firm guidelines for wages and salaries' (reflecting the previous Labour government's approach to the problem of dealing with wage inflation) or 'The government should leave it to employers and trade unions to negotiate wages and salaries alone' (the preferred Conservative approach).

more in sympathy with Tory policy. On inflation the Conservative policy was closely in tune with the views of the average elector, with almost equal proportions lying to the Conservatives' right and to their left, giving a net balance of –3 points. Even at this stage there was less sympathy for Conservative policy on unemployment, with a net balance of –32 points, but the gap was nothing like as large as it subsequently became. The change in the question wording after 1979 severely restricts the comparability of this time series, but there can be little doubt that, once the battle against inflation appeared won and the problems of unemployment loomed larger, the Conservatives' persistence with unchanged policies was not in tune with the priorities of the electorate. Here Ivor Crewe's judgement that the electorate were not converted to a Thatcherite philosophy on the evils of inflation is surely correct.

Trade Union Legislation

The Conservatives' victory in 1979 was probably caused in large part by the industrial discontent of the previous winter. The Labour government's 'social contract', which had been their strategy for industrial peace and control of wage inflation, had collapsed, and stoppages, particularly in the public sector, had caused huge public inconvenience (Shaw 1996 gives a useful account of the social contract and its collapse). Unions and strikes were deeply unpopular.

Previous governments, both Labour and Conservative, had attempted to deal with industrial unrest, but both had failed. Margaret Thatcher proceeded cautiously at first with the Employment Act of 1980, but Norman Tebbit later introduced two Acts which successfully outlawed secondary picketing, which enforced strike ballots, and which gave the courts the power to sequester Union assets for violations of these Acts (the Employment Act of 1982 and the Trade Union Act of 1984). The 1988 Employment Act strengthened the rights of individual trade unionists and the 1990 Employment Act concluded the long process of whittling away at the closed shop. As Hutton has argued:

By 1993 nine major pieces of legislation had been enacted, all but one under Mrs Thatcher's premiership, which transformed British industrial relations. . . . The trade unions' wider powers were systematically reduced in a series of acts, each building on the last. Secondary picketing was banned. Ballots before strike action became mandatory. Individuals not wishing to abide by majority union decisions could violate them freely, without any fear of disciplinary action. Unions could be sued for damages if they went on strike without fulfilling the statutory procedures. Companies were under no obligation to recognise unions, and if they chose to undermine collective bargaining agreements with individual contracts they were free to do so. (Hutton 1995: 92)

In 1984–5 the government was able to resist the year-long miners' strike, in contrast to Edward Heath's government, which had been brought down by the 1974 miners' strike. Industrial unrest declined (probably influenced by the much weaker bargaining position of unions in the labour market as unemployment increased, as well

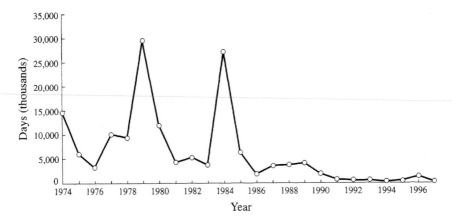

Fig. 3.2. Working days lost, 1974–1997.

Source: Employment Gazette (various years); *Labour Market Trends* (2000)

Table 3.4. Perceptions of trade union power, 1979–1997

Year	Percentage thinking that the trade unions had too much power	
	All respondents	Trade union members
1979	79	69
1983	71	56
1987	46	30
1992	30	16
1997	21	9

Sources: BES 1979, N = 1,849 (541 trade union members); *1983*, N = 3,932 (986 trade union members); *1987*, N = 3,394 (780 trade union members); *1992*, N = 2,842 (473 trade unin members); *1997*, N = 2,685 (416 trade union members).

as by the legislation). As Figure 3.2 shows, strikes have remained at a relatively low level ever since.

The electorate clearly noticed, and approved, of the changes. All the BESs have included a question about trade union power. Respondents were simply asked: 'Do you think that trade unions have too much power or not?'[6] Initially, as Table 3.4 shows, a very large majority of the electorate did indeed feel that the unions were too powerful, and even trade union members shared this view, although not by so large a majority. But as the real world changed, under the impact of Norman Tebbit's reforms and the looser labour market, the animosity towards unions reduced. Whereas in 1979 three-quarters of the electorate felt that unions had too much power, by 1992 less than a third did so.

---

[6] In 1987 this question was asked in the self-completion supplement and respondents were given five agree–disagree response codes. In all the other surveys the question was asked in the main face-to-face interview, and respondents were offered just two responses: 'too much' and 'not too much'.

Table 3.5. Support for stricter trade union laws, 1979–1997

Year	Percentage thinking that the government should introduce stricter trade union laws			
	Should	Doesn't matter either way	Should not	Don't know
1979	70	9	17	4
1983	57	6	31	7
1987	51	12	33	5
1992	36	20	38	7
1997	35	22	39	5

Sources: *BES 1979*, N = 1,856; *1983*, N = 3,941; *1987*, N = 3,808; *1992*, N = 2,843; *1997*, N = 2,686.

The BESs have also regularly asked about trade union legislation. Respondents were asked: 'Do you think the government should or should not . . . introduce stricter trade union laws?' The trends on legislation are very similar to those on trade union power. In 1979 nearly three-quarters of the electorate felt that there should be stricter trade union laws, and there was substantial support for the Conservative position even from trade union members. As on inflation, in 1979 a clear majority of the electorate either agreed with the Conservative position or placed themselves to the right of the Conservatives.[7] Margaret Thatcher was only exaggerating slightly when she said that 'not only did we have huge public support for our policies, but . . . the majority of trade unionists supported them too, because their families were being damaged by strikes which many of them had not voted for and did not want. We were the ones in touch with the popular mood' (1993: 40).

But as the laws did indeed become tougher and the unions were enfeebled, fewer of the electorate felt that stricter laws were called for. Again, then, the electorate responded quite reasonably to the changed circumstances, just as they did in the case of unemployment and inflation. As the laws became stricter, fewer and fewer of the electorate felt that further reforms were necessary.

However, the electorate's view of trade union legislation was probably rather different from their view of measures to deal with unemployment and inflation. In the case of unemployment it is clear that the electorate were out of sympathy with Conservative policies from 1983 onwards and wished to see greater priority given to the reduction of unemployment. But in the case of trade unions it is probably wiser to assume that the electorate approved of the Conservatives' reforms and wished to maintain what had become by 1997 the new status quo. On balance there were more or less equal numbers in 1997 favouring and opposing stricter laws, while the number who were effectively indifferent between the

[7] In the 1979 BES questions 67a, b, c asked for perceptions of party positions as well as for the respondents' own views on trade union legislation. 42.2% placed themselves to the left of the Conservatives, 45.2% in the same place, and 12.6% to the right.

two options had risen to a quarter. In aggregate, this looks like an acceptance of the new institutional arrangements that the Conservatives had engineered. Here, in contrast to unemployment, it does seem that the electorate had no wish to change direction.

The fact, then, that answers to the survey questions shifted in a pro-union direction has to be interpreted in the light of the changes that had been happening in the real world and to which our respondents were reacting. We would not go so far as to argue that Margaret Thatcher had converted the electorate to her own views on union reform; it is much more plausible to suppose that the electorate were already disenchanted by unions before Margaret Thatcher came to power and that this disenchantment was one of the factors that helped her to victory. But the evidence does seem to support New Labour's decision to accept most of the Conservatives' trade union reforms. On this issue at least Margaret Thatcher had been in touch with public opinion.

Privatization

Perhaps the greatest of Margaret Thatcher's institutional changes, and the one that would be hardest for a Labour government to reverse, was the sell-off of publicly owned industries. Much of the programme is well known, although what is perhaps less well known is that privatization actually began in 1977, when the Labour government made a public share offer of their holdings in British Petroleum (BP), reducing the government shareholding from 68.3 to 51 per cent.

Margaret Thatcher proceeded cautiously at first, just as she had done with trade union reform. The first sell-offs were relatively modest, such as tranches of British Aerospace and Cable and Wireless. Thus 5 per cent of BP was sold off in October 1979; 51.6 per cent of British Aerospace was sold in February 1981; the government's 24 per cent shareholding in the British Sugar Corporation was placed with institutional investors in July 1981, and 49.4 per cent of Cable and Wireless was sold in October 1981. The programme picked up momentum during Margaret Thatcher's second administration with the huge privatizations of British Telecom (50.2 per cent sold in November 1984) and British Gas (100 per cent sold in December 1986). The programme peaked in the third Conservative administration, notable landmarks being the sale of British Steel, the ten regional water and sewerage companies, the twelve regional electricity companies, and further tranches of British Gas, BP, and the electricity industries. John Major's administration continued the programme with a final tranche of BT, tranches of National Power and PowerGen, and the dismemberment and sale of British Rail. Figure 3.3 plots the proceeds of these sales over the Conservative years.

How, then, did the electorate respond to these changes? Attitudes towards nationalization and privatization have been asked throughout the BES series. Respondents were asked: 'are you generally in favour of . . . more nationalisation

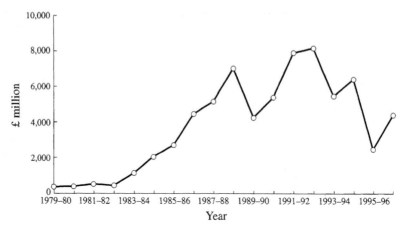

Fig. 3.3. Privatization proceeds, 1979–1997.

Source: Butler and Butler (2000); Her Majesty's Treasury (1998)

Table 3.6. Attitudes to nationalization, 1979–97

Year	Percentage in favour of			
	More nationalization	Same as now	More privatization	Don't know
1979	16	41	38	6
1983	16	35	38	12
1987	17	48	31	5
1992	23	49	23	6
1997	27	55	14	5

Sources: BES 1979, N = 1,863; *1983*, N = 3,937; *1987*, N = 3,761; *1992*, N = 2,784; *1992*, N = 2,685.

of companies by government; more privatisation of companies by government; or—should things be left as they are now?' (*BES 1987*, question 36a).[8]

Table 3.6 shows that in 1979 the balance was clearly right of centre, 38 per cent favouring more privatization against 16 per cent for more nationalization, while 41 per cent actually favoured the then status quo. There was no real change by the end of the first Thatcher administration, reflecting perhaps the relatively modest sell-offs that took place over that period. The balance then gradually shifted over the

---

[8] The question was originally loaded towards nationalization, since that was the institutional context in 1964 when the question was originally designed, the main issue being Labour's plans to nationalize. Thus in the first BES in 1964 respondents were asked: 'Which of the four statements comes closest to what you think should be done, or say if you can't choose any: A lot more industries should be nationalised; Only a few more industries should be nationalised; No more industries should be nationalised, but industries that are now nationalised should stay nationalised; Some of the industries that are now nationalised should become private companies.' To reflect the changed institutional context, in 1987 we adapted the wording to that given in the text above.

next two administrations, and so by 1992 there were equal percentages favouring more nationalization and more privatization, with a larger proportion, virtually half the electorate, favouring the new status quo. In 1997 the balance had tilted towards the left and for the first time since 1979 more people favoured nationalization than favoured privatization.

What this means is that by 1992 there seemed to be broad acceptance of the institutional changes that the Conservative governments had made, just as there had been on trade union reform. The Conservatives had thus taken the electorate with them: the huge programme of privatization was clearly accepted by the electorate in 1992, and there was, on balance, no wish to turn the clock back. In this sense, it is probably correct to suppose that the electorate had moved substantially to the right over the thirteen years of Conservative privatizations. The electorate was effectively content with this crucial part of the Thatcherite project, although they did not want it to go any further. Thus when Margaret Thatcher came into office in 1979 a majority of the electorate were opposed to further privatization. When she left office before the 1992 election, a majority of the electorate were content to leave things in the very different state to which they had now become.

Table 3.7, however, suggests that the Conservatives had always been considerably in advance of the electorate. For example, even in 1979 the net balance was –33 points. In other words there were substantially more electors to the Conservatives' left than there were to their right. The net balance increased further in 1983 and in 1987. However, as Table 3.6 showed, five years later, in 1992, the electorate overall accepted the huge amount of privatization that had actually taken place. In other words, at each election the Conservatives were proposing more privatization than the electorate on balance wanted, but by the end of each Parliament the electorate showed no inclination to reverse the sales that had been accomplished in the life of the Parliament. (The one exception to this is 1997, where rail privatization seems to have been one privatization too far.)

It seems, therefore, that governments do not necessarily need to feel constrained by the electorate's original views. A successful programme of reform can gain public acceptance, even if it goes substantially beyond what the public originally

Table 3.7. Positions relative to the Conservatives on nationalization and privatization, 1979–1997

Year	Percentage who were			
	Left of Conservatives	Same as Conservatives	Right of Conservatives	Net balance
1979	45	43	12	–33
1983	55	29	16	–39
1987	67	22	11	–56
1992	62	21	17	–45
1997	62	19	19	–43

Sources: BES *1979*, min. N = 1,671; *1983*, N = 3,539; *1987*, N = 3,634; *1992*, N = 1,328; *1997*, N = 2,563.

wanted. In this sense Margaret Thatcher's reform programme not only was institutionally successful but also converted the public to her views.

Tax Cuts and Government Spending

Margaret Thatcher saw low rates of direct taxation as a key adjunct to her strategy of increasing competitiveness. High rates of income tax, she argued, acted as disincentives. Perhaps even more important, many on the Conservative side saw tax cuts, and in particular income tax cuts, as an election-winning strategy. This was in tune with the popular academic theory of 'pocketbook voting'—that voters would support whichever party gave them, or was expected to give them, greater material benefits. Margaret Thatcher may or may not have shared this rather materialistic view of voters; in her own speeches she placed great emphasis on the role of incentives and low marginal rates of taxation for stimulating a successful free enterprise economy rather than for bribing voters. For example, she argued that her Chancellor Nigel Lawson's reduction in the top rates of income tax 'provided a huge boost to incentives, particularly for those talented internationally mobile people so essential to economic success' (Thatcher 1993: 674).

New Labour, in contrast, placed more emphasis on the vote-losing aspects of high taxation. Indeed Philip Gould (strategy and polling adviser to Tony Blair since 1994) admitted that tax 'was a fetish for us. We were certain that we had lost elections in the past partly because of tax, and we were determined not to let it happen again this time' (Gould 1998: 7) One of the elections that Gould thought Labour had lost because of tax was the 1992 election, when John Smith had announced at the beginning of the campaign that Labour would increase taxes. However, there is not a shred of evidence that Labour's popularity declined in 1992 in the immediate aftermath of John Smith's shadow budget and the furore over his proposed tax increases (Heath and Clifford 1994). Still, the belief that voters will not tolerate increases in tax has now become a shared article of faith among Conservative and Labour leaders.

At any rate, income tax was cut by Geoffrey Howe in 1979, the basic rate coming down from 33 to 30 per cent, with the highest rate cut from 83 to 60 per cent. Nigel Lawson in 1986 cut the basic rate by a further 1 per cent, and in 1988 cut the basic rate of income tax to 25 per cent and the top rate to 40 per cent. As with the control of inflation, trade union reform, and privatization, New Labour largely accepted these changes. Despite these changes in income taxes, the actual burden of personal taxation changed relatively little. In effect, there was a shift from direct to indirect taxation.

Conservative rhetoric also emphasized the need to cut government expenditure, and there were attempts to limit expenditure on health, education, social services, and defence (but not the police). However, government spending did not change all that much as a proportion of GDP (partly because of the expense of social security payments, entailed by the high rates of unemployment). In the area of taxation and

Table 3.8. Attitudes to taxes and spending, 1979–97

Year	Percentage thinking government should			
	Cut taxes	Leave as they are	Extend services	Don't know
1979	34	25	34	7
1983	22	22	49	6
1987	12	21	61	5
1992	10	20	66	4
1997	7	18	72	3

Source: Gallup, *Political and Economic Index*, quoted by King (1998: 200).

public expenditure Conservative governments thus appear to have been running very fast just in order to remain in the same place, in complete contrast to their highly successful institutional changes on inflation, strikes, and privatization.

As we noted at the beginning of this chapter, the electoral significance of tax cuts and the control of public expenditure is widely debated. Research shows that the electorate consistently expresses a preference for greater government spending rather than tax cuts, and the balance has been steadily shifting towards expenditure. For example, from 1979 onwards Gallup has regularly asked respondents:

People have different views about whether it is more important to reduce taxes or keep up government spending. How about you? Which of these statements comes closest to your view?

Cut taxes, even if this means some reduction in government services, such as health, education and welfare

Things should be left as they are

Government services such as health, education and welfare should be extended, even if it means some increases in taxes.

A similar question, although with slightly different wording, has been asked by the British Social Attitudes (BSA) survey ever since 1983. The BSA trends are shown in Table A3.1. Table 3.8 shows the Gallup time series. The responses are sensitive to the exact question wordings, but the trends from the Gallup and BSA data are the same: the balance shifted more and more in the direction of extending services and away from tax cuts. The Gallup data in particular suggest that the median member of the electorate was reasonably happy with the balance of taxation and spending in 1979, with equal proportions favouring cutting taxes on the one hand and extending services on the other. Since then, the balance shifted much more towards increasing services, and by 1997 over two-thirds of the electorate said that they favoured increasing services.

Since personal taxation had not actually fallen all that much, and since there had been little change overall in government spending as a proportion of GDP, we cannot simply interpret these changes as responses to changes in the real world. However, as we shall see later in this chapter, the electorate certainly believed that

Table 3.9. Positions relative to the Conservatives on taxes and spending, 1979–1997

Year	Percentage who were			
	Left of Conservatives	Same as Conservatives	Right of Conservatives	Net balance
1979	65	23	12	–53
1983	63	20	17	–46
1987	65	22	13	–52
1992	65	23	12	–53
1997	70	17	13	–57

Sources: BES 1979, N = 1,674; *1983*, N = 3,656; *1987*, N = 3,697; *1992*, N = 1,354 (half-sample); *1997*, N = 2,595.

the standard of public provision of health and education had declined, and indeed the proportion of GDP going to education, although not that going to health, had in fact declined under the Tories (Holliday 1997). The electorate may also have been more aware of the reductions in direct taxation than of the increases in indirect taxation. In this sense, then, the electorate may well have been reacting to what they believed to have been the case. We are inclined therefore to interpret these changes in attitudes to taxation and government spending as essentially similar to those in attitudes to unemployment and inflation.

As we might expect, then, the electorate were predominantly to the left of the Conservatives on taxation and spending, just as they were on inflation and unemployment. Interestingly, however, Table 3.9 shows that they appear to have been out of sympathy with Conservative policy even in 1979 and that there has been little subsequent change from election to election.

How are we to interpret these patterns? Is the electorate really willing to pay higher taxes, or at any rate to vote for a party that promises to increase taxes? This question goes to the heart of debates about the motivation of electors. Electors may feel that higher taxes and greater public spending are indeed what the country needs, but in the privacy of the polling booth they may decide to follow their own self-interest. Governments that have increased taxes have rarely been rewarded by a grateful electorate—witness Labour's defeat in 1970 or the Conservatives' defeat in 1997. However, the tax increases in the late 1960s and in 1993 occurred because the governments (or their immediate predecessors) had failed to keep control of the public finances, not because they were trying to raise the standard of public services. Indeed, these tax increases were accompanied by cuts in public services. The historical record does not, then, tell us what would happen if taxes were raised in a principled attempt to improve services rather than in a desperate attempt to balance the books.

However, politicians might be right to approach the survey evidence with a certain degree of scepticism. First, there is evidence from the surveys that most respondents feel that the higher taxes to fund increased spending should be paid by other people—the wealthy—not by themselves. Secondly, even when the surveys ask whether people would be prepared to pay the higher taxes themselves, there is a problem in obtaining adequate validation of the survey measures. Wherever they can, survey researchers like to obtain some external evidence to demonstrate that the respondents' answers to their survey questions have what is termed 'validity'. For example, we can check respondents' reports on their turnout in an election against the official returns. These checks show that about 4 per cent of respondents claim to have voted where the official marked-up registers show that they had not in fact been to the polling booth (Swaddle and Heath 1989). This discrepancy between the respondents' reports and their actual behaviour probably reflects what is called a 'social desirability bias': turning out to vote is felt to be one's civic duty, and so people are reluctant to admit that they failed in their duty. It is also quite likely that a social desirability bias affects answers to the questions on government spending: people may feel that they should consider what is good for the country as a whole, rather than their individual self-interest, and this may incline respondents to say that they would be prepared to pay higher taxes in pursuit of socially desirable goals such as improved public services.

Unfortunately, in assessing the responses to the question on tax cuts and government spending, we have no external evidence comparable to the marked-up registers from the polling booths that could serve as a yardstick for judging the scale of the social desirability bias. Validity is essentially a technical version of the saying 'The proof of the pudding is in the eating', but it is in the nature of this particular pudding that it is rarely placed on the menu. For example, a referendum on tax cuts and government spending would provide a cogent yardstick for measuring the validity of our questions and would enable us to check respondents' answers against their actual behaviour.

There has in fact been one such referendum. In February 1999 the Milton Keynes Council held a local referendum in which electors were given three options: option 1 provided for a 15 per cent increase in council tax and some extra spending on local services; option 2, which was recommended by the council, provided for a 9.8 per cent increase in council tax; option 3 was for a 5 per cent increase in council tax together with some reductions in council spending on services such as education. Option 3 was more or less in line with the central Labour government's recommendations for the national increase in council tax.

The context of these proposals was that a unitary Milton Keynes authority had just been established in 1997 but the council felt that it had not received its proper share of the Buckinghamshire County Council budget when the new unitary council was established. It had therefore been in some financial difficulties and had had to draw on its reserves and various one-off measures. It did not feel that it could stay within the government's guidelines without cutting services. In addition, the central government had the power to 'cap' council tax bills if they felt that local councils were making excessive increases in tax. The Milton Keynes Council felt that, if a local referendum supported an increase in tax greater than that recommended by the government, the risk of being capped would be reduced. (For full details see Snelson 1999.)

A total of 149,241 ballot papers were issued to local electors. 66,647 people voted (by post and by telephone), giving turnout of 44.7 per cent—substantially higher than in recent local council elections in Milton Keynes. 23.6 per cent voted for option 1, 46.35 per cent voted for option 2, and 30.05 per cent voted for option 3. As the *Guardian* newspaper concluded:

Who said electorates only vote for tax increases in opinion polls but change heart once inside the voting booth? Many cynics and most strategists in the two major parties. Hence Labour's promise to refrain from any income tax increase for an entire parliament. Yet last year the Scottish people voted to give their parliament the right to add up to 3p in the pound to income tax. Now Milton Keynes has gone one step further to vote for a 10 per cent increase in their local council tax. (*Guardian*, 24 February 1999)

From a social-scientific point of view the Milton Keynes referendum is not decisive. Ideally what we would have liked is a contemporary opinion poll of the local electorate to check whether the survey responses tallied with the actual votes cast. It is possible that in a survey even more people would have opted for increased spending. The result does not rule out the presence of a social desirability bias in survey responses. But at the very least the Milton Keynes result shows that a majority of electors were prepared, under certain circumstances, to pay higher taxes themselves in order to maintain services. Governments may not be quite as constrained by the electorate's desire for lower taxes as they had imagined.

In addition, governments may also be constrained by the electorate's desire, as demonstrated by the Milton Keynes voters, to maintain the quality of public services. Voters may punish governments for their failures to run public services such as health and education effectively, and in that sense governments may be constrained in the extent to which they can cut taxes. Voters may not vote for a party which promises to increase taxes, but they may take their votes away from a party that they feel does not spend enough on public services. This can be shown by the experience of the Conservative government between 1992 and 1997.

Taxes and Spending 1992–1997

Throughout the 1992–7 Parliament there was a widespread belief among Conservative politicians that cutting taxes was a powerful way to win votes. This had seemed to be vindicated by their unexpected victory in 1992, and there was considerable pressure on the government from their backbenchers to repeat the trick in 1997. As it happens the 1991–2 tax cuts were unsustainable, and taxes had to be raised the year after the election in an effort to balance the books. But this did not stop the Conservatives from attempting to repeat the trick in the run-up to the 1997 election, and they reduced the basic rate of income tax by 1p in the autumn of 1995 and again by the same amount in the autumn of 1996. To make financial room for these tax cuts, the government squeezed the public sector. In a sense this was the direct obverse of the traditional left-wing (and Liberal Democrat) policy of increasing taxes in order to fund better public services. It was hardly an outstanding success in the sense that it failed to stave off the Conservatives' worst defeat this century.

Of course, the mere fact that the strategy failed to save the Conservatives from electoral disaster does not on its own prove that it did not work. It may have helped them avoid an even worse disaster. We do, however, have some evidence from the BES that may shed some light on the role that tax cuts and the squeeze on public spending may have played in the 1997 outcome. The BESs have regularly asked respondents how they think various aspects of the economy, public services, and the like have changed since the previous election. Specifically on the economic side we asked about prices, unemployment, taxes, and the standard of living, and on the social side about crime, and the quality of the health and education services. We asked our respondents:

> Since the last general election in ..., would you say that unemployment has increased or fallen?
> What about prices?
> Taxes?
> The standard of the health and social services?
> Crime?
> The quality of education?
> The general standard of living?
> Your own standard of living?

> (*BES 1997*, questions 309, 311, 313, 315, 317, 319, 321, 323, 324)

Table 3.10 shows the percentage who had a positive view of the changes, that is who thought that unemployment, crime, or taxes had fallen, and the proportions who thought that standards in the NHS, the quality of education, and the standard of living had risen. We compare the figures from the 1997 survey with those obtained in the 1992 survey and in the 1994 round of the panel study. The table shows that in general the electorate were rather reluctant to express positive views about the changes, and were particularly negative about the economy and crime. Of course

Table 3.10. Perceived changes in the economy and welfare state, 1992–1997

Issue	Percentage expressing positive views of changes in			
	1992	1994	1997	Change 1992–7
Unemployment	4	29	44	+40
Prices	4	—	5	+1
Taxes	38	12	12	−26
General standard of living	30	10	33	+3
Own standard of living	34	15	31	−3
Standards of NHS	44	13	11	−33
Crime	6	—	9	+3
Quality of education	36	8	14	−22

Sources: *BES 1992*, min. N = 2,843; *BEPS 1994*, min. N = 1854; *BES 1997*, min. N = 2,728.

we must remember that the 1992 election was called at a time when the economy was deep in recession, and so the absence of positive views on the economy at that time is not altogether surprising.

On the economic side, the electorate overall clearly recognized that there had been some recovery during the second half of the electoral cycle, with big increases in the proportion who took positive views of the changes in unemployment. Thus in 1992 only 4 per cent of respondents felt that unemployment had fallen over the previous Parliament (reflecting accurately the recession at the time of the 1992 election). By 1994, 29 per cent of our respondents felt that unemployment had fallen, and in 1997 the percentage had increased to 44 per cent (again accurately reflecting the trends in the official figures for unemployment). The electorate, then, seemed to have been well informed about the state of unemployment.

In other areas of the economy, however, there was little recovery. It is particularly notable that the reductions in income tax in the run-up to the 1997 general election did not really register with the electorate. Thus 38 per cent of the electorate had felt in 1992 that taxes had fallen, but in 1997 this was down to a meagre 12 per cent. The Labour Party had of course made a great deal of play in their election campaigning about the Conservative government's twenty-two tax increases (although it was never very clear exactly what the twenty-two increases were) and argued that the Conservatives' promises on tax were no longer to be trusted. And indeed the Conservative government had been forced to make substantial increases in indirect taxation such as VAT in order to balance the books in 1993. The electorate seems to have accepted the Labour version.

Turning to the non-economic side, the most striking feature of Table 3.10 is that, over the electoral cycle as a whole, there was a substantial net decline in the proportion expressing positive views of changes in the quality of health and social services. The figure for health was down from 44 per cent in 1992 to 11 per cent in 1997, while on the quality of education positive views were down from 36 to 14 per cent. Judgements of standards and quality are inevitably rather subjective, and it is hard to know how much these negative perceptions were due to people's real experiences of health and education, how much they were caused by the vocal criticisms of Conservative government policy expressed by the British Medical Association and the health professionals, and how far they were brought about by the squeeze on expenditure as opposed to the government's institutional reforms, which tried to introduce a degree of competition into the provision of health and education. The government itself presented evidence that real spending on health and education had increased, but again the electorate does not seem to have accepted the government's version.

Moreover, we need to remember that Table 3.10 simply reports whether the respondents felt that taxes, standards, and so on had changed, and does not on its own tell us whether they attributed responsibility for the changes, if any, to the government. Governments tend to try to take the credit for all improvements that occur over their period of office, and they like to blame external events or circumstances outside their control for all the failures. Teachers and doctors in particular received

Table 3.11. Attribution of responsibility to the government, 1997

Issue	Percentage thinking that the changes were mainly the result of government policies		
	All respondents	Respondents with positive views of the changes	Respondents with negative views of the changes
Unemployment	65	58	74
Prices	67	65	67
Taxes	89	87	91
General standard of living	72	63	89
Own standard of living	44	26	65
Standards of NHS	87	78	91
Crime	51	53	52
Quality of education	78	73	84

Source: BES 1997, min. N for column 1 = 2,486.

a great deal of criticism from the government. To find out where the electorate attributed responsibility we asked a supplementary to each of the questions on their perceptions of the changes in unemployment and so on. We asked our respondents: 'Do you think this is mainly the result of the Conservative government's policies or, for some other reason?'

Table 3.11 shows that our respondents differentiated rather clearly between different areas. For example, almost 90 per cent felt that the government was responsible for whatever changes had taken place in taxes—which seems entirely realistic since it is indeed the government that decides on taxes. In contrast, only 44 per cent felt that the government could take responsibility for changes in their own individual standard of living. Not unreasonably this seems to be regarded much more as a matter of individual responsibility, although it is perhaps surprising that as many as 44 per cent do actually accord the government collective responsibility (perhaps another sign that the electorate was not really converted to Thatcherite values). Standards in the health service and the quality of education come very close to taxes, being seen as government responsibilities with 87 per cent and 78 per cent respectively saying that the changes had been mainly the result of the Conservative government's policies.

In between the two extremes of taxes and one's own standard of living come the other economic issues of unemployment, inflation, and the general standard of living. Crime comes close to individuals' own standard of living, with 51 per cent attributing responsibility to the government. This in itself is quite interesting, given the debates between the parties over the question of the causes of crime: did crime have social causes, such as unemployment, or was it more a consequence of the moral failings of individuals and their families? This time the electorate seems to accept the Conservative version.

However, are people more likely to blame the government when they perceive that things have gone badly than they are to give them credit when things have gone well? To answer this, we can break down the figures for government responsibility according to whether the respondent had a positive or a negative view of the changes that had taken place. Thus in column 2 of Table 3.11 we look at respondents who had positive views of the changes in unemployment and so on (that is, of respondents who felt that unemployment had fallen). In column 3 we look at respondents who took negative views of the changes. We can think of these two columns as indicating respondents' willingness to give the government credit for positive changes and the blame for negative changes.

What we find is a very interesting asymmetry: in general people seem more likely to blame the government for what has deteriorated than to give them credit for what has improved. This is most noticeable in the case of one's own standard of living: thus 65 per cent of people who felt that their own standard of living had deteriorated held the government accountable, whereas only 26 per cent of those who felt their standard of living had improved felt that the improvements were the result of government policies. There is little, if any, asymmetry on crime, taxes, and inflation, but quite marked asymmetry on unemployment and the general standard of living.

These figures suggest that the perceived improvements in unemployment and the standard of living (both general and individual) may not have brought the government as much credit as the figures in Table 3.10 would at first have suggested; conversely, the perceived deterioration in the quality of the NHS will have brought the government a great deal of blame.

To assess the overall impact of the changes in the economy and so on reported in Table 3.10, we need to weight the changes by the attributions of responsibility given in Table 3.11. That is, we weight improvements by the figures in the 'credit' column (column 2 of Table 3.11) and we weight the deteriorations by the figures in the 'blame' column (column 3 of Table 3.11). The detailed calculations are shown in Table A3.2. What they tell us is that an extra 23 per cent of the electorate gave the government credit for the fall in employment in 1997. But this was more than matched by the extra 24 per cent who blamed the government for the rise in taxes, an extra 30 per cent who blamed the government for the perceived fall in the quality of the NHS, and an extra 18 per cent who blamed the government for the fall in the standards of education.[9] As it happens, then, the government managed to achieve the worst of both worlds, with blame for tax increases together with blame for perceived deterioration in health and education.

Moreover, these attributions of blame for deterioration in the standards of the NHS and education do seem to be closely connected with whether respondents defected from the Conservatives or not: people who defected were more likely to believe that standards had fallen, and to blame the government, than were people

---

[9] These calculations assume that attributions of credit–blame have remained constant over time. This is quite a strong assumption but cannot be checked since we did not ask the relevant question in 1992.

who remained loyal to the Conservatives. (For technical details see Appendix 3.2.)

Conclusions

The picture that has emerged from this analysis is that the electorate accepted the Conservative reforms on privatization and trade union legislation and that, on balance, the electorate showed at the end of Margaret Thatcher's period in office little desire to put the clock back. In these two respects Margaret Thatcher not only changed social institutions but won public backing for the changes. On both these topics it should be noted that the electorate was very hostile to collectivism in 1979, with 79 per cent feeling that the unions had too much power in 1979 and only 16 per cent favouring extensions of nationalization (which were being proposed in Labour's 1979 manifesto). Margaret Thatcher recognized the public mood and took advantage of it. New Labour has probably been right to recognize it too.

But in two other respects Margaret Thatcher failed to carry the country with her: once the problem of inflation was apparently solved, the electorate wanted unemployment tackled and did not appear to accept the Thatcherite philosophy. And the electorate showed no enthusiasm for the Thatcherite philosophy of reduced government spending on public services. Whether or not survey questions on willingness to pay higher taxes are to be trusted, it would be wise for governments to recognize that the public do regard both taxes and public services as unambiguously government responsibilities and that the public is prepared to punish governments that do not maintain the quality of public health and education services, which they have been elected to run. If governments can find ways of maintaining public services without raising taxes, the electorate would surely appreciate it. But it was unwise of the Conservatives to assume that income tax cuts would automatically bring electoral benefits, regardless of the costs in deteriorating public services (or at least in perceived deterioration).

But these data also suggest that a political party does not need to be closely in tune with the electorate's policy preferences in order to win an election (or indeed to win several elections). On some of these issues Conservative policies seemed to have been consistently out of line with the public's sentiments. On privatization, for example, even back in 1987, when Margaret Thatcher won a landslide victory, about two-thirds of the electorate placed themselves to the left of the Conservatives; on unemployment and inflation it was again two-thirds, and similarly on taxation and government spending. To be sure, in 1979 the electorate did seem to be more in tune with Thatcherite policy. But once Thatcherism got into its stride, the electorate seemed to have, overall, rather little sympathy with many elements of it. We agree with Ivor Crewe that Margaret Thatcher's crusade to change social values failed, although we would add the caveat that the electorate did accept many of her reforms once they were working successfully.

Margaret Thatcher herself believed that the electorate did support her policies. 'In education, housing and health the common themes of my policies were the extension of choice . . . This was the application of a philosophy not just an administrative programme . . . this approach was successful: it was also popular. Indeed, if it had not been the Conservative Party would have lost the three general elections it fought under my leadership, not won them' (Thatcher 1993: 618). She was probably right about housing and about her policy of council house sales, but she was wrong about education and health, and most spectacularly about the poll tax.

So how did the Conservatives manage to win the three elections of 1983, 1987, and 1992 despite being out of line with public opinion? One part of the answer is simply that the Labour Party obligingly pursued policies that were even more out of line with public sentiment. As we shall see in Chapter 5, on the issues which seem to have had most weight with the electorate Conservative policies were more popular than those of the Labour Party. On this view, it was not so much the popularity of Conservative policies that won Margaret Thatcher her three victories as the even greater unpopularity of Labour policies.

The crucial point is that the electoral marketplace is far from a free market. There are very substantial effective barriers to entry for new competitors in the market (arising *inter alia* from the first-past-the-post electoral system) and so the market much more closely resembles an oligopoly or cartel rather than a perfectly competitive market. In a perfectly competitive marketplace it might well be true that the parties are constrained by the electorate's preferences. In such a marketplace Margaret Thatcher might well have been right to draw the conclusion that her electoral success demonstrated the popularity of her policies. But in the kind of oligopolistic marketplace that British general elections resemble, no such comforting conclusion can be drawn.

Appendix 3.1. Supplementary Tables

Table A3.1. Attitudes to taxes and spending, 1979–1997

Year	Percentage thinking government should			
	Reduce taxes	Keep taxes and spending as they are now	Increase spending	Don't know
1983	9	54	32	5
1987	3	42	50	4
1993	5	28	63	4
1997	3	24	70	4

Sources: BSA 1983, N = 1,716; *1987*, N = 2,762; *1993*, N = 2,941; *BES 1997*, N = 2,729.

Table A3.2. The effects of government record, 1992–1997

Issue	Change 1992–7	Blame–credit weightings	Net effect
Unemployment	+39.7	0.582	+23.1
Prices	+0.1	0.650	+0.1
Taxes	−26.2	0.910	−23.8
General standard of living	+2.6	0.632	+1.6
Own standard of living	−2.8	0.646	−1.8
Standards of NHS	−33.4	0.913	−30.5
Crime	+2.7	0.528	+1.4
Quality of education	−21.9	0.839	−18.4

Sources: BES 1992 and 1997.

Appendix 3.2. Logistic Regression of Credit, Blame, and Vote-Switching

Our aim in this appendix is to explore the relation between defections from the Conservatives in 1997 and voters' attributions of credit and blame for the government's record. We restrict ourselves to the 'risk set' of respondents who reported that they had voted Conservative in 1992. Our 'outcome' measure is whether respondents voted for the Conservatives again in 1997 or defected to one of the other parties. The outcome measure is therefore a binary variable, coded 1 if the respondent reported a Conservative vote in 1997 and 0 otherwise. We conduct a separate analysis of non-voting in 1997.

Our main explanatory variables are the respondents' perception of the changes in unemployment, prices, and so on, as described in the text, together with their attributions of credit and blame. We rescore the perceptions of change so that 'no change' scores 0, increases have positive scores, and decreases have negative scores.

We use two different data sets for the analysis. First we have the 1997 BES, which forms the basis of the tables reported in the text. Use of the 1997 BES means that respondents' reports of how they voted in 1992 are 5 years old, and these retrospective reports are well known to be biased, with respondents tending to bring their reports into line with their current behaviour. Our hope is that these biases will affect the distribution of the reports but not the relationship between these reports and the other variables of interest. We can check on this, to some extent, by comparing the results with those in the panel. The 1992–7 BEPS has the advantage of contemporary reports of the way in which the respondents voted in 1992, although it does have other disadvantages such as attrition. Moreover, the questions on attributions of credit and blame were asked only in the BES and not in the BEPS, and we cannot therefore replicate this aspect of the analysis. We can, however, replicate the relationship between defection and perceptions of the changes in the economy and welfare state.

Since we have a binary dependent variable, we carry out a set of logistic regression models. The results are shown in Table A3.3. In the first model we report the results from the panel study. Here we see that there were significant associations between a Conservative vote in 1997 and perceptions of changes in unemployment, the NHS, and the general standard of living. The signs associated with the significant parameter estimates are all in the expected

Table A3.3. Logistic regressions of defections to other parties from the Conservatives, 1992–1997 (parameter estimates)

	Model 1	Model 2	Model 3
Constant	0.75 (0.19)	0.80 (0.20)	1.11 (0.15)
Change in:			
Unemployment	−0.32 (0.11)	−0.46 (0.08)	−0.49 (0.11)
Prices	−0.10 (0.10)	−0.07 (0.11)	−0.15 (0.11)
Taxes	−0.17 (0.11)	−0.20 (0.09)	−0.22 (0.10)
NHS	0.32 (0.11)	0.37 (0.09)	0.42 (0.09)
Crime	0.14 (0.10)	0.12 (0.09)	−0.18 (0.11)
Education	0.17 (0.13)	0.29 (0.09)	0.34 (0.10)
Respondent's standard of living	0.05 (0.14)	0.12 (0.10)	0.44 (0.18)
General standard of living	0.38 (0.16)	0.62 (0.11)	0.52 (0.13)
Model improvement	71.1	246.2	278.1
N	558	934	934

Notes: Sample consists of respondents who reported that they had voted Conservative in 1992. Standard errors are given in brackets. The wording for the perception of changes was identical in the two sources, except that the panel asked respondents about changes in prices.

Sources: Column 1, *BEPS 1992–7*; columns 2 and 3, *BES 1997*.

direction, with perceptions of increases in unemployment being associated with defections from the Conservatives and perceptions of increases in the quality of the NHS and the general standard of living having positive signs and thus being associated with continued support for the Conservatives.

In the second model we report the results from the analysis of the same items in the BES. The pattern of signs and statistical significance is almost identical. The strongest associations are again with unemployment, the NHS, and the general standard of living. The parameter estimates for taxes and education are also significant in this model. Most of the parameter estimates are also quite close in magnitude to their values in model 1, giving us considerable confidence in the results. It is also comforting that in these first two models the changes for which respondents were relatively less likely to attribute responsibility to the government, notably crime and one's own standard of living, were nowhere near significant.

In the third analysis we then weight these perceptions of change by the respondents' attributions of responsibility. If the respondent felt that the change was not the government's responsibility, the item is weighted by 0. If the respondent felt that the change was the government's responsibility, the item is weighted by 1. In effect then, we disregard perceptions of change where the respondent felt that the change in question was due to factors other than the government, and these perceptions are treated in the same way as 'no change' responses.

The resulting model provides a significant improvement in fit over model 2. However, the pattern of the parameter estimates is largely unchanged. Most of the estimates increase slightly in magnitude, but the only notable change is for one's own standard of living. This now becomes statistically significant and rivals the general standard of living in importance. Again, this is a reassuring result and supports the interpretation that the minor role of perceived changes in one's own standard of living in models 1 and 2 is largely because these changes are felt by many people not to be a result of government policies.

We have explored further models which include controls for the image of the

Table A3.4. Logistic regressions of defections into abstention from the Conservatives, 1992–1997 (parameter estimates)

	Model 1	Model 2	Model 3
Constant	1.49 (0.26)	1.50 (0.26)	1.77 (0.20)
Change in:			
Unemployment	−0.08 (0.15)	−0.37 (0.11)	−0.36 (0.15)
Prices	−0.47 (0.14)	−0.17 (0.16)	−0.25 (0.15)
Taxes	0.03 (0.17)	−0.04 (0.12)	−0.03 (0.13)
NHS	0.13 (0.16)	0.07 (0.11)	0.16 (0.12)
Crime	0.12 (0.14)	0.18 (0.11)	0.00 (0.15)
Education	0.09 (0.17)	0.23 (0.12)	0.32 (0.14)
Respondent's standard of living	0.15 (0.20)	−0.04 (0.13)	0.42 (0.22)
General standard of living	−0.05 (0.23)	0.41 (0.15)	0.30 (0.18)
Model improvement	20.73	44.2	58.31
N	446	733	733

Notes: See Table A3.1.

Sources: Column 1, *BEPS 1992–7*; columns 2 and 3, *BES 1997*.

Conservative government. Inclusion of such controls does not alter the story in any material way.

We have also conducted a separate analysis of Conservative abstention, and the results are shown in Table A3.4. Abstention is only weakly related to these perceptions of change and attributions of responsibility. This is in line with previous research that suggests that abstention is largely due to circumstantial factors. However, the general pattern is similar to that for vote-switching with significant estimates in model 3 for unemployment and education.

4

Margaret Thatcher's Nationalism

While Margaret Thatcher's radical, laissez-faire approach to the economy has been her most important political legacy, she was also distinctive for her style of British nationalism. As Peregrine Worsthorne memorably described her approach, Thatcherism meant 'bitter-tasting market economics sweetened and rendered palatable by great creamy dollops of nationalistic custard' (quoted in Crewe 1988: 32). Did her nationalism have a popularity that compensated for the unpopularity of her economic policies that we saw in Chapter 3?

The main ingredients in this nationalistic custard were strong defence, especially the retention of Britain's independent nuclear deterrent and the deployment of American cruise missiles in Britain, a willingness to take on Argentina and recover the Falklands, and the vigorous pursuit of what she took to be British interests in Europe. On the home front Margaret Thatcher's nationalism took the form of advocacy of unionism and an opposition to devolution and the possible break-up of the United Kingdom.

As on the economic front, under John Major the Conservatives largely followed the same path as Margaret Thatcher. He displayed the same nationalistic instincts, with success in the Gulf War and opposition to devolution for Scotland and Wales. On Europe the Conservatives under John Major were notoriously divided, but the ascendant right wing of the party placed an emphasis on maintaining British sovereignty and became increasingly hostile to further European integration, and in particular were opposed to joining the common European currency.

The Conservatives' brand of nationalism is what James Kellas has called the official nationalism of the British state (Kellas 1991). It is clearly very different from the nationalism of Scottish, Welsh, or Irish separatists, which aims at securing a measure of home rule for the Scottish, Welsh, or Irish nations. It is also different from the nationalism of extremist parties such as the British National Party in Britain, Jean-Marie LePen's Front National in France, or the Vlaams Blok in Belgium. These are parties which are in essence racist, and while some writers have detected signs of racism in Margaret Thatcher's language (notably when she spoke about the danger of being 'swamped' by immigrants in a speech before the 1979 election), the Conservative Party has generally distanced itself from overt racism, notably with Edward Heath's sacking of Enoch Powell after his 'river of blood' speech in 1968. Racism has little to do with the official nationalism that is our main focus in this chapter. In essence, we see Margaret Thatcher's nationalism as a British nationalism that sought to maintain internally the integrity of the British state and externally to fight for British interests, whether through economic means as in Europe or by military means as in the Falklands. It contrasts with a cosmopolitanism or internationalism that would essentially cede some national sovereignty to international bodies such as the United Nations or European Union.

Even more so than her radical free market approach, Margaret Thatcher's nationalism was in sharp contrast with the pro-Europeanism of her immediate predecessor, Edward Heath, and was in many ways a return to an earlier strand of Conservatism such as Churchill's. Her instincts had a great deal in common with the emphasis on the British empire that had marked pre-war Conservative governments and with the even earlier Conservative emphasis on unionism and opposition to home rule for Ireland. The Conservative Party (historically the Conservative and Unionist Party) has a long tradition of distinctive policies on Ireland and on the empire, and its recent approach to constitutional issues in Scotland, Wales, and the EU is in the same spirit.[1]

While nationalism of this sort, like free market ideology, has long-standing historical antecedents on the Conservative side, there is no necessary connection between nationalism and laissez-faire traditions. The connection is a contingent one. In the nineteenth century it was the Liberals rather than the Conservatives who were the free trade party, while it was protectionism that went with Conservative support for the empire. More recently the Labour and Conservative Parties have played leapfrog over Europe, Labour being the Eurosceptic party in 1983 and the Conservatives taking their turn at Euroscepticism in 1997.

Among both voters and political elites what we find is that British nationalist sentiments tend to be only weakly related to socialist or free enterprise ideology (see Heath *et al.* 1999*b*; Evans 1999; Brown *et al.* 1998, ch. 4). British nationalism and free market ideology sometimes go together, as they did in Margaret Thatcher's own political philosophy, but many peoples' views on British nationalism cannot be read off directly from their views on the classic socialist–free enterprise debates. As we shall see when we look at support for the Referendum Party later in this chapter, it is possible to hold extreme nationalist views on Europe while being quite moderate on the traditional socialist/laissez-faire dimension. Since parties in Britain are fundamentally based on groupings of like-minded people on the socialist/laissez-faire dimension, a cross-cutting issue like Europe is quite likely to be divisive—just as nuclear disarmament, another cross-cutting issue, divided the Labour Party in the early 1980s.

To be sure, there are other issues, such as questions of abortion, divorce, and the death penalty, which cross-cut the left–right dimension even more powerfully. Some writers such as Stuart Hall have talked of Margaret Thatcher's authoritarian

---

[1] However, we should also note the important exceptions to this general stance, notably Margaret Thatcher's support for majority Black African rule in the then Southern Rhodesia and her establishment of the Anglo-Irish Agreement which was bitterly opposed by some unionists.

populism, and it is almost certainly correct to argue that in some respects she was indeed authoritarian, for example on the death penalty or control of immigration or family values (Hall 1979). But these are issues which British political parties have historically kept out of party politics. They are ones on which a free vote is typically permitted in the House of Commons, and hence their potential for creating internal party divisions has been rendered relatively harmless. In this respect British political parties overtly operate a cartel, conspiring together to keep certain options from being available to the electorate.

Europe, devolution, and nuclear disarmament, however, are issues which fall half-way between moral questions such as abortion and the death penalty and the economic questions of the left–right domain. Hence it is not so easy to keep them out of party politics. But nor is it easy to keep them within the conventional party framework, as the Referendum Party demonstrated. We shall have rather little to say, then, about moral and family values, since they played relatively little part in the recent story of British electoral politics.[2] Our main concern in this chapter is with the issues that are related to British nationalism. In particular, is British nationalism, as Peregrine Worsthorne implied, some kind of balance for the bitter-tasting economic medicine that, as Chapter 3 has shown, was not especially palatable to the British electorate?

It has not been usual to think of nuclear weapons, devolution, and Europe as belonging to a distinct ideological domain from that of the bread and butter economic issues of British politics. As a preliminary, therefore, it may be useful to show that they do in fact share some important similarities that mark them out from the economic issues. One way of demonstrating this is by looking at the social basis of attitudes towards these three issues. This is done in Table 4.1, which compares attitudes towards the retention of Britain's independent nuclear deterrent, towards devolution for Scotland, and towards European integration.[3] (As with the corresponding table in Chapter 3, we look at the basis of attitudes at the height of Thatcherism in 1987.) The social basis of these three issues can then be compared with that of the classic left–right issues that we discussed in Chapter 3.

Table 4.1 does not show nearly such a strong social basis for the electorate's attitudes towards Britain's independent nuclear deterrent, European integration, or Scottish devolution as we found with privatization, trade union reform, and unemployment. And the basis is not a straightforward class one. The main contrast is not between the middle class and the working class but between the old middle class of the petite bourgeoisie on the one hand and the new middle class of salaried trade unionists on the other. Thus what we find is that members of the petite bourgeoisie were in general the most likely to support keeping Britain's independent deterrent, to oppose devolution and to oppose further European integration. It is

---

[2] The one notable exception was John Major's ill-fated 'back to basics' campaign, which was widely interpreted as support for traditional family values, and which exposed many of his own MPs to ridicule when it was found that their own private extramarital activities accorded rather poorly with the traditional family values they advocated publicly to the electorate.

[3] The questions used are V27 and V41a from the BES 1987, and question V29a from the BES 1992.

Table 4.1. British nationalist attitudes among different social groups, 1987–1992

Social group	Percentage who favour			
	Independent nuclear weapons	No devolution	Reducing EU powers	N
Petit bourgeois	36	43	44	197
Salariat				
Non-union	32	31	44	605
Union members	23	16	33	157
Routine non-manual	31	25	43	494
Working-class				
Non-union, home-owners	33	32	42	412
Non-union, council tenants	34	37	37	213
Union members	35	36	36	216
Other working-class	39	31	49	68
Unemployed	32	31	32	191
All	32	31	40	2,553

Notes: Question on devolution asked only in England and Scotland. Question on EU integration asked only in 1992; all other questions are from the 1987 *BES*. The Ns are for 1992, which is the smaller sample.

Sources: *BES 1987, 1992*.

probably no accident that Margaret Thatcher herself came from petite bourgeois social origins.

The salaried trade unionists, whom we can think of as the new left, are then the group that is most prone to adopt internationalist positions on these three issues, being the most likely to oppose the retention of Britain's independent nuclear deterrent (and in fact the most likely to support unilateral disarmament, although rather few actually go this far, most preferring Britain to keep nuclear weapons as part of a Western defence system). They are also the most likely to support devolution for Scotland, and they are one of the groups most favourable, or strictly speaking least unfavourable, towards Europe.[4]

The crucial opposition, then, although not such a clear-cut opposition as on the left–right dimension, is to be found between the old and new middle classes. Moreover, we can see that on defence and devolution the various working-class groups are actually closer to the old middle class than they are to the new middle class. In this sense it is right to see these aspects of British nationalism as populist. Margaret Thatcher's instincts were populist in the sense that they were in tune not so much with the politically informed members of the 'chattering classes' and of the highly educated but reached down across social class boundaries to the less educated and to the working class. In this respect British nationalist sentiments are very

---

[4] On this latter issue it is worth noting that relatively high proportions of the working-class groups expressed no opinion on Europe, and so the low percentages in the working class of people favouring reduction in EC powers does not imply high percentages favouring integration. The salaried trade unionists were in fact the group most likely to favour European integration.

different from the classic left–right ideological divisions that continue, as we saw in Chapter 3, to have a class basis.

We now turn to more detailed consideration of defence, devolution, and Europe and ask how Thatcherite the electorate was on these issues, and how constrained the parties were by her legacy.

Defence

As Worsthorne implied, Margaret Thatcher's creamy dollops of nationalistic custard may have had much more appeal to the electorate than some aspects of her bitter-tasting economics, especially the monetarist medicine that she liberally doled out to control the evil of inflation. This was certainly true of her intervention and eventual victory in the Falklands in 1982, which gave an immediate boost to her personal popularity and where three-quarters of the electorate approved of her handling of the war.

The role that the 1982 Falklands War played in the 1983 general election victory has been much debated and cannot be unequivocally proved one way or the other. Success in the Falklands almost certainly led to an immediate increase in government popularity, which then gradually decayed, but it may also have had an indirect effect, helping to establish Margaret Thatcher as a forceful and effective leader, as 'the iron lady'. At all events, it is undeniable that both the attempt to regain the Falklands and of course the eventual victory were highly popular with the electorate and that there was very little sympathy for the pacifism that was displayed by some of the Labour backbenchers.

Aside from the Falklands, defence played a major role in the 1983 and 1987 elections, when Labour considerately adopted a policy of unilateral nuclear disarmament—a policy that was highly unpopular with the electorate and a gift to Margaret Thatcher, fresh from triumph in the Falklands. To measure attitudes towards nuclear weapons we asked a question that had originally been asked in the first BESs of 1964 and 1966 but had then been dropped and was only reinstated in 1987:

Which of these statements comes closest to what you yourself feel should be done? If you don't have an opinion just say so.

  Britain should keep her own nuclear weapons, independent of other countries,
  Britain should have nuclear weapons only as part of a Western defence system,
  Britain should have nothing to do with nuclear weapons under any circumstances.

(*BES 1997*, question 331)

While this question was inevitably designed to capture the debates of the 1960s, we can think of the first of these statements as representing support for an independent nuclear deterrent, while the third captures the unilateral disarmament position that played an important role in Labour's internal politics both in the late 1950s and again in the mid-1980s.

Table 4.2. Attitudes towards nuclear weapons, 1966–1997

Year	Percentage feeling Britain should			
	Keep independent nuclear weapons	Keep as part of Western defence	Have no nuclear weapons	Don't know
1966	33	47	14	7
1987	32	46	16	7
1992	34	46	13	7
1997	28	46	24	3

Sources: BES 1966, N = 1,871; *1987*, N = 3,816; *1992*, N = 2,850; *1997*, N = 2,730.

Table 4.2 shows that there was little support for Labour's unilateralist position either in the 1960s, when the Campaign for Nuclear Disarmament had been at its height, or in the late 1980s and 1990s. However, the table also suggests that the electorate as a whole was not all that enthusiastic about Britain's independent nuclear deterrent either and tended towards a somewhat internationalist position, with the modal response being 'have nuclear weapons only as part of a Western defence system'. In this respect, as with the items belonging to the left–right domain, Margaret Thatcher was considerably more extreme than the electorate as a whole. (It is not strictly appropriate to talk of 'right' or 'left' in the context of the British nationalist domain, although the term 'extreme' has overtones that may not be altogether warranted.) The electorate was also less than enthusiastic about her policy of siting American nuclear Cruise missiles in Britain; for example, the 1983 BES shows that more people thought they made Britain less safe (48 per cent) than made Britain safe (37 per cent).

We can also see some hints, somewhat similar to those in chapter 3, that the electorate may have moved somewhat to the 'left', with the proportion favouring the independent deterrent declining to 28 per cent in 1997. Again, as with privatization, this could reflect changes in the real world, as the end of the cold war (in which Margaret Thatcher's own belligerent stance had perhaps played a role) had changed the international context and perhaps led people to feel that an independent deterrent was less necessary for Britain's defence.

We can check the support for the Conservatives' position more precisely from a scale, analogous in construction to the ones we used in the last chapter, which located respondents and parties on the issue of nuclear weapons. We presented respondents with the two contrasting statements: 'We should get rid of all nuclear weapons in Britain without delay'; 'We should increase nuclear weapons in Britain without delay' (*BES 1983*, question 24a). The question was dropped in 1997, as the issue had virtually vanished from political debate with the Labour Party's abandonment of nuclear disarmament and the end of the cold war. But in the years when it played a significant role in debate, notably 1983 and 1987, the perceived Conservative position was considerably more 'hawkish' than that of the average voter, although it must be said that they were not quite as out of touch with ordinary voters as the Labour

Table 4.3. Positions relative to the Conservatives on nuclear weapons, 1983–92

Year	Percentage who were			
	Left of Conservatives	Same as Conservatives	Right of Conservatives	Net balance
1983	72	20	8	–64
1987	67	24	9	–58
1992	57	29	14	–43

Notes: 21-point scale in 1983 and 11-point scales thereafter. 'Don't knows' and 'not answered' are excluded throughout.

Sources: *BES 1983*, N = 3,691; *1987*, N = 3,742; *BEPS 1992*, N = 1,359.

Party was at that time.[5] Interestingly, Table 4.3 also suggests that the Conservatives had come more into line with public opinion in 1992. We suspect that this was largely because issues like the deployment of Cruise missiles had become so much less salient: the party no longer emphasized the issue in their campaigning, and they were therefore seen by the electorate to be more dovelike than before.

There are clear similarities between defence and economic issues like privatization. Margaret Thatcher knew what she wanted, and she did not feel at all constrained by public opinion. Public opinion was probably the last thing that she had on her mind when she made her decision to send the task force to recapture the Falklands. In the event her judgement was proved right, and the British success in the Falklands transformed the standing both of herself and of her government. Nor was she inclined to change her mind on Cruise missiles because public opinion was hostile. Her 'victory' in the cold war could also be seen as vindicating her policy of taking a tough stance on nuclear weapons, although it is doubtful if it brought anything like the political popularity that the Falklands victory had done. The situation was perhaps more akin to her government's success against inflation: once the problem was dealt with, new issues came to the forefront of the political agenda and past successes became a waning asset.

Devolution for Scotland and Wales

Defence, then, has clear parallels with the economic issues: Margaret Thatcher had a clear idea of where she wanted to take the country, her views were well in advance of the electorate's, but she had some notable successes to justify her course of action. On devolution, however, she was largely fighting a rearguard action, trying

[5] Also note that the 1992 American question on defence spending had 45.2% to the left of the Conservatives, 28.3% the same and 26.5% to the right, a net balance of –18.7. This puts a rather different complexion on things, with a majority of the electorate either agreeing with the Tory position or taking a more right-wing view. The difference from the nuclear question probably reflects specific issues such as Cruise missiles which as we have noted above were relatively unpopular with the electorate.

to maintain the status quo. The Conservative Party had been relatively favourable to devolution under Edward Heath, but Margaret Thatcher's nationalism led the party back towards traditional Tory unionism.

Under Margaret Thatcher the Conservatives saw their share of the vote in Scotland (and Wales) steadily decline, falling from 31.4 per cent in 1979 to 17.5 per cent in 1997 in Scotland, and from 32.2 per cent to 19.6 per cent in Wales. In contrast the Conservatives won a much larger share of the vote in England, and maintained that share over time. Margaret Thatcher herself recognized that 'Some part of this unpopularity [in 1992] must be attributed to the national question on which the Tories are seen as an English party and on which I myself was apparently seen as a quintessential English figure. . . . The Tory party is not of course an English party but a Unionist one' (Thatcher 1993: 624).

In many ways Scottish and Welsh nationalisms are the obverse of Margaret Thatcher's British nationalism. Scottish and Welsh nationalisms are paradigm cases of the kind of nationalist movement that Ernest Gellner had in mind. Gellner defined nationalism as

primarily a political principle, which holds that the political and the national unit should be congruent. Nationalism as a sentiment, or as a movement, can best be defined in terms of this principle. Nationalist sentiment is the feeling of anger aroused by the violation of the principle, or the feeling of satisfaction aroused by its fulfilment. A nationalist movement is one actuated by a sentiment of this kind. (Gellner 1983: 1)

As Gellner pointed out, this definition assumes concepts of state and of nation. The former he defined in Weberian terms, as that agency within society which possesses the monopoly of legitimate violence. The latter is defined in subjective terms as groups which share a common culture and which recognize each other as belonging to the same nation. The nation is not a legal concept, therefore, but a cultural one, and this is particularly important in Britain, where we may all share legal British citizenship but may have differing notions of whether we belong to a Scottish, Irish, Welsh, or indeed English nation. Margaret Thatcher in contrast believed that the nation and the state were already coterminous, and that there was a single British nation rather than separate English, Scottish, or Welsh nations.

In this respect she was increasingly out of touch with Scottish and Welsh opinion and there was a general increase in support for some degree of home rule both in Scotland and in Wales over the period of Conservative ascendancy. Questions were asked about support for constitutional change in the Scottish and Welsh election studies of 1979, and broadly comparable questions were asked in the 1997 surveys.[6] In 1997 we asked

[6] In Wales, the 1979 survey asked: 'Forgetting the referendum for a moment, which option from this card comes closest to your view of the ideal form of government for Wales? No change, keeping the government of Wales much as it is now; An assembly as proposed at the referendum; A stronger assembly with its own law-making powers like the one proposed for Scotland; Complete self-government for Wales.' A somewhat similar question was asked in Scotland in the 1979 SES: 'Here are a number of suggestions which have been made about different ways of governing Scotland. Can you tell me which one comes closest to your own view? No devolution or Scottish Assembly of any sort; Have Scottish

Table 4.4. Attitudes towards devolution in Scotland, Wales, and England, 1979–1997

Year	Percentage favouring			
	Independence	Elected assembly	No change	Don't know
Scotland				
1979	8	60	29	3
1992	23	50	24	3
1997	26	51	18	5
Wales				
1979	5	19	71	5
1997	12	43	37	7
England				
1987	6	48	35	10
1992	12	53	29	6
1997	14	55	23	8

Sources: SES 1979, N = 652; 1992, N = 955; 1997, N = 876; WES 1979, N = 858; WRS 1997, N = 686; BES 1979, N = 1,619; 1992, N = 2,384; 1997, N = 2,545.

An issue in Scotland is the question of an elected Parliament—a special parliament for Scotland dealing with Scottish affairs. Which of these statements comes closest to your view . . .

> Scotland should become independent, separate from the UK and the European Union
> Scotland should become independent, separate from the UK but part of the European Union
> Scotland should remain part of the UK, with its own elected parliament which has some taxation powers,
> Scotland should remain part of the UK, with its own elected parliament which has no taxation powers
> Scotland should remain part of the UK without an elected parliament.

(BES 1997, question 420)

An analogous question was asked in the 1997 Welsh Referendum Study (WRS), which was conducted immediately after the referendum held on 18 September 1997. (The WRS surveyed a much larger number of respondents in Wales than did the regular BES and is thus a more reliable source of evidence on Welsh opinion.)

To obtain some comparability over the years we group responses together and simply distinguish preferences for independence, some form of elected assembly or parliament, or no change. Table 4.4 shows the trends between 1979 and 1997. In both cases opinion moved away from the 'no change' option, quite markedly so in the case of Wales, where the percentage favouring the status quo fell by half. These

Committees of the House of Commons come up to Scotland for their meetings; An elected Scottish Assembly which would handle some Scottish affairs and would be responsible to Parliament at Westminster; A Scottish Parliament which would handle most Scottish affairs, including many economic affairs, leaving the Westminster Parliament responsible only for defence, foreign policy and international economic policy; A completely independent Scotland with a Scottish Parliament.'

changes were of course closely in line with the change in the outcomes of the 1979 and 1997 referendums, where in Wales support for devolution went up from 20.9 per cent to 50.3 per cent and in Scotland support on the principle of a Scottish Parliament increased from 51.6 per cent to 74.3 per cent.

These trends are perhaps the first ones we have seen that cannot be linked more or less directly with changes in the institutions and the world around the voters. On unemployment, trade unions, privatization, and even defence, the world had rather clearly been changing, and we can interpret the trends in opinion as being, at least in part, reactions to these changes: trade unions became weaker, so voters saw less need for further legislation; the cold war ended and so voters saw less need for strong defence.

But in Wales and Scotland there had been no major institutional changes to which the voter might have been reacting, although Margaret Thatcher's centraliz- ing tendencies, especially with regard to local government, may have increased Scottish and Welsh feelings that they were becoming progressively more subord- inate to Westminster. While this centralism may well have played some role, our own feeling is that to a large extent the changes in Scottish and Welsh opinion were of a relatively autonomous kind, reflecting a waning of the unifying force of British identity. Margaret Thatcher's British nationalism was largely rooted in the past and in an older generation that remembered the British empire, the Battle of Britain, and the Second World War. These had been shared endeavours that gave a real meaning to Britishness, but as they receded into memory the symbolic identity of being British lost some of its power and thus provided room, particularly among younger generations, for new forms of identity to take root. We do find quite a strong age dif- ference in support for these nationalisms, British, Scottish, and Welsh. To be sure age differences could be caused either by life-cycle effects or by generational effects, but in the present case we strongly incline to the generational interpretation (For further details,see Heath and Kellas 1998; Heath and Park 1997; Heath *et al.* 1999*b*.)

At all events, under Margaret Thatcher and John Major the Conservatives were out of line with Scottish opinion in particular. We asked our respondents in Scotland what they perceived to be the policies of the main parties, using the same items on devolution that we described above. From this information we can construct mea- sures of how many voters were to the left or right of the parties, using the term 'right' to signify a unionist position and 'left' to signify positions that were opposed to unionism. As in the case of nuclear defence, the terms 'left' and 'right' are not strictly appropriate, Labour being the most left-wing party on economic issues whereas on devolution they were of course outflanked by the Scottish National Party.

A net balance of 50 points or more has been a regular occurrence for the Conservatives under Margaret Thatcher, but the net balance of –67 points in 1997 is the highest that we have seen, and considerably higher than anything else under John Major. In principle, this lack of popularity for Conservative policies on the Union might have been compensated by enthusiasm in England for the version of

Table 4.5. Positions relative to the Conservatives on devolution in Scotland, 1979–1997

Percentage who were	1979	1992	1997
Left of Conservatives	59	58	73
Same as Conservatives	31	36	21
Right of Conservatives	10	5	6
Net balance	–49	–53	–67

Note: Samples: residents in Scotland.

Sources: *SES 1979*, N = 563; *1992*, N = 879; *1997*, N = 758.

official British nationalism that the Conservatives espoused. However, Table 4.4 casts some doubt on this. True, there was slightly less support for Scottish devolution among respondents living in England, but even in England there was majority support for the Labour proposal to grant an elected Parliament to Scotland. The Conservatives would not have been quite as out of line with public opinion in England as they were in Scotland, but they were none the less out of line.

On Europe, however, the Conservatives were in line with English public opinion, and it is to this that we now turn.

Europe

Throughout the last quarter-century Europe has been one of the most divisive issues within British political parties. Originally it was the Labour Party that was most divided internally over Europe, and Europe played a major part in the split in 1981 that led to the formation of the SDP (Crewe and King 1995). But the roles were reversed in the 1990s, when the Conservative Party was almost torn apart by Europe.

The Conservatives had been relatively united in favour of Europe when the Conservative prime minister Edward Heath had taken Britain into the European Community in 1973 (after two previous unsuccessful bids by Harold Macmillan and Harold Wilson). At the time Labour was deeply divided, and Tony Benn, one of the leading anti-Europeans on the Labour side, suggested that there should be a referendum on membership of the EC. The Labour leader Harold Wilson came to see the tactical advantages for Labour in a referendum when he succeeded Heath as prime minister in 1974, and he called a referendum in 1975. Wilson preserved the unity of the party by allowing MPs who opposed membership to campaign for a 'no' vote, but he himself joined with the Liberals and many Conservatives in recommending 'yes'. This cross-party alliance demonstrated rather clearly the crosscutting nature of the European question. The 1975 referendum gave a comfortable majority (67.2 per cent) for remaining in Europe, and the issue for a short time disappeared from the political agenda.

When she became prime minister in 1979, Margaret Thatcher vigorously pursued British interests within Europe, notably over British budget contributions, and she successfully renegotiated the terms. Early in her premiership the European agenda was dominated by progress towards the single European market, and this was compatible with Margaret Thatcher's own competitive, free trade ethos. While the aggressive pursuit of national interests within Europe already distinguished the Conservatives' approach in 1983, their Euroscepticism was much less marked than it became subsequently. Thus the 1983 Conservative manifesto recorded the government's success in renegotiating Britain's financial contribution to the Community budget, but concluded that 'Withdrawal [from the European Community] would be a catastrophe for this country . . . It would be a fateful step towards isolation.' The main issue on the European agenda at that time was the creation of a single European market, an issue with which free-marketeers within the Conservative Party could feel at ease.

However, problems later emerged over the exchange rate mechanism (ERM). Margaret Thatcher's instincts were against it, largely because it limited British freedom of manœuvre and perhaps because it threatened British sovereignty, while her chancellor, Nigel Lawson, was in favour of joining the ERM. A protracted dispute followed between the chancellor and the prime minister, eventually culminating in the resignation of Nigel Lawson in 1989. Her next chancellor, John Major, did take Britain into the ERM, but at too high a level of sterling, with eventual disastrous consequences.

The internal divisions within the Conservative Party caused by the ERM were, however, relatively minor compared with the conflicts generated by the Maastricht Treaty of 1991 and the proposed move towards a single currency and European monetary union (EMU). While there were a variety of technical issues at stake, the principle lying behind them concerned national sovereignty. In effect, many Conservatives believed that the Maastricht Treaty entailed moves towards a federal Europe, limiting Britain's national freedom for manoeuvre and infringing national sovereignty. In this way, Maastricht came to symbolize more fundamental concerns over British nationalism and national sovereignty.

The Maastricht Treaty had been signed before the 1992 election, but the business of ratifying the treaty in Parliament dominated the 1992–3 session. The ratification of the Maastricht Treaty exposed these divisions within the Conservatives, with twenty-seven Tories voting against the government. Even after ratification, the issue of Europe did not go away. The whip was withdrawn from eight rebels (joined by a ninth) who abstained over the European Communities (Finance) Bill in November 1994, and the later years of the Parliament were dominated by debates about currency union. In October 1995 Sir James Goldsmith announced the formation of a Referendum Party, which campaigned on the single issue of a referendum to allow the British public to decide whether the United Kingdom should 'be part of a federal Europe'.

The formation of the Referendum Party gave further publicity to Euroscepticism. In his anxiety to appease his Eurosceptic MPs (and ministers) and thus maintain his narrow majority in Parliament, John Major edged slowly closer to a Eurosceptic position, eventually promising to hold a referendum on membership of the EMU if a future Conservative government decided to join the single currency. This promise did not, however, preserve party unity in the way that he might have hoped, and for the rest of the Parliament the prime minister was under pressure to rule out membership of the single European currency.

Over the 1992–7 Parliament as a whole, then, there were vocal disputes within the Conservative Party over Europe, and the party seemed to move in a Eurosceptic direction. The public too seemed to share these concerns over greater European integration (as indeed did the public in many other European countries). Respondents to the BESs have regularly been asked whether they favoured Britain's continued membership of Europe. A majority of the British electorate voted in favour of membership of the European Community in 1975, and this is reflected in the figures for the 1974 BES, with 54 per cent in favour of membership. From then on, support for membership gradually increased until it reached 72 per cent in 1992. Over this period the British seemed to accept their membership of the European Community (later Union), although Eurobarometer data indicate that they still showed less enthusiasm than did most of the other member countries. However, after the Maastricht Treaty support for membership went into decline. By 1997 it had fallen back to 58 per cent, little different from the figure a quarter of a century earlier.

While there was still a majority among the electorate in favour of membership, opposition to further European integration was widespread. To tap these general attitudes towards European integration we asked our respondents:

Do you think that Britain's long-term policy should be . . .

> to leave the European Community,
> to stay in the EC and try to reduce its powers,
> to leave things as they are,
> to stay in the EC and try to increase its powers,
> or, to work for the formation of a single European government?

(BES 1997, question 327)

On the more specific question of a common currency we asked:

And here are three statements about the future of the pound in the European Community. Which one comes closest to your view?

> Replace the pound by a single currency
> Use both the pound and a new European currency in Britain
> Keep the pound as the only currency for Britain.

(BES 1997, question 328)

On the first question, as we can see from Table 4.6, the electorate was fairly evenly divided between Eurosceptics and Europhiles in 1992, but by 1997 the balance had shifted decisively in a Eurosceptic direction, with 66 per cent wanting either to leave outright or to reduce EC powers. While the proportion who actually favoured withdrawal remained low, there were increasing proportions who wanted to reduce EC powers. Similarly, the electorate was distinctly Eurosceptic, and becoming

Table 4.6. Euroscepticism in the electorate, 1992–1997

Percentage agreeing that Britain should	1992	1997
Leave the EC	10	17
Reduce its powers	35	43
Leave as is	13	15
Increase its powers	29	10
Work for single European government	11	7
Don't know	4	8
Replace pound	25	16
Have both ecu and pound	24	20
Only have pound	49	60
Don't know	3	4

Sources: BES 1992, N = 2,852; *1997*, N = 2,688.

more so, on the issue of a single currency. As we can see, even in 1992 keeping the pound on its own was the most popular of the three options, and by 1997 opinion had hardened somewhat.

Euroscepticism, therefore, was on the increase over the course of the 1992–7 Parliament, in contrast to the trends over the Thatcher years. Indeed, it seems to have been the only major issue where popular sentiment was moving in a hawkish direction. It is difficult to tell whether the Conservative and Referendum Party rhetoric (aided by the tabloids) influenced the electorate, or the parties were emboldened by the electorate's increasing Euroscepticism, or both parties and electorate were simply reacting in the same way to the institutional changes in Europe. The fact that rather similar changes had been happening among the electorates in other European countries does, however, suggest that it was the institutional change that was primary rather than specifically British political developments.[7]

So in a sense this shift in a hawkish direction is simply another example of the British electorate's reactions to the changing nature of the real institutions around them which we saw in Chapter 3. The difference is that on the economic front the institutional changes themselves had been moving in a free enterprise direction, whereas in Europe they had been moving in a federal direction. For once Margaret Thatcher had proved relatively unable to move institutions in the way she wanted, and John Major was even less successful. On Europe, then, the Conservatives were essentially opposing change (just as they were on devolution), whereas on the economy they had been promoting change.

The Conservatives were, however, for once closely in tune with public opinion. We can again check the support for the Conservatives' position more precisely from a scale, analogous to those we have used earlier, which located respondents and parties' positions on European integration. We presented respondents with the two contrasting statements: 'Britain should do all it can to unite fully with the European

---

[7] Flickinger (1995) gives a useful account of possible models of change and the evidence in favour of each of them. See also Franklin *et al.* (1994).

Table 4.7. Positions relative to the Conservatives on European integration, 1979–1997

Year	Percentage who were			
	Left of Conservatives	Same as Conservatives	Right of Conservatives	Net balance
1979	15	27	59	+44
1992	33	27	39	+6
1997	37	23	40	+3

Sources: *BES 1979*, N = 1,863, *1992*, N = 1,318 (half-sample); *1997*, N = 2,502.

Community'; 'Britain should do all it can to protect its independence from the European Community' *(BES 1997*, question 413).

What we find is that, unlike every other issue that we have considered, there were more electors to the 'right' of the Conservatives than there were to the 'left'. This was especially true in 1979, when the net balance was 44 points.[8] However, it is doubtful if at this stage the electorate had a clear idea about Margaret Thatcher's own views on Europe, and they were probably basing their judgements more on the behaviour of previous Conservative governments, notably Edward Heath's. At any rate the increase in Euroscepticism in the Conservative Party brought them closer to the electorate over time, and by the 1990s the Conservatives were quite close to the electorate, although still seen as slightly less Eurosceptic than the respondents themselves.

Europe thus seems to be the issue on which the Conservatives were closest to the electorate. However, it is unlikely that it was a substantial vote-winner for them. As Evans (1998) has cogently shown, the disunity of the Conservative Party meant that they gave out confusing signals to the electorate. On the one hand, the more Europhile members of the electorate perceived the Conservatives as being rather Eurosceptic, but on the other hand Eurosceptic members of the electorate thought that the party was relatively Europhile. Disunity therefore meant that there was no clear idea among voters about where the party really stood, and the public disagreements between the Europhile and Eurosceptic wings of the party meant that voters from all parts of the spectrum had some grounds for suspicion about the party's real intentions (or lack of real intentions).

Paradoxically, moreover, getting too close to the centre of the political spectrum can also have its dangers. It leaves huge areas of political territory for other parties to invade, most notably in 1997 the Referendum Party, which outflanked the Conservatives on their right.

---

[8] The question asked in 1979 was: 'Some people think that Britain should be more willing to go along with the economic policies of other countries in the Common Market. Others think that we should be readier to oppose Commom Market economic policies. Which comes closest to your view? If you don't have an opinion on this just say so.' There were seven response codes ranging from very strongly in favour of the first statement to very strongly in favour of the second.

The Referendum Party

The Referendum Party was a creation of the late Sir James Goldsmith, who announced his intention to form it on 27 October 1994, although it formally came into being a year later in October 1995. It campaigned on the single issue of a Referendum on Europe. It eventually published the text of its proposed question for a referendum, namely:

Do you want the United Kingdom to be part of a Federal Europe
or
Do you want the United Kingdom to return to an association of sovereign nations that are part of a common trading market?

Sir James emphasized that his proposed referendum was quite different from those proposed by the Labour and Conservative Parties, which dealt only with the question of joining the single European currency. His was a more fundamental question about the preservation of British sovereignty, and as such it fits rather well into our characterization of British nationalism.

The Referendum Party contested 547 constituencies, standing aside only in seats where the incumbent MP had given explicit support for a referendum. They won a total of 3.0 per cent of the vote in those constituencies where they stood (while the UK Independence Party secured a further 1.1 per cent of the vote in the 194 constituencies where it stood). But the Referendum Party's appeal tailed off noticeably north of the Scottish border, where it secured an average of just 1.1 per cent of the vote. As Curtice and Steed (1997) have suggested, this may reflect the rather higher level of support for Europe in Scotland, or perhaps a feeling that the party's anti-Europeanism was a form of English rather than British nationalism. Its best performances were all in those parts of England where Euroscepticism was at its highest, especially the south of England and East Anglia. It tended to do particularly well in constituencies with a large agricultural or elderly population, the former doubtless a reflection of the controversy surrounding European agricultural policy and the European response to BSE.

It was widely assumed at the time that these votes had largely come from the Conservatives and that they might have cost the Tories as many as nineteen seats. (In nineteen seats the Referendum Party share of the vote was larger than the winning party's majority over the Conservatives.) But it was also a rather remarkable phenomenon in its own right. The conventional wisdom is that foreign affairs play little role in domestic voting behaviour and that bread-and-butter issues from the left–right domain tend to be decisive. But at face value it seems that nearly 3 per cent of voters did vote on the basis of a single non-economic issue.

Voters for the Referendum Party were not a cross-section of the electorate. They were predominantly people who had voted Conservative in 1992 and, to a lesser extent, for the Liberal Democrats. Hardly anyone who had voted Labour in 1992 supported Goldsmith's party. 60 per cent of Referendum Party voters had voted

Table 4.8. Positions of Referendum Party voters relative to the Conservatives, 1997

Issue	Percentage who were			
	More Europhile or left-wing	Same as Conservatives	More Eurosceptic or right-wing	Net balance
European integration	9	15	77	+68
Taxes and spending	76	12	12	−64
Privatization	63	22	15	−48
Unemployment	65	19	17	−48

Note: Sample: responders who reported a vote for the Referendum Party in 1997.

Source: *BES 1997*, N = 44.

Conservative in 1992, about 20 per cent had voted Liberal Democrat, and only about 10 per cent had supported Labour (for further details, see Heath *et al.* 1998).

These figures do not on their own allow us to conclude that Referendum Party voters felt that the Conservatives were insufficiently Eurosceptic. In theory it could have been a more generalized expression of discontent among people with right-wing sympathies on a broader range of issues who were disillusioned by the Tories' poor performance in office but who could not bring themselves to vote Labour. In other words, was the Referendum Party a vehicle for generalized right-wing disillusion with the Tories or a specific protest about their European policies?

We can answer these questions rather easily by looking at the positions of Referendum Party voters relative to the Conservative Party. This is done in Table 4.8.[9] What we find is that Referendum Party voters were in fact highly distinctive in their attitudes towards Europe. Europe stands out as the only issue on which these voters placed themselves to the right of the Conservative Party with three-quarters taking a more Eurosceptic position than the Conservative Party. But they show no sign of being right-wing on the economic issues of the left–right domain. They were not right-wing ideologues. Their vote does not therefore appear to have been either part of a specifically right-wing revolt against the Conservatives or a general diffuse protest vote. Moreover, we have data from the 1992–7 panel study which shows that their ideological profile was long-standing and pre-dated the formation of the Referendum Party (see Heath *et al.* 1998). In attitudinal research there is always the worry that people may bring their attitudes into line with their political behaviour rather than the other way round. However, the panel shows rather clearly that these particular voters brought their party choice into line with their previous beliefs. There can be little doubt about the nature of the causal process. The fact that these voters chose the Referendum Party rather than any of the other options open to them was undoubtedly a result of their specific concerns about Europe.

[9] With so few voters for the Referendum Party in our sample, we have to be particularly cautious in drawing conclusions. However, we can replicate our results with the 1992–7 panel, and although of course the numbers there are also very low, the pattern of results is almost identical. See Table A4.1.

This demonstrates once again how Europe cross-cuts the economic issues. There is little congruence between the attitudes of Referendum Party voters to Europe and their attitudes to the standard economic issues. Their extreme Euroscepticism was not matched by an extreme free market ideology. So in these other respects they were not perhaps natural Tories anyway. Even back in 1992 their support for the Tories might have been conditional on the Tories' Euroscepticism rather than on their general free market policies.

It is a nice paradox, therefore, that the one issue on which the Conservatives were apparently most in tune with public opinion was the one on which they most clearly lost votes—outflanked by the Referendum Party.

Conclusions

Margaret Thatcher's nationalism embraced a range of issues: strong defence, vigorous pursuit of British interests in Europe, the protection of British sovereignty, and the maintenance of the Union. While there has been some tradition in Britain for this sort of British nationalism being associated with right-wing views on economic issues, the economic and the nationalist domains are both conceptually and empirically distinct from one another. They cross-cut each other, and attitudes towards defence, Europe, or devolution cannot be read off from one's views on free enterprise or nationalization.

It is this cross-cutting character that gives the nationalist domain its potential to divide the parties. True, there are long-standing divisions within parties on economic issues, with differences between the 'wets' and the 'drys' under Margaret Thatcher on the Conservative side and between the 'hard left' and the 'soft left' on the Labour side. And these differences have been long-standing bases of internal power struggles within the parties. But defence, Europe, and to a lesser extent devolution have shown an even greater potential to threaten party cohesion. Europe in particular played a major role in the split of the SDP away from the Labour Party in 1981, and at times has seemed close to splitting the Conservatives too.

The distinctive character of the British nationalist domain can also be seen from the social bases of attitudes. Margaret Thatcher's views were populist on many of these nationalist issues, in the sense that they were more popular among some of Labour's core working-class groups than they were among the educated middle classes.

Her victory in the Falklands was also of course immensely popular as well as populist, and in that respect the creamy dollops of nationalistic custard probably did compensate for the bitter-tasting economic medicine. But victory in the Falklands proved to be a waning asset (just as her success on the economic front against inflation was also a waning asset). More generally, as on the economic front, Margaret Thatcher tended to be more extreme than the electorate both on nuclear defence, where the electorate did not share her enthusiasm for Cruise missiles, and on the maintenance of the Union, where the electorate progressively moved away from her brand of British nationalism.

Table 4.9. The changing structure of attitudes, 1979–1997

Correlations of attitudes towards Europe with	1979	1983	1987	1992	1997
Nationalization	0.04	−0.23[a]	−0.10[b]	0.04	−0.01
Unemployment	0.06[a]	−0.18[b]	−0.05[b]	0.05	0.02
Tax cuts	0.15[b]	−0.12[b]	−0.07[b]	0.03	0.00
Devolution	0.02	n.a.	−0.02	0.04	0.09[b]
Defence	0.00	−0.17[b]	−0.04[a]	0.12[b]	0.14[b]
Racial equality	−0.03	0.09[b]	0.14[b]	0.15[b]	0.16[b]
Death penalty	−0.05	0.13[b]	0.15[b]	0.14[b]	0.22[b]
Stiffer sentences	−0.08	0.05[a]	0.12[b]	0.12[b]	0.21[b]

Note: Variables have been recoded so that low scores represent left, Europhile, and liberal views, and high scores represent right, Eurosceptic, and authoritarian views.

[a] Indicates that the correlation is significant at the 0.05 level.

[b] Indicates that the correlation is significant at the 0.01 level.

Source: *BES 1979*, min. N = 1,851; *1987*, min. N = 3,455; *1992*, min. N = 1,347 (half-sample); *1997*, min. N = 2,556.

However, only on Europe could Thatcherite views be said to be popular as well as populist. But paradoxically on Europe the Conservatives proved vulnerable to the Referendum Party. Being close to the median voter did not in the event prove to be a vote-winner. A party that positions itself close to the median voter may therefore run the risk of being outflanked by a more extreme party, or of generating dissension among its more extreme members, or both as in the case of the Conservative Party in the years between 1992 and 1997.

The defection of Eurosceptics from the Conservatives to the Referendum Party is straightforwardly in line with the consumer theory of voting. However, the evidence suggests that the real world is somewhat more complex than this. What we find is that attitudes towards Europe have not shown a particularly stable relationship with the well-established left–right and liberal–authoritarian ideological domains. This can be seen from Table 4.9.

In Table 4.9 we report the correlations between attitudes towards Europe and those towards some of the main items belonging to the left–right and liberal–authoritarian ideological dimensions. The structure of these two main dimensions has been very stable over time (see Appendix 4.2), but the structure of attitudes towards Europe has been rather volatile. As we can see, in 1979 Europe was rather weakly related to the two main dimensions, but there are some indications that Eurosceptic attitudes were associated with right-wing views on unemployment and tax cuts (hence the positive sign for these correlations). It will be recalled that at this point Margaret Thatcher was campaigning vigorously for renegotiating Britain's budget to the European budget.

In 1983, in contrast, Eurosceptic attitudes were significantly associated with left-wing economic views and with pacifist views on defence (hence the negative signs with the correlations). This was of course a time when Labour advocated a left-wing, pacifist, and Eurosceptic package. In 1987, when Labour had somewhat softened its hostility to Europe, these negative correlations persisted but were substantially weaker. They vanished altogether in 1992.

By 1997, however, a completely new structure had emerged, with Eurosceptic ideas being unrelated to the left–right dimension but strongly associated with authoritarian views and opposed to Scottish devolution. Perhaps most interestingly there was a reversal of sign in the case of defence; instead of being associated with pacifist views as in 1983, by 1997 Euroscepticism was associated with support for the independent British deterrent. This structure looks very like the Referendum Party's policy package.

This suggests that parties can themselves shape their supporters' attitudes. The changes in the structure of attitudes towards Europe are very hard to account for on the standard consumer, or 'bottom up', model of voting behaviour. On the standard consumer theory of voting, changes in party policy would simply lead Eurosceptic voters to switch their allegiance, supporting Labour in 1983 but then abandoning them in subsequent elections. This would lead to changing correlations between attitudes and vote over time as the parties changed their policies, but it would not in itself lead to changes in the correlations between one set of attitudes and another.

To be sure, it is conceivable that exogenous processes in the real world had influenced voters: the evolution of the European agenda and the changing nature of the European project might in theory lead to a change in the structure of attitudes (and the way to test this hypothesis would be to see if similar changes in the structure of attitudes had occurred in other European countries). However, the changes in the British electorate do show a striking parallel with the changes in the policy packages put before the electorate. In 1979 the lack of structure in the electorate's attitudes parallels the lack of prominence given to Europe in the parties' packages. In 1983 the electorate's attitude structure parallels the distinctive Labour package. In 1997 it parallels the very different Referendum Party package. We cannot be sure of the causal direction in any of this, but the results are consistent with the 'top down' theory: parties may be able to influence how voters see issues, especially those issues that are not firmly anchored in the two well-established left–right and liberal–authoritarian domains. As Margaret Thatcher would no doubt herself have argued, there may be a significant role for political leadership. The electorate's preferences do not necessarily have to be taken as externally derived.

Appendix 4.1. Supplementary Table

Table A4.1. Positions of Referendum Party voters relative to the Conservatives, 1997

Issue	Percentage who were		
	Left of Conservatives	Same as Conservatives	Right of Conservatives
European integration	3	10	87
Taxes and spending	91	9	0
Privatization	73	9	19
Unemployment	75	22	4

Note: Sample: respondents who reported a vote for the Referendum Party in 1997.

Sources: *BEPS 1992–7*, N = 33.

Appendix 4.2 Changing Ideological Dimensions in the British Electorate

We can use attitudes towards individual issues to see whether the structure of British political attitudes has been undergoing change over time. To explore this, we conduct factor analyses of the relevant issues in the 1979, 1983, 1987, 1992, and 1997 BESs. We score all the
items so that low scores represent left-wing or liberal views (or Europhile views in the case
of attitudes to Europe) and high scores represent right-wing or authoritarian views. 'Don't
knows' have been included (usually merged with the middle value) while 'not answereds'
have been excluded. Where possible we have used identical questions in each survey, but this
was not always possible. In particular, many of the questions in 1979 differ in various ways

Table A4.2. Factor analysis of issues, 1979

Attitudes towards . . .	Factor 1	Factor 2	Factor 3
Nationalization–privatization	0.13	0.73	0.08
Unemployment–inflation	0.09	0.69	0.21
Spending–taxation	0.09	0.13	0.71
Scottish devolution	0.13	0.08	0.25
European integration	–0.27	–0.05	0.70
Northern Ireland	–0.41	0.50	0.01
Britain's defence	0.18	0.62	–0.03
Aid to Third World	0.55	0.18	–0.09
Racial equality	0.53	0.04	0.29
Death penalty	0.71	0.01	0.11
Stiffer sentences	0.62	0.09	–0.06
Eigen value	2.09	1.52	1.11

Note: The questions used are 24a, 25a, 23a, 33, 27a, 38o, 26h, 38e, 26e, 38f, and 38l.

Source: *BES 1979*, N=1,833.

Table A4.3. Factor analysis of issues, 1983

Attitudes towards . . .	Factor 1	Factor 2
Nationalization–privatization	0.67	0.11
Unemployment–inflation	0.62	0.08
Spending–taxation	0.50	0.24
Scottish devolution	—	—
European integration	−0.56	0.37
Northern Ireland	0.45	−0.44
Britain's defence	0.60	0.26
Aid to Third World	—	—
Racial equality	0.09	0.59
Death penalty	0.08	0.72
Stiffer sentences	0.10	0.57
Eigen value	2.03	1.62

Note: The questions used were 36a, 28a, 31a, 43b, 27a, 24a, 45g, 42c, and 42e.

Source: BES 1983, N = 3,541.

from those in later surveys. However, we would argue that they tap the same basic concepts. In each case we use principal component analysis with varimax rotation.

In 1979 there are two main factors corresponding to the libertarian–authoritarian and left–right dimensions respectively. Note that attitudes towards defence load strongly on the left–right dimension. The main items loading on the third factor are attitudes to Europe and, more surprisingly, attitudes towards tax cuts. We should note that the only question on Europe in the 1979 questionnaire concerned Britain's willingness to go along with the economic policies of the EC.

We next turn to the 1983 data. Unfortunately, in 1983 we cannot include attitudes towards devolution since, although the relevant question was included in the questionnaire, it was asked only of respondents in Scotland and hence cannot be used in a general analysis. Nor was the question on aid to the Third World included. We can see from Table A4.3 that the 1983 data yields a two-dimensional solution. We cannot be sure whether this is due to a change in the structure of attitudes or is a methodological artefact of the reduced number of questions.

The natural interpretation of the first factor is that it represents the left–right dimension with high loadings on nationalization, unemployment, and taxation. The second factor can be interpreted as the libertarian–authoritarian dimension with the expected high loadings for racial equality, the death penalty, and stiffer sentences. The item on Britain's nuclear weapons clearly falls on the first, left–right, factor. The other striking, although hardly surprising, finding is that European integration has a negative loading on the first factor. Essentially, this means that pro-European responses tended to be associated with free market attitudes.

The 1987 survey then yields a three-factor solution that is basically similar to the 1979 structure. The first factor is the libertarian–authoritarian one, the same items having high loadings as in 1979. The second factor is the left–right one, and unsurprisingly the same three items load on it as before. The third factor then includes both internal and external aspects of British nationalism, with relatively high loadings for Scottish devolution, the future of Northern Ireland, and European integration. The only ambiguous item is Britain's nuclear deterrent, which loads more or less equally on all three factors.

Table A4.4. Factor analysis of issues, 1987

Attitudes towards . . .	Factor 1	Factor 2	Factor 3
Nationalization–privatization	0.08	0.63	0.22
Unemployment–inflation	0.00	0.74	0.03
Spending–taxation	0.11	0.70	–0.03
Scottish devolution	0.30	–0.11	0.61
European integration	0.28	–0.10	–0.58
Northern Ireland	–0.22	0.20	0.62
Britain's defence	0.39	0.34	0.33
Aid to Third World	0.63	0.20	–0.16
Racial equality	0.62	0.21	–0.05
Death penalty	0.77	0.00	–0.03
Stiffer sentences	0.70	–0.08	0.00
Eigen value	2.43	1.75	1.03

Note: The questions used were V34a, V28a, V29a, V41a, V24a, V26a, V27, V38d, V43f, V121N, and V121L.

Source: *BES 1987*, N = 2,917.

Table A4.5. Factor analysis of issues, 1992

Attitudes towards . . .	Factor 1	Factor 2	Factor 3
Nationalization–privatization	–0.02	0.68	0.19
Unemployment–inflation	–0.02	0.71	–0.08
Spending–taxation	0.12	0.72	0.07
Scottish devolution	–0.03	0.12	0.66
European integration	0.37	0.06	0.13
Northern Ireland	0.01	–0.09	0.72
Britain's defence	0.24	0.12	0.56
Aid to Third World	0.68	0.11	0.00
Racial equality	0.68	0.06	0.08
Death penalty	0.74	0.00	–0.06
Stiffer sentences	0.61	–0.16	0.04
Eigen value	2.18	1.59	1.16

Notes: The questions used were Va37a, Va36a, Va35a, V60a, V29a, V33a, V32, V47b, V50e, V47d, and V47e.

Source: *BES 1992*, N = 1,224 (half-sample).

Once again, however, European integration has the 'wrong' sign. In other words, anti-European attitudes tended to be associated with favourable orientations towards Scottish devolution, which is not the pattern we had expected from our theory of nationalist sentiment. While nationalist issues seem to be distinct, then, from the other major dimensions in 1987, they did not have the ideological coherence anticipated.

In 1992 we have three factors once more. The loadings on and interpretations of the first two factors are similar to those for 1987. Once again the third factor can be interpreted as a British nationalist one with high loadings for Scottish devolution, the future of Northern Ireland, and Britain's nuclear deterrent (which now loads unambiguously on this dimension). European integration fails to load as strongly on this dimension as it did in 1987, while its loading on the libertarian–authoritarian dimension has increased somewhat in size.

Table A4.6. Factor analysis of issues, 1997

Attitudes towards . . .	Factor 1	Factor 2	Factor 3
Nationalization–privatization	–0.06	0.59	0.15
Unemployment–inflation	0.06	0.74	0.00
Spending–taxation	0.04	0.75	0.05
Scottish devolution	0.04	0.07	0.64
European integration	0.48	–0.11	0.28
Northern Ireland	–0.06	0.03	0.72
Britain's defence	0.25	0.13	0.49
Aid to Third World	0.65	0.20	0.07
Racial equality	0.62	0.21	0.01
Death penalty	0.74	–0.06	0.02
Stiffer sentences	0.68	–0.17	–0.08
Eigen value	2.27	1.63	1.10

Note: The questions used were 377, 341, 359, 606, 327, 329, 331, 456, 561, 457, and 458.

Source: BES 1997, N = 2,538.

Finally, in 1997 we obtain a very similar structure to 1992, although Europe now loads even more strongly on the libertarian–authoritarian dimension.

5

Old Labour and the Social Democratic Party

Old Labour went down to defeat in 1979 largely as a result of the industrial unrest during the 'winter of discontent'. This unrest in turn had been in part a consequence of Labour's attempt to impose a social contract as a way of controlling inflation, which as we saw in Chapter 3 had reached 25 per cent in the wake of the 1974 oil shock. The social contract tried to replace individual unions' bargains with employers by a single collective system, but the system was unpopular with the more powerful unions, particularly of skilled workers, who felt that their traditional differentials were being eroded. In the autumn of 1978 the government proposed a 5 per cent limit on annual pay increases, but this limit was quickly broken (for example, by Ford, who offered 17 per cent). There followed a wave of strikes from low-paid public sector workers: 'A million and a half public service workers went on strike, closing hospitals, schools and local authority services across the country. The railways came to a halt' (Donoghue 1987: 171). The Labour government's popularity fell, and it was duly defeated by Margaret Thatcher's Conservatives, although the 37.8 per cent of the vote that Labour won in 1979 was higher than they were to secure at any of the next three elections.

There is every reason to believe that, if the Labour prime minister, Jim Callaghan, had called the election in the autumn of 1978, he would have won. Margaret Thatcher might then have been replaced as leader of the opposition and Thatcherism might never have flourished. Still, even if it had won in 1978, the Labour government would eventually have been crippled by the same tensions over its incomes and prices policy that culminated in the winter of discontent and so sooner or later would have been replaced by a Conservative government.

At all events, Labour's economic and industrial relations policies were in ruins in early 1979, and both the free market right and the socialist left were agreed in rejecting Labour's social contract. From the point of view of the electorate Labour was widely seen to be incompetent in managing the economy and had lost its reputation for managing the trade unions. Labour had lost authority. As we saw in Chapter 3, the failure of collectivist strategies like the social contract gave Margaret Thatcher the opportunity, and the public support, to experiment with her radical free market alternative.

Labour's own reaction, or rather the reaction of one wing of the party, to its defeat was to blame it on an insufficiently socialist programme in government (an argument that had previously been used in the wake of the 1970 defeat). '. . . when defeat came in 1979, one part of the Left then believed that the reason for defeat was that "true" socialism had never been tried, and therefore instead of altering the path of the Left, it decided instead to plunge down the same path much more vigorously' (Blair 1994: 2). The left of the party argued that the Labour government had failed to deliver the goods for its own working-class supporters, and indeed it was true that as chancellor of the exchequer Dennis Healey had used proto-Thatcherite policies for dealing with the financial crisis of 1976 and for balancing the books. These policies had been followed by a substantial increase in unemployment well above the levels that Britain had become accustomed to before the 1974 oil shock. And there was some evidence that the socialist diagnosis was indeed partly correct: working-class support for Labour did drop relatively sharply in 1979. Whether more socialism would actually have delivered the goods that the working class wanted is another matter.

The remedy that the left designed was an alternative economic strategy based on extensive government intervention in the labour market, import controls, and a major programme of nationalization. So on economic issues Labour moved to the left at precisely the time that the Conservatives were moving to the right under Margaret Thatcher.

In order to obtain the room for manœuvre to implement the alternative economic strategy, the party advocated withdrawal from Europe (that is from the EEC, as it was termed at the time). It maintained its commitment to devolution for Scotland and Wales. And at the same time Labour also embraced unilateral nuclear disarmament—a long-running source of contention within the party. Nuclear disarmament had been a controversial issue on the left ever since the days of the Campaign for Nuclear Disarmament (CND) in the late 1950s and 1960s. Unilateral disarmament had briefly become official Labour policy in 1960, a unilateralist resolution being passed at conference that year, but it was speedily reversed as the then leader of the party, Hugh Gaitskell, refused to accept the decision. Subsequent Labour governments consistently maintained Britain's nuclear deterrent. CND had lost much of its vigour in the late 1960s and 1970s, as other issues such as Vietnam dominated the radical conscience, but it made a strong comeback in the 1980s. This time the Labour left were victorious, and it was adopted as official Labour policy.

The party also advocated a number of other radical issues that have been termed the 'new agenda'—issues such as the environment, gender equality, racial equality and rights for gays and lesbians (see Heath *et al.* 1990, Studlar and McAllister 1992 on the new agenda).

The Labour Party of 1983 thus espoused a set of unambiguously socialist and left-wing policies on the economic front together with radical policies on Europe and nuclear disarmament. These can be thought of as, on the one hand, traditional class issues combined with, on the other hand, new issues that were more popular among middle-class activists than among the traditional labour movement. As we saw in Chapter 4, nuclear disarmament was not a traditional class issue but found greater favour among the new middle class of salaried trade unionists. The strategy can be thought of as a coalition of the two lefts: an old left based in the working-class labour movement and oriented to full employment and traditional class issues, and a new left (not to be confused with New Labour) oriented to the 'new agenda' of disarmament, civil liberties and gender issues.

This coalition on the face of it might have been a reasonable strategy for combating the decline in the size of the traditional working class; by appealing to the new middle class Labour was at least reaching out beyond its traditional but declining core (although it is rather doubtful that electoral considerations of this sort played any role in Labour thinking at this time). Moreover, some old-left policies such as greater public expenditure on the welfare state could be expected in theory to appeal to the new middle class, many of whom were employed in the public sector and who stood to gain from increased public expenditure (and conversely who stood to lose from Margaret Thatcher's attempts to curb the public sector).

In the event, however, the Labour Party was hopelessly divided over this radical strategy and was beset by high-profile disputes such as the fight between Tony Benn and Dennis Healey (representing the radical and moderate wings of the party respectively) for the Labour Party deputy leadership in 1981. If anything, the British electorate dislike a divided party even more than they dislike an ideologically extreme party. Some of the biggest defeats in British electoral history have occurred when a party has been split by internal divisions.

Labour's internal divisions were of course given added exposure through the defection in 1981 of a number of prominent centrist MPs to form the Social Democratic Party, a new moderate but left-of-centre formation that was in many respects a precursor of Blair's New Labour. One of the overt issues that led to the formation of the SDP was Labour's commitment to leaving the European Community, but as Crewè and King emphasize in their account of the formation of the SDP,

the Common Market was undoubtedly important in itself—they believed in it and wanted Britain to remain a member of it—but to them it was much more important for what it symbolized. To be in favour of the Common Market, in their eyes, was to be in favour of a Labour Party and a Britain that were internationalist and forward-looking, that had succeeded in coming to terms with the real world; to be against the Common Market was to be parochial and backward-looking, hopelessly wedded to a vision of things that had never been and never could be . . . the European issue was caught up in a much larger—and less rational—argument about the future of socialism and the future of the Labour Party. What really mattered was not Europe in itself but that larger argument. (Crewe and King 1995: 118)

The SDP, in alliance with the Liberals, briefly overtook both the Conservatives and Labour in the opinion polls. By the time of the 1983 election Labour only just managed to beat the Alliance for third place. The 1983 election was in some ways Labour's worst result this century. It achieved fewer votes per candidate than it had done since the party was formed in 1900. Its share of the overall vote was lower than it had been since 1918. Fewer Labour MPs were elected to the Commons than at any time since 1935. The electorate had given its verdict. The strategy of the 'two lefts' had had its chance and had spectacularly failed.

However, it is perhaps worth checking why the strategy was such a dismal failure. Most commentators and certainly subsequent Labour leaderships have taken it for granted that the 1983 strategy was not electorally viable because it was too left-wing for the electorate to stomach. On the other hand, the evidence of Chapter 3 suggests that a party, in that case the Conservatives, could be out of tune with public sentiment on the major issues and still win elections. How was Margaret Thatcher able to win, and continue winning, despite unpopular policies, whereas Labour's unpopular policies led to spectacular defeat?

Labour's Ideological Appeal in 1983

There is no doubt that in 1983 Labour had positioned itself well to the left of the majority of the electorate on some of the major issues, particularly nationalization and nuclear disarmament, that symbolized the radicalism of Labour under Michael Foot. Table 5.1 shows rather clearly that, on nationalization 79 per cent of the electorate felt they were to Labour's right and only 9 per cent felt they were to Labour's left, a net balance of 70 points. This is actually an even larger net balance than any of the Conservative ones that we saw in Chapter 3. Even at its most extreme, under Margaret Thatcher the Conservatives' net balance never went above –61 points (on unemployment and inflation in 1983).

Nuclear disarmament was almost as unpopular a policy in the electorate and among Labour voters as was nationalization, with a net balance of 62 points. Given Margaret Thatcher's success in the Falklands War and her new authority as a patriotic leader, 1983 was a particularly unfortunate time to be trying to sell nuclear disarmament to the electorate. Labour's choice of 'new left' issue was a disastrous mistake. Unilateralism was deeply unpopular, even among the new middle class.

A third issue where Labour was deeply unpopular was law and order. As with the other scales, we gave our respondents two contrasting statements and asked them to place themselves and the parties on the scales. The two statements were: 'Protecting civil rights is more important than cutting crime'; 'Cutting crime is more important than protecting civil rights' (*BES* 1983, question 41).

With its radical pursuit of the new agenda Labour in 1983 placed itself towards the liberal end of this spectrum. Once again, Labour's perceived policies were extremely unpopular, with a net balance of 59 points.

On nationalization, nuclear disarmament, and law and order, then, Labour in 1983 was thought by the electorate to be even more extreme ideologically than the Conservatives. However Labour's policies, even in 1983, were by no means universally unpopular. As we saw in Chapter 3, the electorate had already come to see unemployment as the top priority by 1983; they regarded it as the most important issue and tended to agree with the priority which Labour gave it. As Table 5.1 shows, Labour was not especially out of tune with popular sentiment on unemployment, with a net balance of only 24 points (compared with a Conservative balance on this item of –61. So here they were clearly much closer to the electorate than

Table 5.1. Positions relative to Labour, 1983

Issue	Percentage who were			
	Left of Labour	Same as Labour	Right of Labour	Net balance
Nationalization–privatization	9	13	79	+70
Unemployment–inflation	20	36	44	+24
Spending–taxes	20	21	59	+39
Nuclear disarmament	12	14	74	+62
Law and order	15	26	74	+59

Source: BES 1983, min. N = 3,493.

Table 5.2. Positions relative to the Conservatives and Labour, 1983

Issue	Percentage who were		
	Closer to Labour	Equidistant	Closer to Conservative
Nationalization–privatization	28	17	55
Unemployment–inflation	52	17	31
Spending–taxes	45	17	38
Nuclear disarmament	36	13	51
Law and order	32	27	41

Source: BES 1983, min. N = 3,471.

Margaret Thatcher was. On taxes and government spending on public services, too, Labour was no more out of tune with the electorate than were the Conservatives (a Labour balance of 39 points comparing with a Conservative balance of –46 points).

Looking at these five policy areas, it is not initially obvious, then, that Labour was at a substantial disadvantage compared with the Conservatives. We can easily calculate which of the two parties the voters felt closer to, and Table 5.2 shows that on two issues Labour had the advantage while on three the Conservatives did. So in 1983 Labour was actually rather closer to the electorate on unemployment and taxation than was the Conservative Party. This was more or less balanced by the Conservatives' advantage on nationalization and nuclear weapons. Overall, the Conservatives had a slightly bigger lead on 'their' issues than Labour did on its issues, but the difference was not all that great.

Moreover, Labour's two issues were ones which the electorate said were of higher priority than were their opponents' issues. We asked our respondents: 'Here is a list of six issues that were discussed during the election. When you were deciding about voting, how important was each of these issues to you?' (BES 1983, question 20a). As Table 5.3 shows, unemployment was the issue most likely to be rated 'extremely important', while two of the main 'Conservative' issues—nationalization and defence—received relatively few 'extremely important' ratings.

As we argued in *How Britain Votes* (Heath *et al.* 1985), if voters had made their

Table 5.3. Importance of the issues in deciding one's vote, 1983

Issue	Percentage saying the issue 'extremely important'	Relative weight in predicting vote[a]	Difference between parties[b]
Defence	40	69	12
Unemployment	69	54	7
Inflation	52	—	—
Health and social services	62	47	10
Nationalization	21	100	13
Law and order	63	9	4

[a] Logistic regression coefficients scaled so that the coefficient for nationalization is set at 100.

[b] Distances between parties on the 21-point scales.

Source: *BES 1983*, N = 2,139.

decisions on the basis of the relative importance of the various policies to them, then there would have been a dead heat between Labour and the Conservatives. Of course, there was not, and so scepticism about respondents' answers to surveys may once again be in order. In fact, it seems rather likely that voters do not accurately interpret what influences their own votes. Their answers perhaps tell us what they think are the most important issues facing the country—the policies that *ought* to decide the election rather than those that actually influenced their own private decisions. (As in the case of reported turnout or reported preferences for increased government spending, a social desirability bias may be at work here.)

An alternative way of approaching the importance of policies is to look at the ones which are actually associated with the way people vote. This is done in column 2 of Table 5.3, which reports the relative weights of different policies in a model of Labour and Conservative voting (setting nationalization, the policy which had the largest weight, at 100 and scaling the other policies accordingly). In practice column 2 suggests that the issues most strongly related to Labour and Conservative voting were nationalization and nuclear weapons, while unemployment was relatively weakly related to the way in which people voted in 1983, and law and order was of minimal importance. (For technical details, see Appendix 5.1)

As it happens, the two issues of nationalization and nuclear disarmament were also the ones on which the parties were most polarized, whereas on law and order the voters saw little difference between the parties. As the third column of Table 5.3 shows, on our 21-point scales the average perceived difference between the Labour and Conservative Parties in 1983 was 13 points on nationalization and 12 points on nuclear disarmament, but only 10 points on government spending 7 points on unemployment, and 4 points on law and order. This suggests that it may be the perceived distance between the parties that decides how much weight voters give a particular issue, rather than its importance in some moral sense. This makes good theoretical sense: in rational choice theory there is little point in giving weight to an issue if the parties take basically the same stand: however strongly one feels about an issue, there is little point in including it in one's calculus if the parties are likely to do more or less the same thing about that issue once in office. It will in fact make more sense to vote on the basis of an issue about which one has less strong views but on which the main parties are polarized. In this latter case, it will actually make a difference which party wins—and indeed the evidence we reviewed in Chapter 3 suggests pretty clearly that the Conservative victory in 1983 did make a rather large difference to the progress of privatization. So even though this was not perhaps the most important issue facing the country, it was the one on which the choice of government was likely to make the most difference.

So we would argue that the voters are actually more rational to weight issues like nationalization and nuclear disarmament highly when deciding how to vote, rather than deciding on the basis of an 'important' issue like law and order where the parties (at least in the eyes of the electorate) did not differ so much in their policies. We are not suggesting that individual voters explicitly go through these calculations: they act 'as if' this was what they were doing. Our data simply tell us about the aggregate outcome of many voters' decisions.

So the conclusion is that, although Labour advocated popular policies for unemployment and taxation in 1983, these actually counted for relatively little in voters' calculations since they perceived less difference between the parties on these two issues. If we weight the figures in Table 5.3 above by these party differences, we find that the balance is more firmly tilted in the Conservative direction: on the basis of these weighted figures we find 37.8 per cent of our respondents were closest to Labour, 16.9 per cent were equidistant between the two parties, and 45.3 per cent closest to the Conservatives.

So one crucial problem for Labour in 1983 was that it was unpopular on the issues where the parties were polarized, and its popular issues were ones where there was less difference between the parties. The obverse of this of course is that the Conservatives were able to get away with being quite remote from the voters on key issues partly because Labour was even more remote.

From an electoral point of view, the moral is not that Labour was simply too extreme, but that it was extreme on the wrong issues.

The SDP and the Alliance

However, Labour had the added handicap of having to fight the breakaway SDP, and its alliance with the Liberals, who had taken up position in Labour territory rather than in Conservative territory. As Crewe and King (1995) describe, the SDP was largely composed of former Labour MPs who lay towards the right of the Labour Party on economic issues and who tended to oppose Labour's anti-European policy and their unilateral disarmament policies. Accordingly, the SDP was widely perceived as a moderate, left-of-centre formation.

In the 1983 BES we asked our questions about party placement only about the Alliance, rather than about the SDP itself. But since they fought a common campaign, issued a single manifesto, and did not compete against each other in the

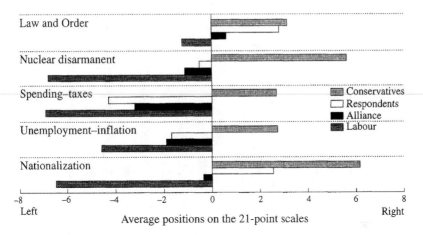

Fig. 5.1. The ideological positions of parties and votes, 1983.
Source: BES 1983. Minimum N = 2,936.

vast majority of constituencies, it is not clear that we can really distinguish the SDP from the Liberals. On four of our five main issues, we find from Figure 5.1 that the Alliance was perceived to be slightly to the left of centre and clearly on the Labour side of the political spectrum. Moreover, on four of the five issues the Alliance lay between the average voter and Labour, hence eating more into Labour support than into Conservative support. And on the fifth issue, taxes and spending, the Alliance was clearly seen to be much closer to Labour than it was to the Conservatives.

Unfortunately, the 1979 BES did not ask respondents where they placed the Liberals, so we cannot test whether the SDP–Liberal Alliance was thought to be more left-of-centre than the old Liberals had been. However, from other questions in the 1979 survey it seems clear that in 1979 voters had thought of the Liberals as being more or less equidistant between Conservatives and Labour. For example, in answer to the question 'considering everything the Conservative, Labour and Liberal Parties stand for, which two of these would you say are closest together?' 41 per cent said Conservative and Liberal were closest together while exactly the same percentage said that Labour and Liberal were closest. In contrast, in 1983 a clear majority of our respondents to the BES thought that the SDP was closer to Labour (49 per cent) than to the Conservatives (22 per cent)—not really surprisingly given that the SDP was largely composed of renegade Labour MPs.

A useful exercise that we can carry out in order to find out how much damage was done to Labour by the SDP is to look at the shares of the vote which the different parties secured from voters located at different places on the ideological spectrum. For this purpose we construct an overall scale which is simply the weighted

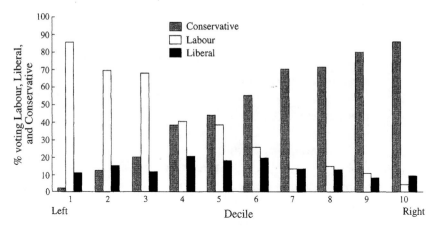

Fig. 5.2. Ideological position and vote, 1979. Each decile has around 125 respondents.
Source: BES 1979

average of the five scales used earlier in this chapter.[1] Since this scale also includes non-economic issues like nuclear disarmament and law and order it should not be thought of as a pure left–right scale *per se*. Strictly speaking, it should be thought of as an Old Labour–Thatcherite scale, but since the economic issues play a much larger overall role in the scale than do the non-economic issues, we can continue to use the terms 'left' and 'right' as shorthand.

We arrange voters according to their percentile position on this scale. That is, we move from the most Old Labour ideological positions on the left (where an Old Labour position favours nationalization, full employment, increased spending on public services, nuclear disarmament, and a liberal approach to law and order) to the most Thatcherite on the right.

Figure 5.2 shows the way in which ideological position was related to vote in 1979.[2] As expected, we find that Labour voting was highest on the left of the scale and Conservative voting highest on the right. There was in 1979 a neat symmetry, with Labour obtaining 86 per cent of the votes of the most left-wing decile while the Conservatives obtained 86 per cent from the most right-wing decile. The Liberal vote was slightly stronger among the moderate-left deciles rather than among the moderate-right, with a plateau of support in the fourth, fifth, and sixth deciles.

There were then some dramatic changes on the left in 1983, as Figure 5.3 demonstrates, but an equally remarkable continuity on the right. The Conservatives continued to maintain their hold on the far right, where they obtained almost exactly

---

[1] We use the perceived differences between the parties, as reported in the third column of Table 5.3, as the weights. This scale corresponds to model 3 described in Appendix 5.1.

[2] For the 1979 scale we use the items on taxes and government services (question 23a), job creation (question 25a), trade union regulation (question 67a), wage control (question 66a) and nationalization–privatization (question 24a). For question wording, see Ch. 3.

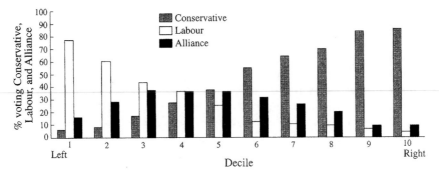

Fig. 5.3. Ideological position and vote, 1983. Each decile has around 290 respondents.
Source: BES 1983

the same share of the vote as they had done in 1979. Their share of the moderate-right deciles was also almost unchanged.

The Alliance, despite the general increase in their share of the vote, failed to make any inroads at all on the far right. They made some gains among the moderate-right deciles (at Labour's expense) but their biggest gains were all among the moderate-left, with gains of 25 points in the 3rd decile, sixteen points in the 4th decile, and 18 points in the 5th decile.

The Labour vote fell correspondingly, especially among moderate-left voters. As we can see from Figure 5.3, in 1983 Labour secured only 77 per cent of the votes among the most left-wing people on the scale, down 9 points compared with the 86 per cent they had obtained in 1979. But they suffered even larger drops in the 3rd, 4th, and 5th deciles, where the average fall was 13 percentage points.

Quite clearly the Alliance ate substantially into Labour's left-of-centre vote. Of course, the decision to vote for the Alliance rather than the Labour Party would not have been decided solely by issue positions. Labour under Michael Foot was widely perceived to be divided, incompetent, and extremist, and was tainted by its past failures in office, whereas the Alliance offered a new start (although it must be said that some of its leaders could also have been said to have been tainted by failure in office since they had been members of previous failed Labour administrations).

It is difficult to disentangle the relative importance of the Alliance's ideological position from that of Labour's perceived incompetence. Even if the Alliance had positioned itself at the centre of the spectrum, at the same position as the median voter, Labour's incompetence is still likely to have enabled the Alliance to pick up more votes from left-of-centre voters than from right-of-centre voters. Only if both major parties were thought to be equally incompetent (as was perhaps the case in the February 1974 election) would a centrist party have picked up equal shares of the vote from left and right. In particular, the drop of 9 percentage points in Labour's support in the most left-wing decile is hard to understand in ideological terms, and it can probably be regarded largely as owing to Labour's perceived incompetence rather than to ideological extremism. More generally, we would expect that reactions to Labour's perceived incompetence would have taken an 'across-the-board' character, whereas reactions to Labour's (and the SDP's) ideological changes would have been specific to particular locations on the ideological scale. On this interpretation we can think of the across-the-board drop of 9 points as due to incompetence, and the additional drop of 4 or 5 points among the centre-left voters as a result of Labour's move to the left and the SDP's emergence as a centre-left force in its own right. Quantitatively, this suggests that incompetence was a much more significant contribution to Labour's defeat in 1983 than was ideology.[3]

Whatever the precise mixture of ideological position and perceived incompetence that led to Labour's failure among left-of-centre voters, it is quite clear that in 1983 Labour did lose disproportionately the support of voters who were ideologically close to the SDP. This establishes the fundamental electoral problem that subsequent leaders of the Labour Party had to deal with: the SDP had effectively squeezed Labour's share of the left-of-centre vote. This was in many ways more important from Labour's point of view than anything the Conservatives got up to on the right of the spectrum. This was where Old Labour suffered its largest losses in 1983 and correspondingly where the party could best expect to make its largest recovery in future.

Whether the reason for these losses was Labour's ideological extremism or its incompetence and divisions is difficult to decide. Our own interpretation is that it probably had more to do with perceived incompetence than with policies *per se*.

The Social Bases of Centre-Left Voters

What was the social profile of these left-of-centre voters that Labour needed to win back from the SDP? How far does this profile correspond with the New Labour diagnosis of Giles Radice?

Table 5.4 shows the proportion of each social group who adopted far-left (the 1st and 2nd deciles), moderate-left (the 3rd, 4th, and 5th deciles), moderate-right (the 6th, 7th, and 8th deciles) and far-right positions (the 9th and 10th deciles). Table 5.4 shows as expected that the petite bourgeoisie and the non-unionized members of the salariat were the two most right-wing groups, while the working-class council tenants and the unemployed were the most left-wing. Again as expected, the new working class fell in between.

Table 5.4 also shows rather clearly the potential attractiveness of the 'two lefts'

---

[3] When we talk of across-the-board changes we need to take account of floor and ceiling effects. We would not,for example, expect Labour's share of the vote to fall by 9 points on the far right of the ideological spectrum, as their share had already been pretty low in 1979. What is needed therefore is to use a technique such as odds ratios or loglinear models which take account of floor and ceiling effects. If we fit a loglinear model to the data for 1979 and 1983 we find that the hypothesis of an across-the-board decline fits the data fairly well ($Chi^2 = 29.3$ for 18 degrees of freedom, $p = 0.045$).

Table 5.4. Social group and ideological position, 1983 (row percentages)

Social group	Far left	Moderate left	Moderate right	Far right	N
Petit bourgeois	11	20	39	31	236
Salariat					
Non-union	11	25	36	28	613
Union members	28	31	23	18	232
Routine non-manual	15	29	36	20	568
Working-class					
Non-union, home-owners	13	34	30	23	436
Non-union, council tenants	31	37	20	12	298
Union members	28	33	25	14	492
Other working-class	28	29	22	21	90
Unemployed	30	35	23	12	281
All	20	30	30	20	—

Source: BES 1983.

strategy to a left-wing party. The new middle class (defined here as union members in the salariat) was by far the most left-wing of all the middle-class groups, with 28 per cent adopting a far-left position and a further 31 per cent adopting a moderate-left position on our overall scale. These figures are not dissimilar from those for Labour's core working-class groups.

Of course, as we noted in Chapter 2, the new middle class was not an especially large group, and so it was not perhaps of key electoral significance. It could, for example, be safely ignored by Margaret Thatcher, who had little but contempt for the new middle class. This is shown in Table 5.5, which gives the column percentages. For example, the first column of Table 5.5 shows what proportion of the far left were to be found in each social group; the second column shows the proportions of the moderate left, and so on.

What we see is that almost half of all far-left respondents were to be found in the core working-class groups, while the new middle class, because of its small size, contributed only 10 per cent of far-left voters. We can also see that the moderate-left voters were more evenly dispersed, with large contingents coming from the working-class homeowners, from the routine non-manual workers, and from the old middle class. Indeed, almost as many moderate-left voters were to be found in the old middle class and lower middle class as there were in the old working class. If we take the moderate left to be the key voters that Labour had to win back, then a strategy like Radice's of focusing on 'middle income, middle Britain' looked likely to be more successful electorally than the two-lefts strategy that Labour adopted in 1983, even if there had been no problem with Labour divisions and incompetence.

However, it is important not to exaggerate the role of ideology in determining how people will vote. Ideological position is not the sole factor in electoral choice, as can be seen from Table 5.6. This table shows that, even when we take account of

Table 5.5. Social group and ideological position, 1983 (column percentages)

Social group	Far left	Moderate left	Moderate right	Far right
Petit bourgeois	4	5	9	11
Salariat				
Non-union	11	16	23	26
Union members	10	7	5	6
Routine non-manual	13	17	21	17
Working-class				
Non-union, home-owners	9	15	14	15
Non-union, council tenants	14	11	6	6
Union members	21	17	13	11
Other working-class	4	3	2	3
Unemployed	13	10	7	5
All	100	100	100	100
N	638	982	969	657

Source: *BES 1983*.

Table 5.6. Social group, ideological position, and support for Labour, 1983 (cell percentages)

Social group	Percentage voting Labour			
	Far left	Moderate left	Moderate right	Far right
Petit bourgeois	—	—	1	2
Salariat				
Non-union	36	12	1	3
Union members	67	17	—	—
Routine non-manual	61	27	7	0
Working-class				
Non-union, home-owners	63	35	10	7
Non-union, council tenants	81	58	44	—
Union members	81	54	23	14
Other working-class	—	—	—	—
Unemployed	84	50	29	—
All	69	35	10	5

Note: Percentages are not reported where the base N is less than 50.
Source: *BES 1983*.

ideological position, there are still substantial differences between the various social groups in their support for Labour. In particular it is noticeable that only two-thirds of far-left voters from the new middle class supported Labour, compared with four-fifths or more from the core working-class groups. The contrast is even more striking among moderate-left voters: less than a fifth of moderate-left voters from the new middle class supported Labour, compared with over half from the core working-class groups. In this respect the two-lefts strategy failed in a fundamental way to deliver votes to Labour in 1983. In other words, Labour was much less successful in converting ideology into vote in the new middle class than it was in the working class.

However, this was a problem that was not specific to the new middle class. In general what we see in Table 5.6 is that substantial class differences in support for Labour persisted even among voters of broadly similar ideological position. Among people with similar ideology, those in Labour's core groups in the old working class and among the unemployed were the most inclined to support Labour; those in the old middle class and the petite bourgeoisie (although here the numbers are too small for reliable conclusions) were the least likely to support Labour, and the three intermediate groups fell in between. In short, class differences in voting cannot be reduced to ideology alone.

There are a number of possible explanations for these persisting class differences. One possibility is that our categorization of ideology into far left, moderate left, and so on is simply too crude: within these broad categories there may be considerable variation, and it is possible, for example, that the new middle-class voters were simply not as radical as those in the old working class and that they therefore found the centrist approach of the SDP and the Liberals more to their taste. Another possibility is that the non-economic issues favoured by the new middle class might not translate into Labour vote quite so effectively as do the economic ones. However, when we check out these possibilities with multivariate analysis, neither receives much support from the data. Whichever alternative formulation we adopt, the kinds of social group differences demonstrated by Table 5.6 remained stubbornly persistent. (See Appendix 5.2 for details.)

The persistence of social group differences, even when we take account of people's ideological positions, is consistent with previous research (Heath 1998; Weakliem and Heath 1994). Part of the explanation for these persisting group differences probably lies in patterns of social interaction and local community relationships. Part of it may also lie in more nebulous links between a party and its supporters. A party's core groups are more likely to be involved in these patterns of social relationship and their associated cultures. Whatever the explanation, it is clear that group differences cannot be reduced to ideological differences: both are important. Fashionable contemporary theories of the electorate tend to emphasize the extent to which it is 'dealigned'—consumerist, individualistic, and open to whichever party makes the best bid for its vote. We do not deny that there may have been some changes in this direction (although we are sceptical of their magnitude), but the electorate has not yet become totally dealigned.

This may have important implications. In the first place, in order to capture an expanding social group it may not be sufficient simply to change ideology: if the target group has its own political loyalties and traditions, it may prove difficult to convert. Ideological change on its own may yield disappointing returns.

Secondly, a party needs to remember that its traditions of loyalty do bring in many votes that it might not get purely on the basis of ideological position (or economic record). Indeed, without these traditions it may well have been that Labour in 1983 would have been overtaken by the Alliance. On the basis of ideological position alone, the Alliance could have been expected to fare even better than it did in 1983, especially among centrist voters (Heath *et al.* 1985), and Labour would have fared even less well.

Conclusions

As we saw in Chapters 3 and 4, Margaret Thatcher was able to win in 1983 despite advocating, and implementing, a set of policies that were in general far to the right of the electorate. She was helped by the fact that Labour took up even more extreme positions on 'her' issues, such as privatization and defence. The problem for Labour was that, although their policies on unemployment were quite popular and were also ones that the electorate said were important, they were not actually ones that formed the major basis for the electorate's decisions. Contrary to the views of commentators and politicians, who all seem to believe that voters will base their decisions on the important issues, the electorate, entirely rationally, give more weight to the issues on which the parties are polarized. It makes much more sense to vote on the basis of an issue where there is a major difference between the parties and hence where the outcome of the election is likely to make a real difference to what happens in the course of the next Parliament.

Unfortunately for Labour in 1983, it was unpopular on the issues where the parties were polarized and which therefore counted a lot, and its popular issues were ones where there was less perceived difference between the parties. From an electoral point of view, therefore, the moral is not that Labour was simply too extreme, but that it was extreme on the wrong issues. This was of course precisely the moral that Neil Kinnock drew when he became leader of the Labour Party after the 1983 debacle.

Labour also lost some votes because the SDP positioned itself to the left of centre, competing for the left-of-centre ground and actually winning as many votes as Labour did from the moderate left. It is arguable, however, how far Labour's losses to the SDP–Liberal Alliance were due to the changes in party position and how far they were the result of Labour's perceived divisions and incompetence; probably both were important, although we suspect that the formation of the SDP probably had rather little direct effect on vote-switching. A large proportion of the Labour losses seem to have taken an across-the-board character and it is therefore quite likely that, even without the SDP, the Liberal Party would have gained substantially among left-of-centre voters. Of course, the formation of the SDP may have been important indirectly by reinforcing Labour's image of division and incompetence.

But whatever the precise mixture of ideological extremism and perceived incompetence that led to Labour's failure at the polls, it is quite clear that in 1983 Labour did lose disproportionately the support of voters who lay on the centre-left of the political spectrum. This established the fundamental electoral problem that subsequent leaders of the Labour Party had to deal with.

Our evidence does, therefore, support many aspects of the New Labour diagnosis of the problems that the party faced after 1983 namely:

- Labour's core groups were small and declining.
- Key policies were unpopular.
- The voters to be won over were to be found in greatest numbers in the new working class and in the middle class.
- Labour's reputation for incompetence and division had lost it support even among left-wingers.

But the evidence of this chapter suggests that competence and policy are not the sole ingredients in the voter's calculus. It is striking that, even among voters who shared the same ideological position, Labour won a larger share of the votes from members of its core groups in the working class than it did from members of the salariat. The New Labour (and fashionable political science) model of the voter is at best a partial one. Voters are indeed quite rational—perhaps even in aggregate more rational than the politicians themselves—but there are other processes of a non-rational kind that seem to be needed to account for the way they vote. Loyalty and tradition and the more affective or emotional ties that link voters to parties have some role to play too.

Appendix 5.1. Measuring the Relative Importance of Issues

To measure the extent to which different issues are related to the way people vote, we carry out a logistic regression where the dependent variable is scored 1 for a Labour vote and 0 for a Conservative vote and the independent variables are the respondents' own positions on the five 21-point scales described in the text. Non-voters and voters for other parties are excluded throughout.

Table A5.1 shows that nationalization had the strongest partial association with vote. This was followed by nuclear weapons, unemployment–inflation, and taxes–spending, with law and order a distant last. Of course, we cannot be sure of the causal relationship between issues and vote: it may well be that voters bring their attitudes and perceptions into line with those of their party. In effect all the regressions can show us is the pattern of partial associations.

We then attempt to reproduce these results using theoretically derived weightings for the issues. First, we give each issue equal weight. We can think of this as our baseline model. Secondly, we weight each issue according to the perceived importance given to it by the respondents themselves. This corresponds to the lay view of decision-making. Thirdly, we weight each issue by the average perceived difference between the two parties. This can be thought of as the rational choice model. And fourthly, we weight each issue according to the directional theory (Rabinowitz and McDonald 1989). The directional model holds that voters vote not for the closest party but for the party that lies on the same side of the political

Table A5.1. Logistic regression of Conservative and Labour voting, 1983

Respondent's position	Parameter estimates
Law and order	−0.17 (0.11)
Taxes and spending	−0.90 (0.13)
Nationalization	−1.92 (0.12)
Nuclear weapons	−1.32 (0.12)
Unemployment	−1.03 (0.11)
Constant	−7.43 (0.94)
Model improvement	1,133.4

Note: Coefficients and standard errors times 10. Standard errors are given in brackets.

Source: BES 1983, N = 2,139.

Table A5.2. Goodness of fit of various models of voting

Model	Model improvement
Equal weights	1,001.8
Weighted by respondents' judgement of importance	873.2
Weighted by distance between parties	1,102.4
Directional model	1,095.8
N	2,139

Source: BES 1983.

spectrum as the voter does. For example, it predicts that a person who lies to the left of centre will vote for a party that lies to his or her left even if there is another, closer party which lies to the right of centre.

The formulas for these four weightings are as follows:

(1) $\text{Score} = (A_i) + (B_i) + \ldots + (E_i)$

(2) $\text{Score} = (A_i \times W_a) + (B_i \times W_b) + \ldots + (E_i \times W_e)$

(3) $\text{Score} = (A_i) \times (A_c - A_l) + (B_i) \times (B_c - B_l) + \ldots + (E_i) \times (E_c - E_l)$

(4) $\text{Score} = (A_i \times A_c) + (B_i \times B_c) + \ldots + (E_i \times E_c)$

where A_i represents the position of voter i on scale A, W_a represents the mean importance ascribed to issue A, A_c represents the mean perceived position of party C on scale A, and A_l represents the mean perceived position of party L on scale A. The scales are all scored from −10 to +10, with a midpoint of 0. Hence, following directional theory, A_i is the distance of voter i from the midpoint of the scale, and A_c is the distance of party C from the midpoint.

The resulting scores are then entered as a single predictor. Table A5.2 shows the goodness of fit of these four alternative predictors. As we can see, the rational choice model (model 3) gives a slightly better fit than the directional model (model 4) and a much better fit than the equal-weights model (model 1). This in turn fares a great deal better than the model in which distances are weighted by respondents' judgements of importance (model 2).

We should note that none of the four models fares quite as well as the model when the five scales are entered separately and the weights are empirically derived (as in Table A5.1). The difference in fit is, however, rather small.

Appendix 5.2. Multivariate Analysis of Social Group, Ideology, and Support for Labour

Table A5.3. Logistic regressions of Labour voting, 1983

	Parameter estimates			
	Model 1	Model 2	Model 3	Model 4
Constant	0.15 (0.13)	1.67 (0.18)	−0.46 (0.16)	−0.43 (0.18)
Social Group				
Petite bourgeois	−2.48 (0.28)	−2.08 (0.31)	−1.99 (0.32)	−1.88 (0.32)
Salariat, non-union	−2.61 (0.21)	−2.32 (0.24)	−2.29 (0.24)	−2.23 (0.24)
Salariat, union	−1.21 (0.18)	−1.42 (0.24)	−1.42 (0.25)	−1.35 (0.25)
Routine non-manual	−1.61 (0.18)	−1.33 (0.21)	−1.34 (0.21)	−1.34 (0.21)
Working-class, non-union, home-owner	−1.25 (0.18)	−0.91 (0.21)	−0.86 (0.21)	−0.85 (0.21)
Working-class, non-union, council tenant	0.12 (0.19)	0.20 (0.22)	0.25 (0.22)	0.23 (0.23)
Working-class, union	−0.22 (0.17)	0.05 (0.20)	−0.02 (0.20)	−0.03 (0.20)
Other working-class	−0.85 (0.29)	0.76 (0.34)	−0.66 (0.35)	−0.66 (0.35)
Unemployed (reference)	0	0	0	0
Ideological position				
Far left (reference)		0		
Moderate left		−1.47 (0.13)		
Moderate right		−2.88 (0.16)		
Far right		−3.53 (0.22)		
Left–right scale (*10)			−3.95 (0.22)	
Individual issues				
Nuclear weapons				−1.00 (0.10)
Unemployment				−0.65 (0.10)
Taxes–spending				−0.53 (0.11)
Nationalization				−1.37 (0.10)
Law and order				−0.02 (0.10)
Model improvement	421.7	1,001.5	1,041.4	1,058.7

Note: Estimates for the left–right scale and the individual issues (measured on 21-point scales) are multiplied by 10. Standard errors are given in brackets.

Source: *BES 1983*, N = 2,670.

As our dependent variable we contrast Labour voting (scored 1) with a vote for any other party (scored 0). In the first model we simply enter the nine social groups, taking the unemployed as the reference category. The parameter estimates therefore show the log odds ratios comparing Labour : non-Labour voting in the reference category with that in the group in question.

In the second model we include ideological position, treated as four categories as in Table 5.6. This results in a very substantial improvement in fit but there is only a modest reduction in the size of the social group parameter estimates.

In the third model we replace the four categories of left–right position with the original scale, and in the fourth model we enter the five issues separately. These two models yield relatively small improvements in fit and lead to small reductions in the size of the social group parameter estimates. Thus, whichever method we use for controlling for ideological position, we find that very substantial social group parameter estimates persist.

6

Labour's Long Road Back

The process of modernization that culminated in Labour's victory in the 1997 general election had its origins in Neil Kinnock's period as leader of the party between 1983 and 1992. As Heffernan (1998) has argued, modernization should be viewed as a gradual process, although with a number of distinct phases. In effect Neil Kinnock laid the foundations for Blair's subsequent reforms and he shared many of the assumptions that Tony Blair and his fellow modernizers espoused so vigorously. He argued, for example, that the 'harsh electoral reality' was that Labour needed to broaden its appeal and hence its electoral base. The party could not rely 'merely on a combination of the dispossessed, the "traditional" and increasingly fragmentary working class and minority groups for the winning of power'. If Labour was to win, it had 'to relate to and draw support from the modern working classes whose upward social mobility, increased expectations and extended horizons are largely the result of opportunities afforded them by our movement in the past' (Kinnock 1985: 2, quoted in Jones 1996: 116).

Kinnock therefore began the gradual process of broadening Labour's appeal by moving it back towards the centre of the political spectrum and attempting to rid the party of its extremist and 'loony left' image. He proceeded cautiously at first, partly because of the weakness of his own position within the party and the strength of the left. At first he concentrated on internal reforms, expelling members of the Militant Tendency (a far-left group that had infiltrated the party) and strengthening the power of the leadership relative to that of the activists. He had some success, but the electoral pay-offs in the 1987 general election were very modest, a mere 3-point increase in Labour's share of the vote, and this gave an added stimulus to his endeavours to reform the party.

After Labour's third successive defeat in 1987, therefore, Neil Kinnock initiated the policy review, which successfully dumped some of Labour's more extreme policies, such as the commitment to nationalize the banks and the commitment to unilateral nuclear disarmament, although he stepped back from repealing Clause IV (see Seyd 1992; Smith and Spear 1992). Nationalization and nuclear disarmament were of course precisely the two areas where, as we saw in Chapter 5, Labour was most out of touch with public opinion and where the gap between themselves and the Conservatives was greatest. Kinnock also quietly reversed Labour's opposition to Europe, and by 1991 Marquand could write that Labour had become 'unmistakably another European social democratic party, committed, like its continental sister parties, to further European integration, continued membership of the Atlantic alliance and a market-oriented mixed economy' (Marquand 1991: 201).

The policy review, and Labour's continued modernization, again brought some electoral benefits, but more modest ones than Kinnock had hoped for. Labour's share rose 4 points to 35 per cent, less than it had achieved in 1979 after the winter of discontent. After the 1992 defeat Neil Kinnock resigned, and John Smith was elected leader. Labour's popularity in the opinion polls rose as the Conservatives' popularity plummeted after Black Wednesday (when the pound was ejected from the ERM and the Conservatives' reputation for economic competence was irreparably damaged). Smith felt little need to make further major changes in Labour's platform, presumably wishing not to endanger Labour's new popularity by any rash initiatives that might split the party. As Shaw has argued, 'He favoured "playing the long game", that is a calm and measured approach to rebuilding support for Labour. The corollary of this was that sudden changes in policy and organization were not required whilst his consensual style of leadership also made him averse to actions that would alienate large sections of the Party' (Shaw 1996: 192–3). Smith did, however, introduce one member one vote (OMOV) for the re-selection of MPs, and reformed the relation between the party and the unions. Again, these provided important further steps in Labour's modernization and made Blair's eventual programme—especially that of distancing Labour from the unions—considerably easier.[1]

Tony Blair, however, and his fellow modernizers such as Gordon Brown were anxious about John Smith's cautious approach. They were not convinced that victory would come so easily as Smith seemed to think. With the benefit of hindsight, we can now see that the Conservatives were set on a self-destructive path with their civil war over Europe, and that Smith's approach would almost certainly have delivered victory in 1997. But in 1994 one might have expected the Conservative instinct for self-preservation to have been stronger. Previous governments had often managed substantial recoveries after mid-term slumps. Moreover, our own evidence at the time suggested that there were many disillusioned Conservative voters who might perhaps have been persuaded to return to their party at a general election. For example, we found that the Conservatives' disastrous performances in the mid-term European and local elections of 1994 were in large part caused by abstention. It was clear that a large number of former Conservatives had stayed at home. Their disillusion with the party was such that they could not bring themselves to go out and vote Conservative, but equally many of them were unwilling to cross party lines and vote for the Liberal Democrats or for Labour, whose acting leader at that time was Margaret Beckett, following John Smith's untimely death.

At that stage of the electoral cycle, in the early summer of 1994, our analysis suggested that Labour should not be complacent. One useful indicator is provided

---

[1] The modernizers were also fortunate that, under Smith, agreement had already been reached that the trade union block vote at the party conference would be reduced from 70 : 30 to 50 : 50 when individual membership rose above 300,000. This was implemented in 1995.

Table 6.1. Flow of the vote in Great Britain, 1992–1994

Vote in the 1992 general election	Vote in the 1994 European elections					
	Conservative	Labour	Liberal Democrat	Other	Did not vote	N
Conservative	34	4	8	4	50	746
Labour	0	57	3	2	37	536
Liberal Democrat	3	15	39	5	38	314
Other	2	15	3	41	41	47
Did not vote	5	10	3	2	80	163
All	15	22	11	4	47	1,806

Sources: BEPS 1992–4.

by the flow of the vote between 1992 and 1994. Table 6.1 shows the pattern of vote-switching that had taken place between 1992 and 1994. The first and most striking feature of the table is the relatively high level of Conservative abstention. Turnout in European elections is of course notoriously low (see e.g. Heath *et al* 1999*a* , and the references cited there), and all parties saw many of their supporters stay at home. The proportion was, however, much higher among the Conservatives in our sample, 50 per cent of whom reported that they had stayed at home compared with 37 per cent of Labour voters.[2] It can be shown that almost half of the 18-point change in the size of the Conservative lead was a result of this differential abstention (McLean *et al.* 1996).

The second crucial feature is that, when former Conservatives did switch to another party, they were much more likely to switch to the Liberal Democrats than to Labour. In particular, for every Conservative who switched to Labour, two switched to the Liberal Democrats. And while the Liberal Democrats were also losing heavily to Labour at this point in the electoral cycle, their gains from the Tories matched their losses to Labour. This also tallied with the experience of 1964 and 1974, when unpopular Conservative governments had seen substantial defections to the Liberals and the Labour victories had proved to be highly marginal, with only a four-seat majority in 1964 and a minority government in February 1974. At this stage of the electoral cycle, then, it seemed quite possible that many former Conservatives might return to the party at the next general election. While the return of the abstainers would not have been anything like sufficient on its own to give the Conservatives victory in 1997, it would have narrowed the gap between the parties to about 7 points (compared with a gap of 20 or more points in the mid-term opinion polls). This

---

[2] Respondents' reports of their turnout are of course notoriously out of line with the official turnout figures. In the present case this will partly reflect response bias, people who were not interested in politics and therefore less likely to turnout in the European elections being more likely to drop out of the panel. It will also reflect some tendency for respondents to over- claim their turnout. However, we should also note that the official figures are likely to be biased downwards, reflecting errors and redundancy in the registers, as well as people leaving the registers either through death or migration. For a detailed treatment of these issues, see Swaddle and Heath 1989.

would have given the Conservatives a base from which to launch a plausible attempt to retain power, perhaps with the aid of some pre-election tax cuts.

So we believe that, back in 1994, the modernizers were right not to take eventual victory for granted. John Smith's death of a heart attack provided the opportunity for the modernizers. Tony Blair succeeded to the leadership and immediately set about his modernizing project. There were several key features of this 'project': institutional, ideological, image. We shall have little to say about institutional changes, since they have been studied in detail elsewhere, but their importance should not be underestimated. In some ways the internal changes, especially consultation of members, were a key to the other policy successes, for example securing the reform of Clause IV of the Labour Party's constitution. (Seyd 1998 provides a detailed account.)

On the ideological side there were three main changes. First, the replacement of Clause IV of the Labour Party's constitution and, as a corollary, the abandonment of plans to renationalize industries that the Conservatives had privatized. Secondly, the abandonment of a Keynesian, interventionist strategy designed to secure full employment and its replacement by a broad acceptance of market forces and a Thatcherite commitment to low inflation. Thirdly, the abandonment of Labour's previous tax and spend commitments, which the modernizers believed had seriously damaged their electoral chances in 1992 (Sopel 1995: 246). In addition, Blair distanced the party from the unions by insisting that no special relationship with the unions should exist and by making no effort to woo trade union leaders; the trade unions would be consulted by a future Labour government only in the same way as other groups. Blair used every opportunity to make it clear that, if Labour came to power, the unions would receive 'fairness not favours' (speech to the TUC, Sept.1995, quoted in Seyd 1998: 62) and the 1997 manifesto made it explicit that the key elements of Margaret Thatcher's and Norman Tebbit's trade union reforms—on ballots, picketing, and industrial action—would not be repealed.

On the positive side, Labour emphasized investment in education: 'absolute priority to education and skills as the means both of enhancing opportunity and creating an efficient economy' (Blair 1994: 6). There was also a radical programme of constitutional change—in particular devolution for Scotland and Wales, an elected mayor for London, reform of the House of Lords, a freedom of information Act, and proportional representation. The constitutional programme was in many ways the most radical aspect of Labour's 1997 manifesto, although it is a little unclear how integral this was to the New Labour project itself. Devolution, in particular, was a topic where Labour was constrained by its Old Labour legacy in Scotland.

To symbolize the changes, Blair and the modernizers talked of the New Labour Party that they now led, in contrast to the Old Labour Party, with its commitment to government intervention and full employment, public ownership, and universal social services funded through taxation. In many ways, of course, the breaks with the past were not nearly as radical as the modernizers sometimes suggested, and they can be seen as an evolutionary step along the path that Neil Kinnock had already charted. But New Labour made it even clearer than Neil Kinnock had done that the party, or at any rate the party leadership, had turned its back on the 'statist socialism' of Michael Foot's Labour Party. Blair talked of social-ism, of social democracy, of left-of-centre politics, but scarcely ever of socialism. As Pat Seyd has argued:

Just fifteen months after his election as leader, Blair was engaged in initiating changes to his party more fundamental than any since Labour adopted a new constitution and programme in 1918. By the time the Labour Party was elected to government in May 1997 it had a new constitution, new policies, new internal structures, and a new image. The party had been changed out of all recognition. A revolution had occurred in British party politics more significant than anything since the Conservative Party's postwar adaptation to social democracy. (Seyd 1998: 49)

The electoral aim of these changes, we assume, was to reach out beyond Old Labour's traditional base in the ever-shrinking working class and among deprived minorities and to gain new recruits in the expanding middle classes and aspiring middle-income groups. As Blair himself said (*Guardian*, 25 Feb. 1995, quoted in Seyd 1998), New Labour's target voters were to be those in 'middle income, middle Britain', a shorthand for a strategy aimed at moving the party away from its traditional concentrations of support among manual workers in northern industrial communities. As Seyd has argued, the strategy was to appeal to voters with economic and social aspirations rather than to the poor and disadvantaged; Labour would aim to represent the great majority of the public, not an assemblage of minorities (Seyd 1998: 60). In many respects this was exactly the same strategy as Neil Kinnock's.

To a large extent, then, New Labour accepted the analysis of social change put forward by Giles Radice. They seemed to accept Lipsey's account of the two-thirds : one-third society described in Chapter 2. However, it is probably also true that the modernizers were genuinely convinced that the Old Labour strategies of government intervention and public ownership would not actually work in practice. The record of interventionist and collectivist strategies when Labour had been in office in 1974–9 was not encouraging. Whereas the left of the party had drawn the conclusion from the failure of Jim Callaghan's Labour government in 1979 that the party had not been faithful enough to its socialist goals, the modernizers drew much the same conclusion that Margaret Thatcher had done: 'Variations in levels of borrowing, taxation and public spending as means of influencing economic performance were no longer realistic options since budget deficits and tax regimes had to be kept broadly in line with those prevailing in other major industrialised countries' (Shaw 1996: 201).

A key aspect of the New Labour project, therefore, was to adopt a realistic approach to the economy in the modern world in place of the utopianism of Old Labour. In this respect the modernizers shared our analysis in Chapter 5 (and expounded earlier in Heath *et al.* 1985) that a large part of Labour's failures in the past had been due to its lack of realism and effectiveness in managing the economy or achieving its own goals. The aim of New Labour was to acquire not only a moderate image but also a reputation for effectiveness. New Labour would attempt less, but it promised that it would actually deliver. Given the Conservatives' economic failures over the ERM and taxation, New Labour had the ideal opportunity to acquire a reputation for competence.

The Economic Issues

Perhaps the boldest, and symbolically most important, change introduced by Tony Blair when he became leader was to revise Clause IV of the party's constitution. The old clause had committed the party

To secure for the workers by hand or by brain the full fruits of their industry and the most equitable distribution thereof that may be possible upon the basis of the common ownership of the means of production, distribution and exchange.

In effect, this had committed the party to a programme of nationalization of industry. It was seen by many on the left as the touchstone of socialism, and it had of course been the focus of a bitter dispute after the 1959 defeat, when a previous modernizing leader of the Labour Party, Hugh Gaitskell, had unsuccessfully attempted to revise Clause IV. Neil Kinnock, presumably wishing to avoid yet more damaging internal strife, had merely watered down the commitment to nationalization rather than abandoning it altogether. The changes which the policy review made were relatively modest. It removed the 1983 proposals to extend public ownership to banks, but it retained, for example, the commitment to return the major utilities to public ownership (although the commitment was hedged with caveats about cost). Essentially it represented a return to the *status quo ante* and still left in policy terms a substantial gulf between Labour and the Conservatives.

Tony Blair decided to go much further. He objected to Clause IV on the grounds that it confused means with ends, that it was outdated, and that it gave the Tories the opportunity to misrepresent Labour's policies.

By reason of the need to distinguish itself from the Liberal reformers, the Labour constitution identified itself with one particular strand of socialist thinking, namely state ownership. This meant that its ideology came to be governed by too narrow a view of democratic socialism. Over time, Clause IV took on the status of a totem. Our agenda was misrepresented. And as statist socialism lost credibility, so did we lose support.

Further, the gap between our stated aims and policies in government fed the constant charge of betrayal—the view that our problem was that the leadership was too timid to tread the real path to true socialism. This did immense harm to the party. (Blair 1995: 4)

A main purpose we presume, then, was to establish with the electorate that Labour really had changed and that the doubts that had perhaps prevented Neil Kinnock from leading the party to success in 1992 should be finally erased. Blair also seems to have been thinking ahead beyond victory and was wishing to avoid the charges of betrayal that had been levelled by the left at Harold Wilson's Labour governments. Blair wanted to get his betrayal in first.

Table 6.2. Positions relative to Labour on nationalization and privatization, 1983–1997

Year	Percentage who were			
	Left of Labour	Same as Labour	Right of Labour	Net balance
1983	8	13	78	+70
1987	12	17	70	+58
1992	17	23	59	+42
1994	17	24	58	+41
1997	26	34	40	+14

Sources: BES 1983, N = 3,493; *1987*, N = 3,532; *1992*, N = 1,633 (half-sample); *BEPS 1994*, N = 1,777; *BES* 1997, N = 2,538.

Did the electorate notice that New Labour had abandoned Clause IV, and did they now believe that Labour really had abandoned socialism? The 1992–7 panel study is particularly valuable here as it enables us to compare the position in 1997 with that in 1994 after John Smith had died but before Blair had won the leadership of the party or reformed Clause IV. In Table 6.2 we report our respondents' positions on nationalization, relative to the Labour Party, at the time of the 1992 defeat, in mid-1994 before Blair had begun his New Labour project, and again in 1997.

Table 6.2 suggests that Neil Kinnock's policy review had had some limited success but still left Labour some way out of touch with the electorate. There was little change in public perceptions between 1992 and 1994 while the party was under John Smith's leadership. A large proportion of the electorate was still situated to Labour's right, 59 per cent in 1992 and 58 per cent in 1994, suggesting that Labour was still vulnerable on the question of public ownership. Tony Blair's repeal of Clause IV made a more substantial change after 1994, and the net balance shrank from 41 points to 14 in 1997. New Labour had indeed positioned itself much closer to the median voter.

Neil Kinnock's policy review was also fairly modest in the changes it sought in other areas of economic strategy. It retained an Old Labour commitment to full employment; it explicitly rejected a Thatcherite approach and by inference it advocated an interventionist strategy involving public–private collaboration in local consortia that would receive some public funding. New Labour in contrast dropped the commitment to full employment and largely abandoned an interventionist strategy. As Seyd has argued,

Brown's economic strategy [as shadow chancellor] was predicated on the assumption that the party was constrained by two factors: one international, globalization; the other domestic, taxpayer revolt. Globalization would restrict a Labour government's ability to control and direct capital and, in particular, to use public expenditure to stimulate growth in employment. . . . Brown was more intent on controlling inflation in order to improve Britain's economic competitiveness than on expanding employment. (Seyd 1998: 61)

Table 6.3. Positions relative to Labour on unemployment and inflation, 1983–1997

Year	Percentage who were			
	Left of Labour	Same as Labour	Right of Labour	Net balance
1983	20	36	44	+24
1987	19	38	43	+24
1992	27	32	41	+14
1994	23	32	45	+22
1997	25	39	35	+10

Sources: BES 1983, N = 3,738; *1987*, N = 3,655; *1992*, N = 1,672; *1997*, N = 2,609; *BEPS 1994*, N = 1,804.

Globalization meant the end of the kind of Keynesian interventionist strategy that Labour had previously advocated in order to reflate the economy and reduce unemployment. In essence New Labour's strategy for dealing with unemployment and inflation seemed little different from Margaret Thatcher's. And like Margaret Thatcher, the new Labour leadership felt that there was no alternative. Any attempt to intervene would be speedily punished by the markets, a view incidentally shared by many economists who have studied the politico-business cycle. Indeed, the Tories' own attempts at government intervention in order to boost consumer purchasing power in the run-up to the 1992 election were savagely punished by the markets after the election.

Table 6.3 shows relatively little change in the electorate's position relative to Labour over the whole of the period, the net balance falling by a rather modest 14 points from 24 in 1983 to 10 in 1997. To be sure, as we saw in Chapter 5, this was an area where Labour had previously been fairly close to the electorate, but the remarkable thing is that the electorate did not perceive New Labour to hold anything like a Thatcherite position on the control of inflation and unemployment. We saw in Chapter 3 that in 1997, 65 per cent of the electorate had been to the left of the Conservatives and only 15 per cent to their right, giving a net balance of –50 points on unemployment and inflation. This contrasts with a Labour net balance of +10 points. The parties were still seen to be well apart, and there were a great number of voters who saw the Conservatives to be on their right on this issue and Labour on their left.

New Labour, then seems to have managed a remarkable feat: they had stolen the Tories' clothes but the electorate thought that they looked a great deal more presentable in them than the Tories ever had done.

Why? First, New Labour had not done anything dramatic and symbolic like the reform of Clause IV to bring home to the electorate how much they had changed from their Keynesian and interventionist past. As Seyd points out, there had been some evolution of Shadow Chancellor Gordon Brown's thinking, and it would hardly have been surprising if the electorate were less than fully informed about the exact state of Labour thinking. Perhaps also the electorate found it hard to believe that a Labour government would be able to ignore the problem of unemployment in the same ruthless way that the Conservatives had appeared to ignore it over the previous eighteen years. After all, there was now plenty of hard evidence over an extraordinrily long period that Thatcherite governments had tolerated high levels of unemployment. There were also of course some differences in policy: thus one of New Labour's five key election pledges was to take 250,000 young people off welfare and into work. New Labour rhetoric thus seemed to have a more compassionate tone than Thatcherite rhetoric had ever done.

The third major area of New Labour reform was taxation. Despite the academic evidence to the contrary, New Labour believed that it was constrained by the likelihood of taxpayer revolt against any increase in taxes. As we argued in Chapter 3, the evidence for this proposition is inevitably contestable, given the difficulties of validating survey measures of the electorate's attitudes towards taxation. In the policy review Neil Kinnock had written: 'We will not spend, nor will we promise to spend, more than the country can afford,' but there was still an implicit commitment to increased spending as economic growth allowed. Gordon Brown in contrast made a clear and public commitment to remain within the Conservatives' spending plans for the first two years of a new Parliament and not to increase the basic rate of income tax.

Table 6.4 indicates that the electorate appear to have registered this change in policy, unlike the changes in economic policy on unemployment and inflation. From 1983 until 1994 about 20 per cent of the electorate had been to Labour's left and well over 50 per cent to Labour's right, with little election-to-election variation. But after 1994 there was a clear-cut shift in the distribution, with the percentage to Labour's right falling by 19 points. The upshot of this was that, as with nationalization, Labour had now positioned itself very close to the median voter.

It is also rather remarkable that, as with economic strategy on unemployment and inflation, New Labour had explicitly adopted key elements of Conservative policy but they were still perceived by the electorate to be some way to the left of the Tories. Thus, while the net balance for Labour on taxation and unemployment was +3 points in 1997, for the Conservatives it was a massive −58 points. In some ways this is even more surprising than the similar discrepancy on unemployment and

Table 6.4. Positions relative to Labour on taxes and spending, 1983–1997

Year	Percentage who were			
	Left of Labour	Same as Labour	Right of Labour	Net balance
1983	20	21	59	+39
1987	18	25	57	+39
1992	19	24	57	+38
1994	20	27	53	+33
1997	31	34	34	+3

Sources: BES 1983, N = 3,600; *1987*, N = 3,573; *1992*, N = 1,677 (half-sample); *1997*, N = 2,594; *BEPS 1994*, N = 1,794.

Table 6.5. Positions relative to the Conservatives and Labour on the economic issues, 1983–1997

Issue	Closest party, 1983			Closest party, 1997		
	Labour	Equidistant	Conservative	Labour	Equidistant	Conservative
Nationalization	28	17	55	61	19	21
Unemployment	52	17	31	55	24	22
Spending, taxes	45	17	38	62	20	18

Sources: *BES 1983*, min. N = 3,471; *1997*, min. N = 2,502.

inflation. An explicit commitment to Conservative plans, for the first two years of the Parliament at least, was still seen to be a substantially different policy position from the Conservatives' own. Maybe this was part of a general 'halo' effect, whereas the Conservatives were suffering from what we have termed the 'forked tail' effect. That is to say, after the debacle of sterling's ejection from the ERM, the Conservatives were generally seen in a bad light, and this may have extended from the narrow area of financial competence to the whole of range economic policies. Many of the electorate came to hold a poor view of the party in general, and this extended to a poor view of their policies as well, with the electorate tending to distance themselves from Conservative positions. Conversely, the Labour Party was seen in a much rosier light, and so the electorate came to feel sympathetic to their policies as well. In this respect, we suspect that judgements of policy are not in fact all that divorced from judgements of competence.

At any rate, between 1983 and 1997 there had been a complete transformation in the ideological relationship between the electorate and the two main parties. As Table 6.5 shows, the positions had not merely been reversed between 1983 and 1997: by 1997 Labour had a bigger lead on all three issues than the Conservatives had enjoyed in 1983.

The Non-Economic Issues

On privatization, unemployment, taxation, and government spending Labour had essentially adopted Thatcherite policies, although, as we have seen, the electorate seemed to be much happier with the New Labour version of Thatcherism than they were with John Major's (or indeed with Margaret Thatcher's own version). Moreover, on the economic issues New Labour made a sharp break not only from the Old Labour of 1983 but also from Neil Kinnock's policy review. However,there was much more continuity, at least with Neil Kinnock, on the main non-economic issues. On these issues it was Neil Kinnock who had made the radical break with Labour's recent past. Correspondingly, on these non-economic issues some substantial policy differences remained between New Labour and the Conservatives. Whereas on the economy New Labour largely accepted the Thatcherite dispensation, on the constitution Labour was diametrically opposed to many Conservative policies.

Table 6.6. Positions relative to Labour on nuclear weapons, 1983–1992

Year	Percentage who were			
	Left of Labour	Same as Labour	Right of Labour	Net balance
1983	12	14	74	+62
1987	11	14	75	+64
1992	25	14	62	+37

Notes: For details of question wording, see Ch. 4.

Sources: *BES 1983*, N = 3,663; *1987*, N = 3,635; *BEPS 1992* N = 1,524. The 1992 data come from the 1987 to 1992 panel study, not from the *BES*.

First, Neil Kinnock's policy review abandoned Old Labour's commitment to unilateral nuclear disarmament and replaced it with a commitment to multilateral negotiations aimed at removing all nuclear weapons by the year 2000. In the absence of multilateral agreement Britain's existing nuclear weapons were to be maintained, but nuclear testing would be stopped and some of the Tories' plans for expanding Britain's nuclear capabilities would be scrapped. New Labour made little change in policy.

Table 6.6 shows the electorate's changing positions on nuclear weapons relative to Labour over the 1983–92 period. As we noted in Chapter 4, questions on nuclear disarmament were dropped from the BES in 1997 as the issue had largely disappeared from the political agenda with the end of the cold war. However, Table 6.6 shows clearly enough that Neil Kinnock's policy review had substantial success in bringing Labour more in tune with the electorate on disarmament: between 1983 and 1987 there was no real change in the net balance, but after the policy review the net balance fell by almost half. Labour was still seen as being to the left of a majority of the electorate, but the electorate clearly recognized that there had been a major change in position.

Secondly, devolution was another part of the New Labour inheritance from Old Labour that Tony Blair and the modernizers decided not to reject. The policy review had promised a directly elected Scottish Assembly or Parliament, with substantial legislative powers, including tax-varying powers. New Labour added the requirement for a referendum, but apart from this there was little change in policy. Table 6.7 shows that in 1979 there were more members of the Scottish electorate who placed themselves to the left of the Labour Party on devolution than to the right. It will be recalled that this was shortly after the failure of the 1979 referendum: a majority of the Scottish electorate had voted in favour of devolution, but the Labour government had added the proviso that 40 per cent of the eligible electorate, and not simply a majority of those who actually voted, needed to support devolution if the measure was to be implemented. In the event, only 33 per cent of the eligible electorate voted in favour, and the measure therefore failed. It would not be surprising if, at this time, the Scottish electorate felt that the Labour Party was relatively unsympathetic to devolution.

Table 6.7. The Scottish electorate's positions relative to Labour on Scottish devolution, 1979–1997

Year	Percentage who were			
	Left of Labour	Same as Labour	Right of Labour	Net balance
1979	39	33	28	−11
1992	29	43	28	−1
1997	38	39	23	−15

Notes: For details of question wording, see Ch. 4.

Sources: *SES 1979*, N = 841; *1992*, N = 854; *1997*, N = 742.

Kinnock's policy review removed the requirement for a referendum, and so in 1992 we find that Labour's policies were more closely in touch with the preferences of the Scottish electorate. New Labour reinstated the need for a referendum (although, unlike 1979, a simple majority of votes cast in the referendum would be sufficient). Table 6.7 suggests that this New Labour proposal was not quite as popular with the Scottish electorate as the policy review's had been.

Thirdly, Neil Kinnock also quietly reversed Old Labour's hostility to Europe. He in fact dropped the commitment to withdraw from Europe before the policy review, and the review itself was very like Labour's 1997 manifesto, with a pragmatic approach to Europe, opposing the idea of a 'federal superstate' (Blair) or 'superpower' (Kinnock), favouring enlargement, and adopting the social chapter. In policy terms this left Labour still some distance from the active hostility to Europe of the Eurosceptic wing of the Tories. Table 6.8 suggests that, despite its largely unchanged policies, New Labour seemed to be further away from the electorate on Europe than the party had been under Neil Kinnock, the net balance rising from 7 to 34 points. As we saw in Chapter 4, the electorate had been moving to the right between 1992 and 1997, and so in effect the electorate had been moving away from the more Europhile position that Kinnock had adopted.

It looks at first sight, then, as though New Labour might have been unwise, at least from an electoral point of view, to have remained with the European policies bequeathed by Neil Kinnock. They were, however, rescued by the Conservatives. The Conservatives were of course greatly divided over Europe, and, as we described in Chapter 4, this meant that the electorate too were divided in their perceptions of Tory policy: Eurosceptics tended to see the Tories as being some way to their left, whereas Europhiles saw them as being some way to their right.[3]

Table 6.9 summarizes the changes between 1979 and 1997 on these non-economic issues. The picture is quite different from the one we saw on the economic

---

[3] If we calculate closest party based not on the individual respondent's own perception of where the two parties stood but on the basis of the average perceived position, the figures become 37% closer to Labour and 64% closer to Conservatives (with none equidistant).

Table 6.8. Positions relative to Labour on European integration, 1979–1997

Year	Percentage who were			
	Left of Labour	Same as Labour	Right of Labour	Net balance
1979	31	26	43	+12
1992	36	21	43	+7
1994	26	23	51	+24
1997	19	27	53	+34

Notes: For question wording, see Ch. 4.

Sources: *BES 1992*, N = 1,557; *BEPS 1994*, N = 1,743; *BES 1997*, N = 2,522.

Table 6.9. Positions relative to the Conservatives and Labour on the non-economic issues, 1979–1997

Issue	Closest party in 1979–83			Closest party in 1992–7		
	Labour	Equidistant	Conservative	Labour	Equidistant	Conservative
Nuclear weapons	36	13	51	37	14	49
Devolution	36	49	15	62	19	19
Europe	44	20	36	45	26	29

Notes: The figures on Europe for 1979–83 come from *BES 1979* as the relevant questions were not asked in 1983. The figures on nuclear weapons for 1992–7 come from *BES 1992* as the relevant questions were dropped in 1997. The figures on devolution for both periods relate to Scottish respondents only.

Sources: *BES 1979*, N = 1,404; *SES 1979*, N = 831; *BES 1983*, N = 3,611; *1997*, N = 3,282; *SES 1997*, N = 727; *BES 1992*, N = 1,249 (half-sample).

issues: whereas on the economic issues Labour had substantially improved its position *vis-à-vis* the Conservatives, there was little change in the balance of advantage on two of the three non-economic issues. Only on Scottish devolution had Labour substantially improved its position, but this had little to do with New Labour.

Nuclear disarmament, devolution, and Europe fall on a different ideological dimension from the socialist/laissez-faire one on which the economic issues are located. As we have argued elsewhere, this dimension can be thought of as reflecting aspects of British national sentiment, and it partly cross-cuts the socialist/laissez-faire one (Heath *et al.*, 1999*b*). Hence Labour's move towards Thatcherite economic policies was quite compatible with an active pursuit of non-Thatcherite policies on devolution, Europe,and defence. In a sense, then, these three issues are not really part of the Blair 'project' strictly defined.

The Squeeze on the Liberal Democrats

By moving back towards the centre of the left–right spectrum New Labour was also, and perhaps most importantly, squeezing the Liberal Democrats. As we saw in Chapter 5, the alliance between the SDP and the Liberals ate deeply in 1983 into the ranks of the left-of-centre voters, although the precise roles of Labour divisions and incompetence and of Labour ideological extremism in this are hard to disentangle. At any rate, a return to the centre, and the more responsible image that was likely to be associated with this, could be expected to reverse much of the damage done in 1983.

Figure 6.1 shows how Labour had closed the gap on their side of the spectrum by 1997 and had positioned themselves closely adjacent to the Liberal Democrats just to the left of centre. The most dramatic case was nationalization, where in 1983 the Alliance had been roughly equidistant between the two main parties, 6.1 points to Labour's right and 6.5 points to the Conservatives' left. By 1992, after Neil Kinnock had brought Labour back towards the centre, the Labour–Liberal Democrat gap had shrunk to 3.6 points while the Conservative–Liberal Democrat gap was little

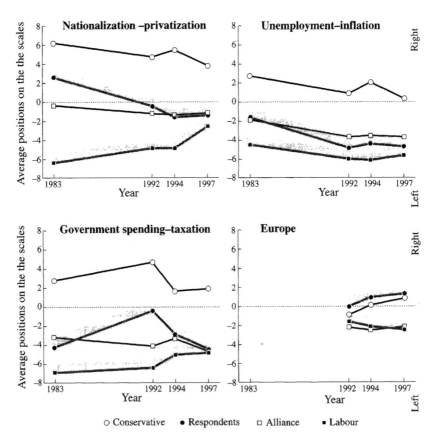

Fig. 6.1. Positions on the issue scales, 1983–1997. The scales have been rescaled with mean zero and range –10 to +10.

Source: BES 1983, BES 1992, minimum N = 1,190; *BEPS 1994,* minimum N = 1,681; *BES 1997,* minimum N = 2,413.

changed. But after 1994 New Labour were seen by the electorate to have moved even closer to the Liberal Democrats, with the gap now down to 1.5 points in 1997.

As our previous analysis has led us to expect, the changes on unemployment and inflation were much smaller, but there were, on the other hand, some major changes with respect to taxation and government spending. From an initial 3.5 points in 1983, the Labour–Liberal Democrat gap shrank to 1.8 points in 1994 and by 1997 had become vanishingly small at 0.2 points. In this latter case, however, the gap closed largely because the Liberal Democrats were seen to have moved left, and here of course the electorate were right: the Liberal Democrats had promised in their manifesto to increase taxes in order to fund greater government spending on health and education.

Interestingly, content analysis of the party manifestos (Budge 1999) suggests that the Liberal Democrats' manifesto in 1997 was somewhat to the left of Labour's. Our respondents, however, continued to place Labour to the left of the Liberal Democrats on all four of the major issues which we covered. Perhaps some of our respondents did not believe that Labour had changed quite as much as the official pronouncements implied (as we noted above in the context of economic policy). They were, however, quite clear that the gap between Labour and the Liberal Democrats had been sharply reduced.

This new close proximity between Labour and the Liberal Democrats had a number of important consequences, not least the changed pattern of tactical voting in 1997. People are most likely to cast a tactical vote when their own preferred party has little chance of winning their constituency, and when they are more or less indifferent between their first and second choice parties (Heath *et al.* 1991; Niemi *et al.* 1992). The close ideological proximity between Labour and the Liberal Democrats meant that a larger proportion of the electorate, particularly those in the centre of the ideological spectrum, regarded these two parties more or less equally favourably.[4]

As Evans and his colleagues have shown, the result was that the pattern of tactical switching in 1997 was considerably different from that in 1992 (and in previous elections). In the 1992 election the Liberal Democrats had lost rather more tactical votes to the Conservatives than to Labour (1.8 per cent of all voters switched tactically from Liberal Democrat to Conservative and 1.5 per cent to Labour). In contrast, in 1997 the Liberal Democrats were much more likely to lose tactical votes to Labour than they were to the Conservatives (a ratio of 1.3 per cent to 2.2 per cent) (Evans *et al.* 1998.)

---

[4] As Evans and his colleagues have found: 'In 1992 Liberal Democrat supporters were if anything slightly more opposed to Labour than they were to the Conservatives. By 1997 they were much more favourably disposed towards Labour. Moreover, with their opinion of their own party little changed, the gap between their feelings towards the Liberal Democrats and their feelings towards Labour had narrowed significantly. The views of Labour supporters changed too. The average rating they gave to the Liberal Democrats rose by 0.32, greater than the 0.10 increase in the score they gave to their own party. In short, Labour supporters came to see less of a gap between Labour and the Liberal Democrats as well' (Evans *et al.* 1998: 75–6).

This increased level of tactical switching between Labour and the Liberal Democrats in turn had major consequences for the share of the seats which the two parties won, and, for example, allowed the Liberal Democrats to win a much increased number of seats despite a fall in their share of the vote. New Labour's squeeze on the Liberal Democrats by moving close to the centre of the ideological spectrum thus almost certainly deprived the latter of votes that they might otherwise have won, but at the same time allowed the Liberal Democrats to capture seats that the Conservatives might have held in the absence of tactical voting.

New Labour's move to the centre also, not surprisingly, changed the ideological profile of its voters. Figures 6.2 and 6.3 show the changing ideological pattern of support for Labour in 1992 and 1997. In 1992 the picture was not unlike that in 1979, with Labour support falling as we move from left to right along the ideological spectrum and Conservative support rising. However, the Conservatives were stronger on the right, securing 83 per cent of the 10th (the most right-wing) decile, than Labour were on the left, where they could manage only 68 per cent of the 1st (most left-wing) decile—a much lower proportion than they had obtained in 1979 or 1983. The gradient of Labour support was accordingly rather flatter in 1992 than it had been earlier: presumably Neil Kinnock's move towards the centre had already increased Labour's appeal to voters located in the centre and on the right, while inspiring less enthusiasm among the more left-wing members of the electorate.

It is also notable that in 1992 the Liberal Democrats had a rather symmetrical profile, obtaining almost as many votes from right-of-centre voters as they did from left-of-centre voters. This of course was quite unlike the 1983 picture, when the Alliance were especially strong on the left of centre, capitalizing on Labour's extremism, divisions, and perceived incompetence at that time. By 1992 they had

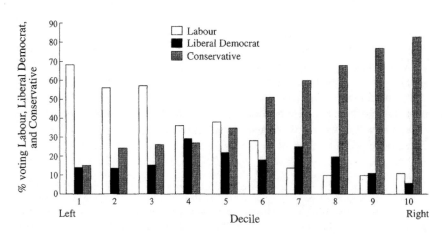

Fig. 6.2. Ideological position and vote, 1992. Percentages do not sum to 100 as voters for other parties are not reported in the figure. Each decile has about 200 respondents.

Source: BES 1992

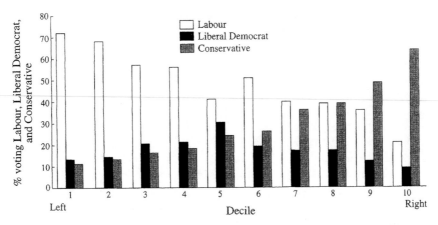

Fig. 6.3. Ideological position and vote, 1997. Percentages do not sum to 100 as voters for other parties are not reported in the figure. Each decile has about 200 respondents.
Source: BES 1997

already been driven back by Neil Kinnock's move towards the centre and his efforts to make the party electable. However, they had managed to make some compensating gains on the right.

By 1997, however, New Labour's further move towards the centre under Tony Blair had produced a much more radical change in the ideological sources of Labour support. The Conservatives of course made huge losses at all points in the ideological spectrum, just as Labour had done in 1983, the Conservative share of the vote falling by 20 points or more in the 6th, 7th, 8th, 9th, and 10th deciles between 1992 and 1997. Interestingly, however, Labour in 1983 did considerably better among the far left, with 77 per cent of the vote of the 1st decile, than the Conservatives did in 1997 among the far right, where they were down to 63 per cent of the 10th decile. Under Michael Foot and his left-wing manifesto Labour managed to retain the enthusiasm of their fellow ideologues much better than the Conservatives did under John Major in 1997. It is important therefore not to draw too close a parallel between the Labour rout in 1983 and the Conservative rout in 1997: the Labour rout was at least in part ideologically driven, but the Conservative rout was almost wholly a matter of perceived incompetence not ideology.

The most remarkable feature of Figure 6.3, however, is that despite Conservative unpopularity on the right of the political spectrum, the Liberal Democrats failed to strengthen their position on the right. Virtually all the net gains went to Labour. As a result the Labour profile in 1997 took on quite an extraordinary shape: Labour strengthened its position only slightly on the left—up from 68 to 72 per cent in the 1st decile, from 56 to 68 per cent in the 2nd decile, and from 56 to 57 per cent in the 3rd decile. But New Labour made huge gains on the right, with increases of over 20 percentage points in the 6th, 7th, 8th, and 9th deciles.

Table 6.10. Labour share of the vote under John Smith
(1992–4) and Tony Blair (1994–1997) (%)

Respondents' ideological position (decile)	1992–4	1994–7
1	+5	−2
2	+14	−2
3	+2	−1
4	+17	+2
5	+6	+9
6	+3	+20
7	+16	+10
8	+12	+18
9	+3	+22
10	−3	+13

Notes: The figures for 1994 are based on current vote intention not on actual votes in the European or local elections.

Source: *BEPS 1992–7*.

Given the tactical switching between Labour and the Liberal Democrats, it is of course possible that some of these Labour gains on the right were tactical ones rather than 'sincere' ones. But if we exclude tactical voters from the analysis, the picture on the right of the spectrum is largely unchanged. (See Table A6.2.)

How much of this was actually due to Tony Blair and New Labour? Would much the same kind of process have happened if John Smith had continued to lead the Labour Party? While it may seem obvious that Labour gains on the right of the political spectrum must have had a great deal to do with New Labour's move to the centre, it is always worth checking on the obvious. Table 6.10 shows the Labour gains at each point on the ideological spectrum under John Smith, that is between the 1992 general election and the 1994 European elections. It then compares the Smith gains with Tony Blair's gains between 1994 and the 1997 general election.

What stands out clearly is that Labour under John Smith (and under Margaret Beckett, who was acting leader in 1994) made substantial gains more or less right across the ideological spectrum (except among the furthest-right decile). The gains were a bit uneven, probably reflecting sampling error, but they were quite substantial both on the centre-right and on the centre-left, and were not trivial on the left itself in the 1st and 2nd deciles. So even without any ideological repositioning, John Smith managed to make substantial gains on the right of the spectrum.

In contrast, between 1994 and 1997 Tony Blair and New Labour lost ground somewhat on the left, made only modest gains on the centre-left, and had their largest gains on the right of the spectrum. Unlike the 1979–83 and the 1992–4 periods, when gains and losses tended to take an across-the-board character, the 1994–97 gains were highly unevenly distributed and we have no hesitation in attributing them to New Labour's ideological shift rather than to its perceived competence (or to the Conservatives' perceived incompetence).

It follows from this evidence that New Labour must have drawn many new

Table 6.11. Flow of the vote in Great Britain, 1992–1997

Vote in the 1992 general election	Vote in the 1997 general election					
	Conservative	Labour	Liberal Democrat	Other	Did not vote	N
Conservative	59	16	11	4	10	883
Labour	2	80	6	2	11	850
Liberal Democrat	4	26	52	5	13	266
Other	0	25	8	58	10	52
Did not vote	11	21	10	2	56	398
New voters	18	39	22	2	20	128
All	24	40	14	4	18	2,577

Notes: Respondents' reports of their vote in 1992 are a recall measure from 1997. See Table A6.1 for figures based on the panel.

Source: BES 1997.

recruits directly from the Conservatives. Whereas in the first part of the electoral cycle, as Table 6.1 showed, the Liberal Democrats had received the lion's share of Conservative defectors, in the second part it was Labour that benefited most from Conservative defections.

The flow of the vote matrix given in Table 6.11 shows a very different pattern from that of Table 6.1, which looked at the flow of the vote between 1992 and 1994. The first point of course is that, at the 1997 general election, the abstention rates were very similar among former Conservatives, Labour, and Liberal Democrat voters. Whereas in the European (and local) elections of 1994 the Conservatives had suffered more severely than the other parties from abstention, this was no longer true in the 1997 general election. The claim that some Tories made (e.g. Critchley and Halcrow 1997)—that their voters had stayed at home rather than vote for one of the opposition parties at the general election—was simply not true. Or at least, it was no more true than it was for the other parties. Tory abstention cannot explain the Tory defeat. (We look in more detail at the question of abstention in Chapter 8.)

The second major point is that Conservative defectors were in 1997 more likely to switch to Labour than to the Liberal Democrats, reversing the pattern that had been true in virtually all previous elections for which we have the relevant data (Heath *et al.* 1991). (The only exception was in 1970, another election when Labour was seen to be rather close ideologically to the centre.)

In a thinly veiled attack on our previous work[5] Philip Gould wrote:

As Labour stumbled from defeat to defeat it was never quite alone. The psephologists were always there . . . dedicated followers of failure, always wanting to make sense of yet another defeat, always willing to speculate that, yes, it was possible that one day Labour might win.

Not that we took their advice. In the aftermath of 1992 we were advised that leadership

---

[5] The book which we assume Gould was attacking was *Labour's Last Chance?* (Heath *et al.* 1994c). He seemed to be singling out the chapters by Crewe and King on leadership, Curtice and Semetko on newspapers, and Heath, Jowell, and Curtice on switching.

had not been a decisive issue, that tabloid attacks had had no effect, that we could raise tax without fear of electoral damage, that few Conservative voters would switch directly to us without stopping first at the Liberals. Needless to say we based our strategy on precisely the opposite precepts and just managed to scrape home. (Gould 1998: 3)

If John Smith had lived, our advice might well have been vindicated, but the evidence of this chapter shows rather clearly that the New Labour strategy did contradict our predictions (although in self-defence we should point out that what we actually said was that 'if Labour were simply to rely on the government's misfortunes it could well be the Liberal Democrats who gain the most votes from disillusioned former Conservatives' (Heath *et al.* 1994c: 290). Of course, the correct formulation is that the greater the ideological distance between any two parties, the less likely voters are to switch between them. When the Liberals are ideologically much closer to the Conservatives than is Labour, we would expect Conservative defectors to be more likely to switch to the Liberals. By repositioning itself so much closer to the Liberal Democrats, New Labour ensured that it was ideologically as attractive a destination for disillusioned former Conservatives as were the Liberal Democrats. To that extent, the pattern of vote-switching between 1992 and 1997 was entirely consistent with standard theory.

Conclusions

Through the policy review Neil Kinnock had begun the process of modernization and making Labour electable. In many respects Tony Blair's New Labour was merely a continuation of what Neil Kinnock had already undertaken, and indeed it is doubtful whether Tony Blair could have been successful without Neil Kinnock's groundwork.

On the non-economic issues such as disarmament, Europe, and devolution Tony Blair made little change from Neil Kinnock's settlement. In these areas Blairism was largely a continuation of Kinnockism not of Thatcherism.

However, it was on the economic issues that New Labour made the clearer break with its old Labour inheritance. On nationalization, unions, government spending, and taxation New Labour went much further than Neil Kinnock had done, and adopted many Thatcherite precepts. Rather remarkably, however, Tony Blair's version of Thatcherism was much more favourably evaluated by the electorate than was the Thatcherism of John Major. The electorate placed themselves much closer to the Labour position than to the Conservative one, despite the formal similarity of their manifesto commitments. As we have suggested, this may have been a consequence of a New Labour 'halo' effect or conversely of a Conservative 'forked tail' effect.

At any rate, the decisive move of New Labour towards the centre on the economic issues did have major electoral benefits. It squeezed the Liberal Democrats' share of the vote on the centre-left, but it also captured ground on the centre-right from the Conservatives. So whereas in 1983 we felt that Old Labour's losses largely took the form of an across-the-board decline due to their incompetence and division, between

1994 and 1997 New Labour's gains did not take the usual across-the-board character but were much more marked on the right of the spectrum than on the left.[6]

New Labour's move to the centre also disrupted the usual patterns of vote-switching, more Conservatives than usual switching directly to Labour rather than to the Liberal Democrats. It also disrupted the usual patterns of tactical voting and led to an increased volume of tactical switching between Labour and the Liberal Democrats—to their mutual benefit in terms of seats. From a political science point of view, however, neither of these consequences was at all surprising.

Appendix 6.1. Supplementary Table

Table A6.1. Flow of the vote in Great Britain, 1992–1997: panel data

Vote in the 1992 general election	Vote in the 1997 general election					N
	Conservative	Labour	Liberal Democrat	Other	Did not vote	
Conservative	59 (58)	13 (14)	12 (14)	4 (4)	11 (11)	633
Labour	2 (2)	83 (80)	4 (6)	2 (2)	9 (9)	473
Liberal Democrat	6 (6)	31 (34)	50 (48)	6 (5)	8 (8)	267
Other	0 (1)	39 (37)	11 (9)	42 (44)	9 (9)	39
Did not vote	19	27	10	2	42	121
All	28 (27)	40 (39)	16 (17)	5 (5)	12 (12)	1,533

Note: Figures in parentheses give the percentages for preferred party in 1997; that is, tactical voters are assigned to the party that they 'really preferred' in place of the one that they reported voting for in 1997.

Sources: BEPS 1992–7.

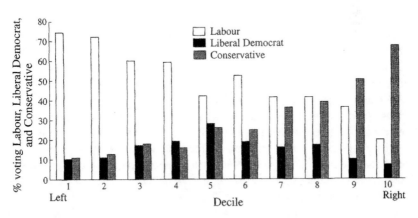

Fig. A6.2. Ideological position and vote, excluding tactical voters, 1997. Percentages do not sum to 100 as voters for other parties are not reported in the figure.

Source: BES 1997

[6] If we fit a loglinear model to the cross-tabulation of vote by ideological position (deciles) for 1992 and 1997 we find that the model of across-the-board change does not give a good fit to the data. Chi^2 is 65.6 for 9 degrees of freedom, $p < 0.001$.

7

The Changing Social Basis of Party Support

In this chapter we turn from the ideological to the social bases of support for the parties. While many of the changes that Margaret Thatcher or Tony Blair engineered in their own parties were primarily ideological, their own analyses were often sociological in character. Margaret Thatcher, for example, believed the essence of her success was that her policies appealed to the middle classes and those that aspired to join them, and she suggested that the Tories' electoral difficulties under John Major were in part because of his government's failure to look after these groups. Similarly, much of the New Labour analysis, as we described in earlier chapters, was based on a sociological account of Labour's contracting social base and its need to appeal to the aspiring members of the working class.

One of the central claims made about Margaret Thatcher's victories—and one that also lay behind Giles Radice's analysis of Labour's 'southern discomfort'—was that her victories were based on the successful recruitment of 'Essex man'. The term 'Essex man' was coined by Simon Heffer to refer to men (and women) from the upper working class or lower-middle classes in the south-east; these voters were believed to be instrumental and materialistic, ambitious for economic advancement, and attracted by the Conservatives' policies of low taxation and economic opportunity (for example, the opportunity to buy one's own home). These voters were believed to have abandoned the Labour Party in large numbers, particularly in south-eastern constituencies like Basildon.

It was precisely these voters that New Labour set out to win back. Much of Giles Radice's analysis that we described in Chapter 2 was geared towards these voters, now redescribed as 'middle income, middle Britain', and much of Tony Blair's reforms of the Labour Party since 1994, such as the commitment to stay within the Conservatives' spending plans, were designed to win these voters back. However, we should remember that another set of theories, such as those of Will Hutton, suggested that these voters might already have been disillusioned by the long recession of the 1990s which hit the south-east relatively hard, by the increased number of house repossessions, and by the growing level of economic insecurity as the pressures of globalization increasingly brought the threat of redundancy and unemployment to groups that were unused to these risks.

At any rate, one central question for us is the voting behaviour of this supposedly key group variously described as Essex man, the aspiring working class, or middle-income middle Britain. The changing voting behaviour of this group may give us at least some clues to the plausibility of the theories underlying New Labour's reforms. Incidentally, we should note that, while the notion of Essex man was very much a catchphrase developed by commentators in the 1980s and taken up by politicians, rather than a theory with solid academic backing, it has many similarities with an earlier, more academic literature on the affluent worker and the phenomenon of 'embourgeoisement'. In that respect the theory was not new, and possibly the phenomenon (as we suggested in Chapter 2) was not all that new either.[1]

While the Conservatives were believed to have successfully recruited Essex man to their side, Old Labour was widely felt to have been too concerned with, and too dependent on, the votes of disadvantaged and declining groups within the working class. At the same time, we need to remember that Old Labour was partly based on a coalition of the two lefts: the traditional old left in the unions and working class and a new left of post-materialists, highly educated, often working in middle-class jobs in the public sector and active in the peace and feminist movements. These groups had been anathema to the Conservatives, who had made various reforms of the health and education services that were especially unpopular with workers in those services. New Labour did not explicitly try to dissociate itself from these groups in the way that it had done with the trade unions and disadvantaged minorities, although equally it did not go out of its way to court them: for example, New Labour clearly rejected any spending commitments that would have been popular with workers in health, education, and social services generally.

The key questions for us in this chapter, then, are how these various groups responded. In particular did Margaret Thatcher win over Essex man, and did Tony Blair win him back? But in doing so did New Labour alienate the disadvantaged groups and the new middle class? Commentators have frequently postulated that 'class dealignment' has occurred in late twentieth-century Britain, but these theories of Essex man and the like are really postulating a process of class *realignment*, not dealignment. Dealignment can be thought of as a process whereby the classes converge in their patterns of support for the parties so that there becomes less and less difference between, for example, the petite bourgeoisie and the old working class in their support for Labour or the Conservatives. Realignment, on the other hand, is a process whereby a particular group, such as Essex man, shifts its support from one party towards a different one. Dealignment, therefore, can be thought of as a general process of convergence between the classes, whereas realignment is a class-specific movement. Both these processes can be contrasted with across-the-board movements, where parties become more or less popular in all social groups alike.

---

[1] Some of the key contributions to this earlier academic literature on the affluent worker were Zweig (1961), Abrams *et al.* (1960), Goldthorpe *et al.* (1968), Crewe (1973), and Hope (1975).

The Parties' Appeal to Different Social Groups

The parties' connections with different social groups is as well known to the electorate as it is to politicians (although often disputed by political scientists). The electorate shares a sociological view of the link between parties and their supporters, as is clear from the BES. In 1997 we reintroduced a question that we had previously asked in 1987, namely:

Some people say that all political parties look after certain groups and are not so concerned about others. How closely do you think the Conservative Party looks after the interests of

  . . . working class people
  . . . middle class people
  . . . unemployed people
  . . . big business
  . . . trade unions
  . . . black people and Asians in Britain

And the Labour Party—how closely do you think the Labour Party looks after [these groups]?

(*BES 1987*, self-completion suppl., questions 23 and 24)

There were four response codes: 'very closely', 'fairly closely', 'not very closely' and 'not at all closely'. We have combined the last two.

Table 7.1 shows how our respondents perceived the Conservative Party and compares the results we obtained in 1997 with those from a decade earlier in 1987. It shows that the electorate had a remarkably clear picture of the nature of the Conservatives' concern for different social groups. There was a widely shared view that they were very concerned with big business, and an almost equally prevalent view that they were not closely concerned with the interests of working-class people, trade union members, or the unemployed. More surprisingly, most respondents felt that the Conservatives looked after the middle classes 'fairly closely' rather than 'very closely'. In this respect, the party was seen as primarily the party of big business rather than the party of ordinary people.

The table also shows considerable continuity over time in these perceptions (just as there was considerable continuity in the perceptions of the Conservatives' ideological position). Most of the changes between 1987 and 1997 were very small, but the overall pattern is that our respondents' views of the Conservatives tended to become more negative: there were increases in the proportions who felt the party was not concerned with the interests of the various social groups. This suggests some hardening in perceptions of the Tories: they were felt to be even less concerned with the working class, the unemployed, or trade unions than they had been earlier.[2]

---

[2] The BES has also regularly asked the question 'Would you describe the Conservative Party as good for one class or good for all classes?' The trend in this question is given in Table A7.1.

Table 7.1. The Conservatives' perceived concern for different social groups, 1987–1997

Social group	Percentage thinking the Conservatives looked after the interests of each group		
	Very closely	Fairly closely	Not closely
Working-class people			
1987	5	34	61
1997	4	26	70
Change, 1987–97	−1	−8	+9
Middle-class people			
1987	19	69	13
1997	16	67	16
Change, 1987–97	−2	−2	+3
Unemployed people			
1987	5	26	68
1997	3	20	76
Change, 1987–97	−2	−6	+8
Big business			
1987	73	24	2
1997	75	21	3
Change, 1987–97	+2	−3	+1
Trade unions			
1987	5	18	77
1997	4	15	81
Change, 1987–97	−1	−3	+4
Blacks and Asians			
1987	9	41	50
1997	6	40	54
Change, 1987–97	−3	−1	+4

Sources: *BES 1987*, min. N = 3,331; *1997*, min. N = 2,159.

These changes are by no means surprising given, on the one hand, the general disillusionment with the Conservatives and, on the other hand, the public concern with 'fat cats'—the senior executives in the newly privisatized corporations who were being awarded huge pay increases. In some ways it is more surprising that the changes were so small. In essence, the Tories under John Major were seen to be little different in the groups they represented from the Tories under Margaret Thatcher.

In contrast, Labour's image shows some large and remarkable changes, as we can see from Table 7.2. In 1987 the Labour image was almost the exact obverse of the Conservative one: the party was widely perceived to be very closely concerned with trade union interests and to be unconcerned with big business; it was seen to be more concerned with working-class people and the unemployed than with the middle class; and just as the Tories were seen to be more concerned with big business than with the middle class in general, so Labour was seen to be more concerned with the unions than with the working class as a whole. In 1987, then, both parties were seen as highly sectional and selective in the interests they represented.

Table 7.2. Labour's perceived concern for different social groups, 1987–1997

Social group	Percentage thinking the Labour Party looked after the interests of each group		
	Very closely	Fairly closely	Not closely
Working-class people			
1987	47	44	9
1997	34	59	6
Change, 1987–97	−13	+15	−3
Middle-class people			
1987	6	53	40
1997	10	75	15
Change, 1987–97	+4	+22	−25
Unemployed people			
1987	42	45	13
1997	28	57	14
Change, 1987–97	−14	+12	+2
Big business			
1987	8	31	60
1997	16	53	30
Change, 1987–97	+8	+22	−30
Trade unions			
1987	67	28	4
1997	31	58	11
Change, 1987–97	−36	+30	+7
Blacks and Asians			
1987	30	51	18
1997	15	65	19
Change, 1987–97	−15	+14	+1

Sources: BES 1987, min. N = 3,329; *1997*, min. N = 2,191.

However, unlike the lack of change in the Tory image, there were some very clear and striking changes between 1987 and 1997 in Labour's image, changes exactly of the sort that we imagine New Labour was trying to achieve. The biggest change was in relations with the trade unions, where the percentage of our respondents who thought that Labour looked after the unions 'very closely' more than halved, falling from 67 per cent in 1987 to 31 per cent in 1997. To be sure this was balanced by an increase from 28 per cent to 58 per cent in the percentage who thought that Labour looked after the unions 'fairly closely'. But Labour's especially close relationship with the unions was clearly thought to have been broken by 1997.

There were also falls, although not quite such large ones, in the percentages who thought that Labour looked 'very closely' after the working class, the unemployed, and Blacks and Asians. Again, these falls were largely balanced by increases in the percentage who thought that Labour looked after these groups 'fairly closely'.

A different pattern emerges with the groups that Labour has traditionally been opposed to, namely the middle class and big business. Here there was little change in the percentage who thought Labour looked after these groups very closely; but there were large reductions in the percentages who thought Labour did not look after these groups and corresponding large increases in the percentage who thought Labour looked after them 'fairly closely'. For example, the percentage who thought Labour did not look after the interests of big business fell from 60 per cent in 1987 to 30 per cent in 1997.

The upshot of all this is that in 1997 New Labour was thought to be much less a party of sectional interests than it had been before. New Labour's profile was therefore much 'flatter', and perhaps blander, than it had been before. It was seen as concerned fairly closely with almost all groups, but not especially concerned about any. There is still a gradient, but it is much flatter, ranging in 1997 from the 34 per cent of respondents who thought Labour was very concerned with the working class down to the 10 per cent who thought Labour was very concerned with the middle class. This compares with a 1987 gradient which ranged from 67 per cent for the unions down to 6 per cent for the middle class. It was not yet seen to be a classless party or wholly independent of the unions, but it had very substantially reduced its sectional character.[3] In this respect Tony Blair did seem to have achieved his objective of making Labour represent the great majority of the public, not an assemblage of minorities.

The consequence of these changes was that the Labour and Conservative profiles were no longer mirror images. In 1997 the Conservatives continued to be seen as a highly sectional party, whereas Labour was now a party that was seen by a majority of our respondents to be concerned with the interests of the social groups that constituted the Conservatives' traditional core voters as well as with the interests of its own traditional core.

Moreover, this changed perception was shared more or less equally by all groups alike. The most deviant group were the unemployed respondents, who were rather more sceptical of New Labour than was the electorate as a whole (see Table A7.2). Thus 26 per cent of unemployed people in 1997 thought that New Labour did not look closely after their interests, whereas only 14 per cent of the electorate as a whole were as negative. Trade unionists were also slightly more sceptical of New Labour than was the electorate as a whole, while respondents in big business (defined here as owners of or managers in large private sector enterprises) were slightly more enthusiastic.[4] In general, however, there was a high degree of consensus on the

---

[3] As on the Conservative Party, the BES has also regularly asked the question 'Would you describe the Labour Party as good for one class or good for all classes?' The trend over time in this question is shown in Table A7.1.

[4] In Table A7.2 we show the percentages of each group who thought that the Labour Party looked closely after their own group. The middle-class–working-class distinction has been constructed by collapsing the Goldthorpe classes 1, 2, 3, 4, 5, 7 into the middle class, and 6, 8, 9, 10, 11 into the working class. Note that on this procedure own-account workers are included in the working class not the middle class. In constructing the measure of trade union membership we treat former members of trade unions and members of staff associations, whether past or present, as non-union members. In constructing the measure of unemployed we include all those who defined themselves as unemployed, including those not looking for work, i.e. categories 5, 6, 7 of the variable Reconact. The measure of big business is constructed from socio-economic groups 1.1 and 1.2, i.e. large employers and managers in large enterprises.

nature of Labour's changes. In essence New Labour had made itself more appealing to its traditional opponents without alienating its traditional supporters, although this also meant that New Labour was no longer distinctively associated with any particular group. It had successfully become a catchall party.

The Conservatives and Essex Man

The 'Essex man' thesis held that Margaret Thatcher had made special inroads among the aspiring manual workers in constituencies like Basildon in Essex. This was the group that had deserted Labour, it was widely assumed, and this was the group that Labour had to win back—the so-called 'swing' voters. And these were the voters on whom politicians such as Giles Radice had focused in their discussions of Labour's 'southern discomfort'. Incidentally, there never was any good evidence from proponents of the Essex man thesis that working-class men in the south-east were any more likely to swing to the Conservatives than working-class women. The notion of 'Essex man' is one of those slogans that are never clearly defined and are therefore never clearly tested.

To test the Essex man thesis we begin by looking at the changing levels of support given by the aspiring members of the working class (whom we equate with the home-owning, non-unionized members of the working class) to the Conservatives over time.[5] We use the same basic classification of social groups that we employed in Chapter 2 when we investigated processes of social change, and we begin by looking at the national picture. Clearly, to test the Essex man thesis rigorously we will need to examine more closely patterns in the south-east. We shall move on to this, but an initial overview of the country as a whole will be useful (not least because our sample sizes are larger and therefore give more reliable estimates of change).

We begin with the picture in October 1974, when Edward Heath was still leader of the Conservative Party, since it is possible that Margaret Thatcher had already won over Essex man in 1979 with her appeals to lower personal taxation in the 1979 manifesto (although the manifesto emphasized the importance of cutting 'the absurdly high marginal rates of tax both at the bottom and top of the income scale' rather than the tax burden of middle-income Britain). Table 7.3 shows how our various social groups voted over this period.

Table 7.3 shows that, although there were considerable fluctuations in the overall levels of Conservative support at the beginning and end of our period, the social basis of their support was remarkably stable. Throughout, Conservative voting was highest among the petite bourgeoisie and among the non-unionized salariat. Throughout, the groups giving least support to the Conservatives were the working-class council

---

[5] As we noted earlier, we have no direct measure of aspirations in the BES. We use home ownership as a proxy. Alternative ideas might be to look at social and political attitudes, although there is a danger here of circularity: attitudes may reflect partisan choice rather than be a cause of them.

Table 7.3. The social basis of Conservative voting, 1974–1997

Social group	Percentage voting Conservative					
	1974	1979	1983	1987	1992	1997
Petit bourgeois	71[a]	77	72	65	68	42
Salariat						
Non-union	54	67	62	61	63	44
Union members	33	43	36	35	31	19
Routine non-manual	42	50[a]	53	52	55	32
Working-class						
Non-union, home-owners	43	45	48	43	46	23
Non-union, council tenants	19	30	22	26	15[a]	7
Union members	12[b]	25	28	26	26	10
Other working-class	31	49	35	54	44	21
Unemployed	—	—	21	18	19	13
All	35	47	45	45	47	30

[a] Residual larger than 1.96.

[b] Residual larger than 2.51, when the loglinear model of 'across-the-board' change is fitted to the data.

Source: *BES Oct. 1974 to 1997*. No percentages are reported when the base N is less than 50.

tenants, union members, and the unemployed. The aspiring working class of non-unionized home-owners within the working class, and the new middle class of union members in the salariat, both tended to hold an intermediate position. These two groups tended throughout to be close to the overall national average (given by the bottom row of Table 7.3) in their support for the Conservatives.

Is there any sign that the working-class home-owners were more likely than other social groups to swing to the Conservatives under Margaret Thatcher, or that they were more likely than other groups to abandon the Conservatives under John Major? It is hard to detect anything distinctive about their swings over time in Table 7.3. Indeed, if anything, the evidence runs directly counter to the Essex man thesis at the beginning of the period: Conservative support among this group in 1974 had been rather above the national average (43 per cent compared with 35 per cent), but in 1979 it was almost exactly the same as the overall average. Moreover, the figures for 1983 and 1987, the elections which marked the apogee of Thatcherism, again show that levels of Conservative support among these aspiring manual workers remained very close to the national average. The variations lie well within the range expected in representative random samples of this size.

The striking feature of this period, then, is how closely levels of Conservative support in different groups tended to move in unison. In general Margaret Thatcher's victories were built on increased levels of support across the board and were not specific to any of the particular groups distinguished in Table 7.3. The only large group which seems to have swung more than the average to Margaret Thatcher were the working-class trade unionists. However, we have to remember the context in which our baseline election, October 1974, took place. The year 1974 had seen the miners' strike and the three-day week, which had brought down Edward Heath's government earlier that year. Labour under Harold Wilson had immediately settled the miners' strike, on rather favourable terms for the miners; it had repealed the Conservatives' Industrial Relations Act (which had been fiercely opposed by the union leaderships); and it had lifted the Conservatives' statutory incomes policy. At the time of the October 1974 election, then, the votes of trade union members are likely to have reflected the recent history of unsuccessful Conservative attacks on unions and successful Labour defence of union powers. In fact, it appears to be the October 1974 figure that is the 'deviant' one: if we look at the voting behaviour of this group in earlier years, we find distinctly higher levels of support for the Conservatives (22 per cent in 1970 and 18 per cent in February 1974) than in October 1974.

To check on these, and other, apparent deviations such as that among the petite bourgeoisie, what we can do is to fit a statistical model which allows for across-the-board changes and see if any particular groups deviated significantly in their support from this general pattern. This notion that changes usually take the form of across-the-board movements that affect all groups alike is the one that we have repeatedly emphasized in our previous work (e.g. Heath *et al.* 1985, Heath *et al.* 1991), although it is also one that British commentators seem to have been remarkably reluctant to grasp.[6] What we find is that the model postulating across-the-board changes in support for the Conservatives gives a reasonably good fit to the data for the 1979–97 period.[7] None of the deviations for the aspiring working class (that is, for the non-union home-owners in the working class) is anywhere near statistically significant. That is, the over-time changes for this group are in line with the hypothesis that support for the Conservatives rose and fell more or less in unison in all social groups alike. Experiments with alternative ways of categorizing aspiring workers leads to exactly the same conclusion. This result is a robust one and does not depend on the precise way we have defined this group. (For a multivariate analysis of these data, see Appendix 7.2.)

Now of course the Essex man thesis did focus on the south-east rather than on the national picture, and it is certainly true that regional differences were accentuated during the 1980s. The growth of regional differences in support for the parties was one of the most striking features of the 1970s and 1980s, and it is one of the few examples where change did not take an across-the-board character: support for the Conservatives did not rise as much in Scotland and the north as it did in the south-east.

---

[6] Our analysis has, however, been closely followed in America by, for example, Hout *et al.* (1995), in Germany by Mueller (1999), and in France by Cautres and Heath (1996).

[7] We fit the loglinear model which postulates constant log odds ratios in Conservative: non Conservative voting to the data of Table 7.3. This model in effect postulates that changes in levels of support for the Conservatives took an across-the-board form. We find that the deviance from this model is 63.7 with 40 df, $p = 0.01$. This is not a particularly good fit and suggests that the hypothesis of constant odds ratios should be rejected. However, the main source of deviance is the voting of the working-class trade union members in the Oct. 1974 election, where the adjusted standardized residual exceeds 3.0. If we restrict ourselves to the 1979–97 period, the deviance of the model becomes 43.9 for 32 df, $p = 0.079$. This is an acceptable fit to the data.

Table 7.4. Conservative support in the regions, 1974–1997

Region	Percentage voting Conservative					
	1974[a]	1979	1983	1987	1992	1997
Wales	23.9	32.2	31.0	29.5	28.6	19.6
Scotland	24.7	31.4	28.4	24.0	25.7	17.5
North	34.1	40.7	38.4	36.6	36.9	26.3
Midlands[b]	39.1	48.6	46.8	47.8	46.6	35.1
South-west	43.1	51.3	51.4	50.6	47.6	36.7
South-east	42.1	51.5	50.4	52.2	51.2	37.8
All GB	36.7	44.9	43.5	43.3	42.8	31.5

[a] Figures refer to Oct. 1974 election.
[b] The Midlands include East Anglia.

Sources: Butler and Kavanagh (1974, 1979, 1983, 1987, 1992, 1997).

This phenomenon has been studied in detail by Johnston and his colleagues, and it appears likely that it was related to the unequal geographical spread of economic growth, particularly during the Lawson boom of the late 1980s (Johnston *et al.* 1988; Pattie and Johnston 1990).

Table 7.4 shows the levels of Conservative support in six broad regions. As with the other social bases of support shown in Table 7.2, there is a clear and consistent pattern throughout the period: Conservative support was greatest in the south-east and south-west and then declines as we move north. It was also low in Wales throughout.

However, although the pattern remains basically similar over time, the magnitude of the regional differences increased between 1974 and 1987. Thus the gap between the north and the south–east was only 8 percentage points in 1974, but it widened to 11 points in 1979 and then to 16 points in 1987. It should be noted, though, that the south-east was not all that different in its pattern of change from the south-west or midlands: the south-east/south-west differential remained almost constant, while the south-east/midlands differential grew only slightly. In general all three of these regions moved together and away from the north and Scotland. So in this respect Blair and New Labour were probably right to focus on middle Britain, if that is taken to be a geographical reference to the midlands, rather than specifically on the south-east.

There is of course a crucial difference between the thesis of 'Essex man', interpreted as referring to aspiring workers in the south-east, and the more general argument that the south as a whole, and all groups alike in the south, moved towards the Conservatives. As Table 7.4 implies, there was indeed considerable 'southern discomfort' for Labour in the 1980s. In that sense, Giles Radice and New Labour were of course right to worry. But Labour's 'southern discomfort' was not specific to the aspiring working class. More detailed analysis suggests that the increase in Conservative support in the south and midlands was shared by other social groups in those regions; it was not a distinctively working-class phenomenon.[8] As is often the way with political myths, the Essex man thesis was based on a half-truth.

Still, whether or not their diagnosis was based on a half-truth, it must be recognized that New Labour did suffer much less 'southern discomfort' in 1997 than they had done before. Between 1987 and 1992 the north–south gap narrowed slightly, and then between 1992 and 1997 it fell quite sharply, down from 14.3 points in 1992 to 11.5 points in 1997. However, the crucial point for our present concerns is that, just as the widening of the north–south gap was not specific to any particular class, so the narrowing of the gap in 1997 operated across the board and not simply among the aspiring members of the working class.

John Major's Conservatives and the Growth of Middle-Class Insecurity

As we have shown earlier, John Major's administrations were largely seen by the electorate as a continuation of Margaret Thatcher's in their policies and ideology. Under John Major the Conservatives made little attempt to change the basis of their appeal. However, there was widespread discussion after 1992 of the impact of the long recession on the middle classes, who were being exposed for the first time, it was claimed, to the insecurity brought about by globalization. There were also highly publicized problems of house repossessions, and in this respect Margaret Thatcher's ambition to create a property-owning democracy appeared to have turned sour.

As we noted earlier, Margaret Thatcher herself appeared to advance a sociological account of the Conservatives' troubles under John Major, arguing that the party was failing to look after the middle classes and those that aspired to join them. And a casual reading of Table 7.3 suggests that John Major disproportionately lost support among his core groups of the petite bourgeoisie (down 26 points between 1992 and 1997) and the salariat (down 19 points) However, we have to be particularly careful here because of the presence of 'floor' and 'ceiling' effects. Conservative

---

[8] The Essex man hypothesis perhaps should be interpreted as postulating a distinctive increase in support for the Conservatives among the new working class in the south-east, over and above the general increase in support for the Conservatives in the South-east. To test this, we fit the model which postulates constant odds ratios over time among the different social groups in support for the Conservatives, restricting our analysis to the South-east region only. This model gives a reasonable fit to the data with deviance of 56.8 for 32 df, $p = 0.04$. There were two significant residuals from this model for the new working class. In 1983, in line with the Essex man thesis, there was a positive residual (i.e. more than expected Conservative support) of 2.18. However, in 1987 there was a negative residual of −2.95. If Essex man did swing to the Conservatives in 1983, then, he promptly swung away in 1987. If there was an Essex man phenomenon, it was highly transient.

For contrary interpretations of the link between class dealignment and the changing political geography of Britain, see Johnston and Pattie (1992) and Weakliem and Heath (1995). Our own interpretation of these results is that, contrary to the Essex man thesis, there were greater signs of class dealignment in Scotland and Wales than in the south of England.

Table 7.5. Insecurity and defections from the Conservatives, 1997

Social group	Percentage defecting			
	Very confident	Fairly confident	Not confident	All
Employees	37 (210)	36 (121)	31 (23)	36
Self-employed	26 (47)	28 (32)	33 (9)	27
Unemployed	—		—	
Retired	18 (62)	29 (112)	39 (23)	27

Notes: Sample: respondents who reported that they had voted Conservative in 1992. Figures in parentheses give the base N.

Source: BES 1997.

support was of course notably high in these core groups in 1987, and so there was more room for it to fall. Indeed, a fall of 26 points in Conservative support among the unemployed would have been mathematically impossible, since support was only 19 per cent to start with! If we fit the statistical model which takes account of these floor and ceiling effects, we get considerable support for the hypothesis that changes between 1992 and 1997 took an across-the-board form and were not specific to particular groups.[9] What this suggests, then, is that John Major's failure was due to factors such as the more or less universal perception of Conservative divisions and incompetence rather than factors that were specific to particular groups. In this sense Margaret Thatcher was wrong to advance a sociological account of her successor's failure; the reason was political, not sociological.

The categories used in Table 7.3, however, are not ideal for testing theories of growing insecurity. What we can do, however, is to use our respondents' subjective feelings of insecurity, which we described in Chapter 2 when we first looked at Will Hutton's theory. It will be remembered that employees were asked how confident they felt that they would be able to keep their jobs, while corresponding questions were asked of the self-employed, the unemployed, and the retired.

In Table 7.5 we explore whether these feelings of subjective insecurity were related to defections from the Conservatives in 1997. That is, we restrict our analysis to people who said that they had voted for the Conservatives in 1992 and we report how many defected to one of the other parties in 1997. Thus among employees as a whole 36 per cent defected, among the self-employed 27 per cent defected, while among the retired it was again 27 per cent overall who defected. (We do not report any figures for defections among the unemployed as there were simply too few unemployed who had voted Conservative in 1992 for us to draw any reliable conclusions.)

The central question is whether these defection rates varied according to people's

[9] The loglinear model which postulates constant social group odds ratios in support for the Conservatives between 1992 and 1997 yields Chi^2 of 19.8 with 18 degrees of freedom, $p = 0.342$. None of the residuals from this model was anything near significant either.

levels of subjective insecurity. What we find is that, among the employees and the self-employed, there was no association between levels of subjective insecurity and the likelihood of defection from the Conservatives. About one in three Tories defected, and this was unrelated to their feelings of insecurity. However, there is a difference in levels of defection among the retired; as we can see, defections were rather low among retired people who felt very confident about their prospects; they were about average among people who felt fairly confident; and they were really rather high among retired people who did not feel confident about the future.[10]

Why did insecurity lead to disproportionate levels of defection only among the retired and not among employees or the self-employed? The most likely explanation is that the egocentric theory of voting on which our initial expectation was based is simply wrong. As our evidence showed in Chapter 3 when we looked at perceived changes in standards of health, education, and of living, people were more likely to blame the Conservatives for those failures that were the direct responsibility of government than for ones where responsibility could be attributed to individuals or outside forces. In so far as insecurity was believed by the electorate to be a product of wider economic forces, outside the government's control, then voters probably gave it little weight in their decisions how to vote. But the level of state pensions (although not of occupational pensions) is directly under the government's control, and it was the state pensioners who were particularly likely to feel insecure. State pensioners could reasonably blame the government for failures to increase their pensions, and accordingly might defect from the Conservatives.

Labour Support among the Two Lefts, 1979–1983

As we argued earlier, the Old Labour from which Blair and the modernizers set out to distance themselves was in many ways a coalition of two lefts: an Old Left that was rooted in the working-class Labour movement and was largely concerned with traditional class issues, and a New Left rooted in what has been called the new middle class of the cultural and social specialists (see Kriesi 1989). As we saw in Chapter 4, members of the New Left, while quite radical on economic issues, were particularly concerned with social and moral issues such as nuclear disarmament and the environment. This group tended to be younger and better educated than their working-class colleagues. They also had self-interested reasons for opposing Thatcherism, because many were employed in the public sector in health and education, where wages were squeezed and disruptive reforms introduced.

Just as Essex man went under various aliases—the new working class or affluent workers, for example—so the new middle class also went under various guises—post-materialists, social and cultural specialists, and public sector employees.[11]

---

[10] The difference in defection rates among the retired was statistically significant only at the 10% level, $Chi^2 = 4.8$ for 2 df, $p = 0.092$.

[11] The literature on the new middle class is now vast. See for e.g. Butler and Savage (1995).

However, there is considerable overlap between these various definitions, and our category of salaried unionists captures the essentials reasonably well. (See Appendix 7.2 for some more detailed models of the social bases of Labour support in 1979 and succeeding elections.)

We know that Labour's experiment with radical socialism in 1983 was not a resounding electoral success. But did it prove relatively more appealing in the traditional socialist stronghold of the working-class labour movement than elsewhere? And how far did the radical socialism of Michael Foot's 1983 Labour Party appeal to the new left in the salariat? Did Neil Kinnock's gradual first steps towards the modernization of the party show signs of a trade-off between winning middle-class votes and losing working-class ones? And what was the impact of New Labour on the voting patterns of our various groups? Was their less sectional image reflected in a growth of cross-class electoral support?

Table 7.6 shows that, on the whole, despite the radical experiments with socialism in 1983, Neil Kinnock's policy review after 1987, and Tony Blair's New Labour after 1994, the social basis of Labour support has remained surprisingly stable. In every single election from October 1974 to April 1997 Labour's three core groups of working-class council tenants, union members, and the unemployed gave Labour the highest level of support. In every single election the petite bourgeoisie and the non-unionized members of the salariat gave Labour the least support; and in every election the salaried trade unionists and the new working class of home-owning non-unionists have been rather similar to each other and have taken an intermediate position. This pattern is evident under Tony Blair in 1997 just as it was under Michael Foot in 1983.

It is important to recognize this astonishing degree of continuity. As we shall see,

Table 7.6. The social basis of Labour voting, 1974–1997 (% voting Labour)

Social group	1974	1979	1983	1987	1992	1997
Petit bourgeois	12[a]	13	12	14	13	37[a]
Salariat						
Non-union	20	16	8[a]	11	14	32[b]
Union members	39	35	27	30	30	52
Routine non-manual	32	32	19	24	28	46
Working-class						
Non-union, home-owners	38	40	25	34	38	55
Non-union, council tenants	61[a]	58	58[a]	53	69[a]	79
Union members	74[b]	58	49	48	60	72
Other working-class	44	40	36	34	42	56
Unemployed	—	—	54	63[a]	61	67[b]
All	43	38	29	30	34	48

[a] Residual larger than 1.96.
[b] Residual larger than 2.51, when the loglinear model of 'across-the-board' change is fitted to the data.

Sources: BES Oct. 1974–1997.

there have been changes in the relative levels of support which different groups gave Labour, but these changes have taken the form of widening and closing differentials rather than groups swapping position. Moreover, one of the biggest changes happened right at the beginning of our period, among working-class trade unionists, and can have had little to do with Labour's later ideological changes. Thus in 1974 working-class trade unionists overwhelmingly supported Labour but their support fell by 16 points, from 74 per cent to 58 per cent, in 1979. As we argued earlier in this chapter, it is probably the 1974 figure that is the deviant one, reflecting the political conditions of the 1973–4 miners' strike and its aftermath.

The radical experiment with socialism in 1983 was of course associated with a collapse in Labour's share of the vote. Moreover, Table 7.6 suggests that this fall was not altogether evenly spread. We can see that Labour lost badly among the working-class owner-occupiers, where their share fell by 15 points, and among the routine non-manual workers, where it fell 13 points, in both cases by considerably more than the overall drop of 9 points. In contrast Labour's vote in 1983 held up relatively well among the working-class council tenants, where it stayed constant, and among the unemployed. So radical socialism of the 1983 variety was perhaps rather less unappealing, if you will forgive the double negative, among the more disadvantaged groups such as council tenants and the unemployed than it was among the intermediate groups.

However, there is no sign that the radical strategy of the two lefts appealed to the salaried unionists in the same way that it appealed to the disadvantaged minorities in the working class. Among the salaried unionists Labour's share of the vote fell by eight points between 1979 and 1983, almost exactly in line with the overall fall in Labour's share of the vote. There is no hint here, then, that the radical New Left agenda found any special favour with the new middle class. In this sense the coalition of the two lefts failed to deliver. There is little evidence of any realignment here, of the sort that seems to have happened in America and France, where the new middle class moved closer to the working class in their patterns of party support.

The 1983 general election, therefore, can best be thought of as demonstrating a modest widening of the conventional differentials between the various social groups rather than any major realignment of the social groups. In general, the deviations from the general pattern of across-the-board losses were relatively small. In this respect, then, our analysis of the changing social basis of Labour support in 1983 exactly parallels our analysis of the ideological basis which we reported in Chapter 6: the main losses took an across-the-board character, but there were some modest additional losses among the left-of-centre voters.

Neil Kinnock and the Policy Review

After 1983, as we have seen, Neil Kinnock began his own attempts to make Labour electable once more, and Labour was gradually coaxed back towards the centre. As we saw in Chapter 6, Kinnock quietly dropped the party's opposition to Europe and, in the policy review after the 1987 defeat, he modified Labour's most radical old-and new-left policies. In essence, Neil Kinnock turned his back on the strategy of the two lefts and began a proto-New Labour strategy of moving back to the centre.

Neil Kinnock's changes did indeed make the party more electable, and Labour's overall share of the vote gradually increased, but they seem not to have involved any radical realignment of major social groups. At first sight Table 7.6 suggests that Labour's move back towards the centre between 1983 and 1992 was associated with larger gains among the main working-class groups than among the various white-collar groups, but Labour was of course starting from a lower level in the salariat or petite bourgeoisie. We therefore once again need to take account of floor and ceiling effects. When we do so, we find that the statistical model postulating across-the-board increases in the Labour share of the vote between 1983 and 1992 gives an excellent fit to the data of Table 7.6. None of the changes in the relative support given by different groups to Labour proves to be statistically significant. In short, Labour's gains between 1983 and 1992 were pretty uniform, and virtually all the changes in Table 7.6 during the Kinnock years can be accounted for by sampling variation.[12]

By and large, then, Neil Kinnock seems to have managed the rather remarkable feat of moving Labour back towards the centre without greatly disturbing the social bases of Labour support. In this sense there was no break with the past. Council tenants, trade unionists, and home-owners all seemed to have increased their support for Labour at similar rates as the middle classes did.

Neil Kinnock, then, demonstrated that a move towards the centre does not necessarily involve any major trade-offs. Despite maintaining the continuities with the past, no doubt because he feared reopening the damaging divisions of 1983, he successfully increased Labour's appeal both in the salariat and in the working class. He did not of course do enough to win—perhaps precisely because he had not made a decisive break with the past—but at least he showed that a strategy of pursuing ideological moderation and electability need not alienate Labour's traditional bases of support.

Tony Blair and New Labour

As we have seen, New Labour made a determined effort both to improve their general reputation for unity and competence but also to appeal to middle-income middle Britain. Whereas the appeal of Neil Kinnock's Labour Party to the various social groups had been the mirror image of the Conservatives in 1987, by 1997 Tony Blair had established a major asymmetry with a much less sectional appeal than either Neil Kinnock or John Major had had. Did this transformation in Labour's perceived appeal translate into a transformation in the pattern of Labour's support?

[12] If we fit the model which postulates that the odds ratios of support for Labour remained constant between 1983 and 1992, we obtain a very good fit to the data, with Chi^2 of 18.2 for 16 degrees of freedom, $p = 0.313$.

Table 7.6 shows that in 1997 New Labour made gains in all social groups alike, but they tended to be larger in the petite bourgeoisie (up 24 points), among the non-union members of the salariat (up 18 points), and among the salaried unionists (up 22 points) than they were in the working class. Within the working class the gains were largest among our group of aspiring workers who owned their own homes (up 17 points). Smaller gains were registered among the working-class council tenants and among the unemployed, where the Labour vote went up only by 6 points in 1997.

We still have to remember the likely impact of floor and ceiling effects: since Labour was already strong among council tenants or the unemployed, we would not expect the gains to be quite so large. However, the model which postulates uniform change between 1992 and 1997 does not fit the data especially well. Moreover, when we take account of floor and ceiling effects in this way, the group that stands out is the non-unionized salariat, which clearly switched to Labour much more than would have been expected by chance (given the overall increase in Labour support). Conversely, the small increase among the unemployed cannot be explained purely by floor and ceiling effects: it was a significantly smaller increase than expected. The other working-class groups of council tenants and trade unionists also increased their support less than expected (although not significantly so). A more detailed multivariate analysis confirms this picture. (See Appendix 7.2.)

This again parallels our analysis of the changing ideological basis of Labour support which we undertook in Chapter 6. In ideological terms, Labour made unusually large gains on the right of centre, where it picked up votes that might have been expected to go to the Liberal Democrats. Similarly, in social terms, New Labour made unusually large gains among the advantaged groups in the salariat, in territory that we normally think of as belonging to the Conservatives and Liberals. In this sense there was a clear-cut case of class dealignment in 1997.

New Labour's continuation of Neil Kinnock's strategy, therefore, does seem to have had rather different social implications. Neil Kinnock's more cautious modernization of the party did not involve any appreciable class dealignment but allowed him to make across-the-board gains. New Labour's more dramatic moves towards the centre did not take quite the same across-the-board character but involved bigger electoral gains in the salariat than among Labour's traditional sources of support.

The implications of these disproportionate gains in the salariat, together with the declining size of Labour's traditional core groups, means that there was a considerable change in the character of Labour's voters. Thus, as Table 7.7 shows, in October 1974, Labour's last victory before the Thatcherite ascendancy, Labour got over half its vote (56 per cent) from its traditional core of the working-class council tenants, union members, and the unemployed. In contrast it received less than a tenth (9 per cent) from voters in the core Conservative social groups. In 1983, despite a reduction in the overall size of its core in the electorate as a whole, Michael Foot's Labour Party slightly increased the proportion of its vote coming from its traditional social bases, which now provided 58 per cent of Labour's vote. It is also

Table 7.7. The changing social composition of the Labour vote, 1974–1997

	Percentage voting Labour					
	1974	1979	1983	1987	1992	1997
Petit bourgeois	2	3	3	4	3	8
Salariat						
Non-union	7	7	5	8	10	19
Union members	6	7	7	6	6	7
Routine non-manual	14	12	12	15	16.	17
Working-class						
Non-union, home-owners	9	13	12	16	18	19
Non-union, council tenants	17	20	20	16	16	11
Union members	36	30	24	19	15	11
Other working-class	6	5	3	2	3	4
Unemployed	3	3	14	14	12	6
N	647	539	849	882	743	926

Sources: BES Oct. 1974–1997.

remarkable that at this time one in seven of Labour's voters was either unemployed or the non-working partner of an unemployed person.

Under Neil Kinnock the party gradually saw an increasing proportion of its voters coming from the various intermediate groups, largely of course as a result of social change rather than political realignment. In 1997, however, the picture was transformed. Under Tony Blair the party received only 27 per cent of its vote from its traditional core groups, a figure that was matched by the proportion coming from the Conservative heartlands of the petite bourgeoisie and the non-unionized salariat. By far the largest proportion, however, now came from the intermediate groups (the new working class, the routine non-manual workers, and the salaried trade unionists). These now gave Labour 43 per cent of its vote. In this sense Labour had indeed become the party of middle-income middle Britain.

The Centre Parties

The centre had also seen some radical experiments in our period, with the formation of the SDP in 1981 and its alliance with the Liberals to fight the 1983 and 1987 elections. As we saw in Chapter 6, the Alliance did eat into the left-of-centre vote in 1983. Did this also go with a new social profile in 1983?

As with the Conservative and Labour Parties, there is substantial continuity over time in the social basis of Liberal voting. Not surprisingly, the Liberals tended to be weakest among Labour's core groups in the working class and among the Conservatives' core in the petite bourgeoisie. Instead they tended to be relatively strong in the intermediate groups, such as the new working class or the lower-middle class, where the other main parties did not have such a strong hold. But in every

Table 7.8. The social basis of Liberal voting, 1974–1997

	Percentage voting Liberal					
	1974	1979	1983	1987	1992	1997
Petit bourgeois	15	10	16[a]	19	16	16
Salariat						
Non-union	23	15	29	27	20	20
Union members	26	20	36	31	35[a]	24
Routine non-manual	24	17	27	22	16	18
Working-class						
Non-union, home-owners	19	14	25	23	14	17
Non-union, council tenants	14	10	19	20	11	8
Union members	8[a]	14	22	24[a]	10	12
Other working-class	21	10	22	12	9	20
Unemployed	—	—	23	18	14	9
All	18	14	25	24	17	17

Note: Liberal includes SDP in 1983 and 1987 and denotes Liberal Democrat in 1992 and 1997.

[a] Residual larger than 1.96.

Sources: BES October 1974–1997.

single election that we cover, the group that was most likely to support the Liberals or their successors was the new middle class of salaried union members. And this to some extent may account for the failure of Labour's two-lefts strategy: the new middle class seem to find the Liberals' softer version of progressive politics at least as appealing as Labour's version. (And in 1983, 1987, and 1992 the centre parties actually secured more votes from this group than Labour did.)

The centre parties were also relatively strong among the non-unionized members of the salariat, even though we have generally thought of this as one of the Conservatives' core groups. More detailed multivariate analysis (see Appendix t7.2 shows that it was particularly the highly educated members of the salariat who preferred the centre parties to the Conservatives.

This pattern of support for the centre parties is one that we have found in our previous research. However, what is perhaps more surprising is that this profile hardly changes at all over the course of the six elections, despite the advent of the SDP in the 1983 election and then the merger of the SDP and Liberals to form the Liberal Democrats for the 1992 election. There are hints that the Alliance made slightly greater than expected gains in 1983 both among the unionized (up 16 points) and non-union (up 14 points) members of the salariat than they did among the petite bourgeoisie (up 6 points) or working-class council tenants and unionists (up 9 and 8 points respectively), but none of these changes reaches statistical significance. In general, the model of across-the-board changes in support for the centre parties gives a rather good fit to the data.[13]

[13] The model which postulates constant log odds ratios over time in support for the Liberals yields $Chi^2 = 39.3$ for 32df, $p = 0.176$ for the 1979–97 period.

Nor at a first glance do there appear to have been any significant changes between 1992 and 1997 in the pattern of support for the Liberal Democrats. New Labour did not seem to have made any special inroads into the social bases of Liberal Democrat support. However, a more detailed analysis does suggest one interesting development in 1997. If we conduct a multivariate analysis that distinguishes the separate effects of class, education, housing tenure, region, and union membership on vote, we find an interesting picture of continuity and change. In general, we find that factors like education and union membership played much the same role in 1997 on support for the three parties as they had done in previous years. Social class, however, showed a very different pattern in 1997. Essentially, social class differences in support for Labour and the Liberal Democrats were sharply reduced between 1992 and 1997, while class differences in support for the Liberal Democrats and the Conservatives sharply increased.

What this means is that the Liberals and Labour had tended to converge in social class terms, while the Liberals and Conservatives had tended to diverge. We can think of this as a realignment of the parties rather than a general dealignment which would have brought all three parties closer together. Again, then, this parallels our analysis in Chapter 6 of the changing ideological bases of support for the parties in 1997.

Conclusions

Whereas in the 1980s the electorate thought that the two main parties were mirror images of each other in the groups they represented, this was no longer the case in 1997. In 1997 the Conservatives continued to be seen as a highly sectional party, whereas Labour was now a party that was seen by a majority of our respondents to be concerned with the interests of the social groups that constituted the Conservatives' traditional core as well as with the interests of its own traditional core. This also meant that New Labour was no longer distinctively associated with any particular group. It had successfully become a catchall party.

This continuity in the Conservatives' image is paralleled by the continuity in the social bases of their support. Almost all the variations in Conservative support (apart from the regional one) took the form of swings that affected all social groups alike. This is hardly surprising since there were no major changes in Conservative ideology over this period. Despite the talk of Essex man, the Conservative gains in 1979 and their losses in 1997 did not seem to be specific to particular social groups. There is not a hint in our data that groups such as the home-owning members of the working class are the crucial 'swing' voters who decide elections. It takes rather exceptional circumstances for a particular group to deviate significantly from the general pattern of across-the-board changes. Elections are rarely won or lost because a crucial group of 'swing' voters behaved differently from the other groups. Possibly the working-class unionists did win Harold Wilson the

October 1974 general election, but none of the other election outcomes depended upon one particular group.

There were, to be sure, some exceptional circumstances in 1997. Under Tony Blair New Labour did manage to change its appeal and did manage to secure larger than expected gains from the salariat, but even under New Labour the usual pattern of support continued—it was simply muted. Furthermore, the outcome in 1997 clearly did not depend on the large swing in the salariat: if Labour had simply secured the usual across-the-board swing of the same magnitude that it actually won among its core social groups, it would still have won a convincing victory.

While it is not our purpose here to revisit the great debate about class dealignment at any length, it is worth noting that the changes that did occur in 1997 surely have a political rather than a sociological explanation. Many writers have suggested that general social processes are leading to a blurring of class boundaries and a weakening of the social cleavages (e.g. Clarke and Lipset 1991; but see also Hout *et al.* 1993). If this were the case, then we would have expected to see a similar pattern of reduced social differences on the Conservative side as well as on the Labour side. We would also have expected the changes to have taken a gradual character instead of the abrupt one that actually occurred. The fact that the changes in 1997 were so specific to Labour provides strong support for a political explanation.

Appendix 7.1. Supplementary Tables

Table A7.1. Trends over time in party image, 1983–1997

Year	Percentage thinking the Conservative Party was				
	Good for one class	Neither or both	Good for all classes	Don't know	N
1983	58	3	35	3	3,951
1987	59	3	35	2	3,816
1992	55	4	39	3	2,851
1997	68	7	24	2	2,687

Year	Percentage thinking the Labour Party was				
	Good for one class	Neither or both	Good for all classes	Don't know	N
1983	54	8	34	4	3,948
1987	56	8	31	5	3,816
1992	54	7	35	4	2,846
1997	19	8	69	5	2,686

Sources: BES 1983, 1987, 1992, 1997.

Table A7.2. Labour's image among different social groups, 1987–1997

Respondents	Percentage thinking Labour looks closely after their own group			
	Very closely	Fairly closely	Not closely	N
Working-class				
1997	35	58	7	918
Change since 1987	–9	+14	–5	1,464
Middle class				
1997	9	74	16	1,231
Change since 1987	+5	+24	–30	1,448
Unemployed				
1997	23	50	26	80
Change since 1987	–20	+8	+11	189
Respondents in big business				
1997	7	56	37	130
Change since 1987	+5	+34	–39	128
Respondents in trade unions				
1997	23	65	12	452
Change since 1987	–39	+31	+9	772
Black and Asian				
1997	7	66	24	106
Change since 1987	–13	+17	–4	82

Sources: BES 1987 and 1997.

Appendix 7.2. Multivariate Analysis of the Social Basis of Vote, 1979–1997

In Tables A7.3 and A7.4 we give the results of logistic regressions of vote on a range of social structural variables. In Table A7.3 the dependent variable is Conservative voting (coded 1 for Conservative, 0 for all other parties). In Table A7.4 the dependent variable is Labour voting (coded 1 for Labour, 0 for all other parties). In Table A7.5 we use a multinomial logistic regression contrasting centre-party voting with Labour and Conservative voting (minor parties being excluded).

The explanatory variables are class, housing tenure, unemployment, union membership, region, and educational qualifications. Class has four categories, petite bourgeoisie, salariat, routine non-manual, working (the reference category), with a further category for missing data. Housing tenure distinguishes owner-occupiers, local authority tenants (the reference category), and other. In the case of region we contrast the north (including Scotland and Wales) with the midlands, south-east, and south-west. Unemployed includes inactive (not retired) respondents whose spouses were unemployed. Trade union membership contrasts current members of trade unions (excluding members of staff associations) from all others. Educational qualifications distinguishes holders of degree-level qualifications from those with intermediate qualifications (A level, O level, and their equivalents such as HND and OND), and those with low or no qualifications (the reference category). Low qualifications are CSE, RSA qualifications, and their equivalents.

A category for missing data is used in the case of the class variable because of the large

Table A7.3. Logistic regressions of Conservative vote, 1979–1997 (parameter estimates)

	1979	1983	1987	1992	1997	1979–97
Class						
Petite bourgeoisie	1.32	1.19	0.84	0.95	0.87	0.98
	(0.24)	(0.17)	(0.15)	(0.18)	(0.19)	(0.06)
Salariat	0.69	0.56	0.67	0.77	1.02	0.73
	(0.16)	(0.11)	(0.11)	(0.13)	(0.15)	(0.06)
Routine non-manual	0.36	0.54	0.47	0.59	0.62	0.53
	(0.17)	(0.11)	(0.11)	(0.13)	(0.16)	(0.06)
Working-class	0.00	0.00	0.00	0.00	0.00	0.00
Missing	0.45	0.28	−0.24	0.03	0.26	0.10
	(0.22)	(0.14)	(0.15)	(0.17)	(0.19)	(0.07)
Tenure						
Owner	0.87	1.08	1.02	1.36	1.29	1.08
	(0.14)	(0.16)	(0.11)	(0.14)	(0.22)	(0.06)
Other	0.60	0.82	0.67	1.01	1.05	0.77
	(0.19)	(0.16)	(0.17)	(0.20)	(0.26)	(0.08)
Council tenant	0.00	0.00	0.00	0.00	0.00	0.00
Union member	−0.73	−0.71	−0.74	−0.83	−0.84	−0.76
	(0.13)	(0.09)	(0.10)	(0.12)	(0.16)	(0.05)
Unemployed	0.03	−0.85	−0.96	−1.19	−0.69	−0.89
	(0.39)	90.18)	(0.20)	(0.22)	(0.36)	(0.11)
North	−0.34	−0.58	−0.54	−0.65	−0.60	−0.55
	(0.11)	(0.08)	(0.08)	(0.09)	(0.11)	(0.04)
Qualifications						
Degree	−0.51	−0.55	−0.70	−0.77	−0.52	−0.61
	(0.26)	90.18)	(0.16)	(0.19)	(0.19)	(0.08)
Intermediate	0.30	0.19	0.09	0.01	0.14	0.13
	(0.14)	(0.09)	(0.09)	(0.10)	(0.11)	(0.05)
Low–none	0.00	0.00	0.00	0.00	0.00	0.00
Constant	−0.78	−0.94	−0.94	−1.20	−2.31	−1.16
	(0.13)	(0.11)	(0.12)	(0.15)	(0.23)	(0.06)
Chi^2	228.2	497.0	458.4	408.8	246.3	1,988.1
N	1,543	3,173	3,185	2,980	2,695	13,576

Notes: Figures in parentheses give the standard errors.
Sources: BES 1997.

proportion missing. Much smaller proportions are missing of the other variables, and these are deleted.

In the case of the 1979–97 model a control is included for year (which thus adjusts for the varying sample sizes). Deviation contrasts are used for the year variable, and so the other parameter estimates can be thought of as representing the general effect of these variables rather than the effects in any particular year.

These multivariate analyses confirm the story told by the cross-tabulations in the text. On the Conservative side we can see that there is considerable stability from election to election in the magnitude of the parameter estimates. There is no general tendency for their magnitude to decline over time. Nor is there any indication that the pattern (or

Table A7.4. Logistic regressions of Labour vote, 1979–1997 (parameter estimates)

	1979	1983	1987	1992	1997	1979–97
Class						
Petite bourgeoisie	−1.40	−1.22	−0.97	−1.27	−0.59	−1.01
	(0.24)	(0.17)	(0.15)	(0.22)	(0.18)	(0.09)
Salariat	−0.87	−1.15	−1.17	−1.09	−0.79	−1.03
	(0.18)	(0.14)	(0.14)	(0.14)	(0.13)	(0.06)
Routine non-manual	−0.46	−0.81	−0.54	−0.67	−0.42	−0.59
	(0.18)	(0.13)	(0.12)	(0.13)	(0.14)	(0.06)
Working-class	0.00	0.00	0.00	0.00	0.00	0.00
Missing	−0.23	−0.18	0.06	−0.31	−0.21	−0.18
	(0.22)	(0.15)	(0.15)	(0.17)	(0.16)	(0.07)
Tenure						
Owner	−0.96	−1.25	−1.08	−1.16	−0.90	−1.10
	(0.14)	(0.10)	(0.11)	(0.13)	(0.15)	(0.05)
Other	−0.57	−0.93	−0.56	−0.81	−0.79	−0.75
	(0.19)	(0.16)	90.16)	(0.19)	(0.19)	(0.08)
Council tenant	0.00	0.00	0.00	0.00	0.00	0.00
Union member	0.58	0.72	0.72	0.78	0.59	0.68
	(0.13)	(0.10)	(0.11)	(0.12)	(0.13)	(0.05)
Unemployed	−0.19	0.70	0.90	0.93	0.42	0.74
	(0.39)	(0.17)	(0.17)	(0.20)	(0.26)	(0.09)
North	0.30	0.73	0.88	0.56	0.54	0.64
	(0.12)	(0.09)	(0.090	(0.10)	(0.09)	(0.04)
Qualifications						
Degree	0.24	0.24	0.38	−0.14	−0.07	0.12
	(0.28)	(0.22)	(0.19)	(0.22)	(0.17)	(0.09)
Intermediate	−0.47	−0.44	−0.20	−0.44	−0.42	−0.37
	(0.16)	(0.11)	(0.10)	(0.11)	(0.10)	(0.05)
Low–none	0.00	0.00	0.00	0.00	0.00	0.00
Constant	0.25	−0.06	−0.19	0.51	1.01	0.32
	(0.13)	(0.10)	(0.11)	(0.13)	(0.16)	(0.05)
Chi^2	248.6	683.9	640.5	477.8	244.9	2,466.7
N	1,541	3,173	3,185	2,980	2,695	13,576

Notes: Figures in parentheses give the standard errors.

Sources: *BES 1979–1997.*

magnitude) of the estimates is different (or reduced) in 1997 compared with the overall estimates. Of the eleven estimates, only three are actually lower in 1997 than for the period as a whole.

On the Labour side there is again considerable continuity in the pattern of parameter estimates, but they are generally lower in 1997 than they had been previously. Thus, of the eleven estimates, seven are lower in 1997 than they are for the period as a whole.

The relationship of the centre parties to the Labour and Conservative Parties respectively is particularly interesting. The biggest changes involve the social class parameter estimates. The estimates became bigger in 1997 (compared with the overall estimates for the period as a whole) in the case of the centre–Conservative contrast, while they became smaller in the

Table A7.5. Multinomial logistic regressions of Liberal vote, 1979–1997 (parameter estimates)

	Liberal v. Labour		Liberal v. Conservative	
	1979–97	1997	1979–97	1997
Class				
Petite bourgeoisie	−0.53	−0.15	0.63	0.75
	(0.12)	(0.26)	(0.10)	(0.26)
Salariat	−0.80	−0.42	0.28	0.73
	(0.08)	(0.18)	(0.07)	(0.15)
Routine non-manual	−0.44	−0.17	0.24	0.49
	(0.08)	(0.20)	(0.07)	(0.22)
Working-class	0.00	0.00	0.00	0.00
Missing	−0.19	−0.13	0.07	0.16
	(0.09)	(0.23)	(0.10)	(0.26)
Tenure				
Home-owners	−0.72	−0.89	0.51	0.53
	(0.07)	(0.23)	(0.08)	(0.30)
Other	−0.40	−1.00	0.41	0.20
	(0.10)	(0.28)	(0.11)	(0.35)
Council tenant	0.00	0.00	0.00	0.00
Union member	0.26	0.31	−0.52	−0.62
	(0.07)	(0.17)	(0.06)	(0.21)
Unemployed	0.36	0.62	−0.58	−0.10
	(0.12)	(0.17)	(0.13)	(0.50)
North	0.62	0.75	−0.10	0.01
	(0.05)	(0.14)	(0.05)	(0.15)
Qualifications				
Degree	−0.30	−0.63	−0.86	−0.95
	(0.11)	(0.23)	(0.10)	(0.24)
Intermediate	−0.37	−0.56	−0.14	−0.24
	(0.06)	(0.15)	(0.06)	(0.16)
Low–none	0.00	0.00	0.00	0.00
Intercept	1.16	2.00	0.41	−0.10
	(0.07)	(0.24)	(0.08)	(0.31)

Notes: Figures in parentheses give the standard errors. The N for 1979–97 is 12,172, and the model improvement is 2,378.0 (with 11 degrees of freedom). The N for 1997 is 2,044 and the model improvement is 352.9 (with 11 degrees of freedom).

Source: *BES 1979–1997*.

case of the centre–Labour contrast. This pattern appears to be specific to social class and is not repeated for tenure, trade union membership, unemployment, region, or qualifications. This suggests a pattern of realignment between the three parties rather than one of general dealignment.

8

Were Traditional Labour Voters Disillusioned with New Labour?

As Przeworski and Sprague have argued, when a formerly socialist party moves towards the centre in the search for middle-class votes, 'The workers who would otherwise have voted for a Socialist Party have three avenues open to them: they can vote for bourgeois parties; they can abstain from voting altogether, and in some countries, they can vote for other parties that appeal to them as workers' (Przeworski and Sprague 1986: 61). As we have seen, after Tony Blair became leader in 1994, the Labour Party provided a classic example of a formerly socialist party moving towards the centre in search of votes (although in many ways this was the culmination of a process that had begun with Neil Kinnock's policy review in 1987). This move towards the centre was rewarded at the 1997 general election with especially large gains among the middle-class voters that Tony Blair and New Labour had targeted. Working-class voters also increased their level of support for Labour, but not at the same rate as among the middle class. There was thus a sharp reduction in class voting which fell to its lowest level in the post-war period (Evans *et al.* 1999; see also Chapter 7). The trade-off that Przeworksi and Sprague expected did thus materialize, albeit in a relative rather than absolute form.

The third option described by Przeworski and Sprague—voting for other parties that appealed to workers—did not, however, materialize to any great extent. The Socialist Labour Party and the Scottish Socialist Party secured only a handful of votes, while the Referendum Party (which did manage to secure nearly 3 per cent of the vote) proved more attractive to people who had previously voted Conservative or Liberal Democrat than it did to Labour voters (Heath *et al.* 1998; see also Chapter 4).

The second of Przeworski and Sprague's options—abstention—does warrant closer investigation, and this is the primary focus of the current chapter. The central hypothesis is that Labour's traditional constituency in the working class did not respond with enthusiasm to New Labour's apparent lack of concern with their interests and may have shown some reluctance to turn out and vote for the party. Accordingly, while class voting may have declined, there may have been some increase in class non-voting. Weakliem and Heath have suggested that in America the gradual move of the Democrats away from the interventionist policies of the

New Deal to the centrist postion occupied by leaders such as Clinton (one of Blair's models) was accompanied by long-run declines in class voting but increases in class differences in abstention (Weakliem and Heath 1999). Is there any sign of a similar process occurring in Britain?

Abstention was in any event one of the most interesting aspects of the 1997 election. The election saw a striking fall in turnout from the relatively high level of 77.9 per cent in 1992 to 71.6 per cent in 1997. We have discussed the overall fall in turnout in detail elsewhere (Heath and Taylor 1999; see also Denver and Hands 1997). Essentially, we found a number of pieces of evidence which suggested that turnout is higher when the election is expected to be a close one, and lower when it is expected to be an easy victory for one or other party. In 1997 the opinion polls were certainly suggesting an easy victory for Labour, whereas in 1992 the opinion polls suggested a very close race. Other major landslides such as 1935 and 1983 have also seen low turnouts, while close races such as 1950 and 1951 saw very high turnouts. It is important to emphasize that our theory relates to the closeness of the race nationally rather than to the closeness of the race in the individual constituency. The relationship between the marginality of the constituency and the turnout there is conceptually distinct from that between the closeness of the national race and the national turnout.

Our concern here, however, is not with the overall decline in turnout but with the possibility that the decline was greater among traditional Labour voters than it was among other groups. Did Labour's move to the centre and its wooing of new recruits from the middle classes mean that traditional supporters were less inclined to turn out? Curtice and Steed (1997) produced some highly suggestive figures from their analysis of the aggregate data. They found that turnout was especially low in Labour seats. Commenting on the 1997 result they wrote, 'On average just 68 per cent turned out to vote in the average Labour seat, compared with 74 per cent in the typical Conservative one, a larger gap than ever before. Labour's heartlands, then, were distinctly lukewarm about their party's surge to victory' (Curtice and Steed 1997: 299). They pointed out that 'This is in sharp contrast with 1945 when Labour first swept to a major Commons victory. Turnout then was highest in Labour strongholds in northern cities, in Wales and in the mining and textile areas of Yorkshire and Lancashire' (Curtice and Steed 1997: 322).

Curtice and Steed based their analysis on aggregate data (that is, on the constituency results). One difficulty with the aggregate data is the so-called ecological fallacy: we cannot know for sure that it was actually Labour voters who abstained in the Labour seats. It is logically quite possible that the low turnout in Labour seats arose because Conservatives in those seats saw no point in casting their ballots. Another difficulty is that electoral registration may not be equally accurate in the different sorts of constituency. Registration officers in Labour seats might have carried over more names from previous registers, thus leading to more redundancy in the registers. As a result, the denominator used when calculating the aggregate turnout in a constituency may have been subject to systematic error.

Most importantly, however, we cannot from the aggregate data distinguish a

Table 8.1. Abstention in Conservative and Labour seats, 1997 (%)

Winning party in 1992	Self-report data	Official records
Conservative	16.2 (1,435)	17.1 (1,207)
Labour	20.0 (1,123)	22.4 (930)
Other	22.9 (130)	23.2 (114)
Difference	3.8	5.3

Note: Figures in parentheses give the base Ns.

Source: *BES 1997*.

hypothesis of disillusion with New Labour from one of complacency. Were Labour supporters in these constituencies simply more confident than those in other constituencies that Labour would win easily? Or were safe Labour seats ones where there happened to be large numbers of disillusioned traditional voters?

Survey data can help with some of these problems. First, we can avoid the ecological fallacy by comparing the turnout of Conservative and Labour supporters. Secondly, we can control for registration differences by looking at the turnout of people who actually were on the register. Finally, we can check directly on the subjective feelings and perceptions of the electors.

However, there is one well-known problem with the use of survey data for studying turnout. Election surveys the world over tend to show much higher levels of reported turnout than are found in the official data. The discrepancy is likely to have three components: errors and redundancy in the register (which in effect means that the 'true' turnout rate will be higher than that shown by the official data); non-response bias in the surveys, with non-voters also tending to be non-participants in election surveys; and actual overclaiming by respondents of their turnout (Swaddle and Heath 1989). We cannot do much about the first two of these problems, but we can deal with the third by validating the data against the official records.[1] In this chapter we report both self-report and validated results wherever possible. (The turnout data were validated in the 1997 BES but not in most of the earlier ones. When we compare 1997 data with earlier patterns, therefore, we have to rely on the self-report material.)

We begin by checking whether our survey data replicate Curtice and Steed's finding that turnout was lower in Labour seats. This is done in Table 8.1. Following usual practice, we define a Labour seat as one that Labour won at the previous election.

It is heartening that survey and aggregate results tell the same story. Both self-report and validated turnout data indicate that abstention was higher in 1997 in the seats that Labour had won in 1992 than in the seats that the Conservatives had won at that election: the self-report data show a difference of about 4 points, while the

---

[1] The marked-up registers indicating whether individuals voted or not are retained for a period after each election and are available for public consultation. We can check these marked-up registers against our survey respondents' own reports of whether they voted.

Table 8.2. Social characteristics and abstention, 1979–1992

Social group	Percentage who abstained (self-reported)				
	1979	1983	1987	1992	Average 1979–92
Petit bourgeois	12	15	17	11	14
Salariat					
Non-union	12	13	10	9	11
Union members	7	8	11	5	8
Routine non-manual	14	15	11	10	12
Working-class					
Non-union, home-owners	13	18	14	13	15
Non-union, council tenants	14	22	16	17	18
Union members	16	17	13	8	14
Other working-class	24	25	23	19	23
Unemployed	27	20	23	21	22
All	14	16	14	11	14

Sources: BES 1979–92.

validated data show a slightly larger difference of 5 points. Moreover, these differences are close to the gap of 6 points found in the aggregate data by Curtice and Steed.

However, one reason why abstention might be higher among electors in the Labour seats could simply be that these were more likely to be working-class electors: the working class generally tends to have slightly lower turnout than do middle-class electors, and hence seats that Labour won in 1992 were likely to have had larger proportions of working-class electors. In other words, the social geography of Conservative and Labour voting could well explain differences in turnout between the different types of constituency.

The general relationship between social characteristics and abstention can be seen in Table 8.2, which gives the self-report figures for 1979 to 1992. The table shows a familiar pattern of turnout differentials: the middle class groups tend to have higher turnout than the working class, and in turn the unemployed usually have lower turnout than the working class as a whole. This pattern is more or less evident in all the years covered by the table. In general, the core Conservative groups (the petite bourgeoisie together with the non-unionized salariat) have lower abstention rates than the core Labour groups (working-class council tenants, trade unionists, and the unemployed), with the mixed groups lying in between. Hence social geography could in principle explain the lower turnout in Labour seats. The crucial question, therefore, becomes whether these turnout differentials became magnified in 1997 as New Labour moved away from its traditional supporters. Curtice and Steed, for example, emphasized that the gap was larger in 1997 than it had been before. However, it was only 1 percentage point larger, so we are looking for very small changes.

Table 8.3. Social characteristics and abstention, 1997

Social group	Percentage who abstained		
	Official records	Self-report data	Difference of 1997 self-report from 1979–92 average
Petit bourgeois	19	20	+6
Salariat			
Non-union	14	13	+2
Union members	11	9	+1
Routine non-manual	17	17	+5
Working-class			
Non-union, home-owners	19	17	+2
Non-union, council tenants	29	24	+6
Union members	24	23	+9
Other working-class	25	26	+3
Unemployed	30	31	+9
All	19	18	+4

Sources: Table 8.2 and *BES 1997*.

Table 8.3 shows the differences between the level of abstention in 1997 and the average for the period as a whole. All the differences are positive, reflecting the low turnout in 1997. But abstention does seem to have been higher in 1997 than was usual for the period as a whole among the working-class council tenants, the trade unionists, and the unemployed. For these three groups the 1997 abstention figures are 6, 9, and 9 points higher respectively than the 1979–92 average. Table 8.3, there-fore, gives an indication that in 1997 abstention was rather larger in Labour's core groups than it had been in the earlier years. The differences do not quite reach sta-tistical significance at the 0.05 level, however, so we should treat the results as sug-gestive rather than conclusive.

We also need to check whether these possible changes in rates of abstention were specific to former Labour voters or were common to both Labour and Conservatives in these working-class groups. If abstention in the working-class groups had increased among both Labour and Conservative supporters alike, we could hardly attribute the increase to disillusion with New Labour. A more plaus-ible explanation would be that these were seats with large expected Labour major-ities. Hence supporters of both parties might have felt that the result in these constituencies was a foregone conclusion and not bothered to turn out.

To check on this argument, we need to distinguish Labour and Conservative sup-porters and to look at their turnout separately. However, cross-tabulating Table 8.3 by previous vote would lead to many very small categories: so to explore this ques-tion we aggregate our groups into three broad categories—the Conservative core, consisting of the petite bourgeoisie together with the non-unionized salariat; the Labour core, consisting of the working-class council tenants, trade unionists, and

Table 8.4. Previous vote and abstention, 1979–1992

Social group	Percentage who abstained (self-reported)				
	1979	1983	1987	1992	Average 1979–92
Former Conservative voters					
Core Conservative groups	7	9	7	6	7
Mixed groups	7	11	8	6	9
Core Labour groups	10	18	13	8	13
Former Labour voters					
Core Conservative groups	17	17	12	8	14
Mixed groups	6	13	11	5	9
Core Labour groups	12	12	8	7	10

Sources: BES 1979–92.

unemployed; and an intermediate group, comprising all the other categories with more mixed voting traditions.

Table 8.4 shows a rather interesting pattern. In general, former Conservatives show a clear gradient, with the lowest abstention occurring in the core Conservative groups in the middle class and the highest abstention occurring in their opponents' core groups in the working class. In the 1979–92 period as a whole, we find that Conservative abstention was only 7 per cent in their middle-class core, rising to 9 per cent in the intermediate groups and 13 per cent in Labour's core groups in the working class. Labour abstention, in contrast, shows a relatively flat profile, although there are hints that it was the obverse of the Conservative pattern. Thus Labour abstention was slightly lower on average, at 10 per cent, in its core working-class groups than it was in the middle-class core, where it was 14 per cent on average.

Again we must emphasize that the differences are small, but the pattern makes good intuitive sense. In effect there were probably two processes occurring. First, abstention generally tended to be higher in the working class; this probably reflected the tendency of the working class to have a weaker sense of political efficacy. Secondly, abstention by a party's supporters tended to be lowest in its own core group and highest in its rival's core; this may well have been due to social norms within each core supporting the core's 'own' party. People who deviated from these norms may have felt under cross-pressure and have taken refuge in abstention.

At any rate, these two processes led to a relatively steep class gradient among Conservative supporters, where they reinforced each other, and to a weaker gradient in the opposite direction among Labour supporters, where the two processes tended to cancel each other out.

Did 1997 demonstrate the same pattern? Table 8.5 shows that the Conservative pattern in 1997 was a straightforward repeat of the Conservative pattern in the previous four elections, although, as expected, in all three groups abstention was

Table 8.5. Previous vote and abstention, 1997

Social group	Percentage who abstained (self-reported)		
	Official records	Self-report data	Difference of 1997 self-report from 1979–92 average
Former Conservative voters			
Core Conservative groups	11	8	+1
Mixed groups	14	11	+2
Core Labour groups	21	14	+1
Former Labour voters			
Core Conservative groups	9	9	–5
Mixed groups	17	9	0
Core Labour groups	17	14	+4

Sources: Table 8.4 and *BES 1997.*

somewhat higher in 1997 than it had been previously. The Labour pattern, however, was rather different in 1997 from previous years: Labour abstention was actually lower in the middle-class core in 1997 than it had been previously, down by 4 points, while it rose by 4 points in the working-class core. The net result was that in 1997 Labour abstention showed a very similar class gradient to the Conservative one. The inverse pattern that had characterized previous elections completely disappeared.

Of course there are many problems with the use of retrospective measures, and indeed of contemporary measures of turnout. So this cannot be conclusive evidence. However, the results do make a lot of sense. In 1997, unlike all previous years, the patterns of abstention on the Labour side looked identical to the pattern on the Conservative side: there was a modest but definite class gradient, with the highest abstention being in the Labour core groups. The process whereby a party's core group tended to promote the turnout of its supporters seems to have disappeared on the Labour side. By turning its back on the working class, New Labour seems to have undermined one of the processes that encouraged the civic incorporation of the working class.

To check on these conclusions we can look at strength of partisanship, which is closely related to turnout (Heath and Taylor 1999, Table 9.7) and which is also a more direct measure of enthusiasm for one's party. This measure also has the advantage of including both voters and non-voters, so it gives a fuller picture. (We use the standard BES item on strength of partisanship, combining the categories 'very strong' and 'fairly strong'). In Table 8.6 we cross-tabulate this measure by the respondent's current party identification, not by their previous vote.

In the years from 1979 to 1992 the same clear patterns are evident as with abstention: there tended to be stronger partisanship for a party within its own core group. Thus among Conservatives in 1979, 82 per cent in their core middle-class groups were strong supporters, compared with 76 per cent in their opponents'

Table 8.6. Social characteristics and strength of partisanship, 1979–1992

Social group	Percentage with strong or very strong partisanship				
	1979	1983	1987	1992	Average 1979–92
Conservative identifiers					
Core Conservative groups	82	80	81	77	80
Mixed groups	77	75	76	74	75
Core Labour groups	76	68	65	68	69
Labour identifiers					
Core Conservative groups	71	68	67	66	68
Mixed groups	75	72	68	71	71
Core Labour groups	85	72	76	75	76

Sources: BES 1979–92.

Table 8.7. Social characteristics and strength of partisanship, 1997

Social group	Percentage with strong or very strong partisanship		
	Average 1979–92	1997	Difference between 1997 and 1979–92
Current Conservative supporters			
Core Conservative groups	80	66	−14
Mixed groups	75	66	−9
Core Labour groups	69	59	−10
Current Labour supporters			
Core Conservative groups	68	72	+4
Mixed groups	71	73	+2
Core Labour groups	76	71	−5

Sources: Table 8.6 and BES 1997.

working-class core. The reverse pattern held for Labour, with 85 per cent of their supporters in their core working-class groups being strong supporters, falling to 71 per cent in their opponents' core. These differences are not all that large, but they persist in every single study from 1979 to 1992.

The 1997 data present a challenge to this general pattern, but once again only on the Labour side. The Conservative side shows a sharp dip in strength of support, but the dip happens in all social groups alike. So even though Conservative supporters in the party's core middle-class groups were less enthusiastic than usual in 1997, they remained more enthusiastic than Conservative supporters in their opponents' core.

The year 1997, however, sees quite a marked turnaround on the Labour side. In 1997, for the first time since 1979, there was no gradient at all in enthusiasm for the party: enthusiasm increased in the core middle-class groups, up 4 points from its previous average to 72 per cent, but declined 5 points in the core working-class groups from its previous average of 76 per cent to 71 per cent. This thus corroborates the story told by the abstention data. There was a definite weakening, both absolutely and relatively, of enthusiasm for New Labour among its traditional core.

Conclusions

Once again, we must emphasize the smallness of the changes that occurred in the patterns of abstention and strength of partisanship in 1997. It would be far too strong to argue that supporters in Labour's traditional core social groups were disillusioned by New Labour's move towards the centre of the political spectrum; after all, Labour enthusiasm in its traditional core in 1997 was actually stronger than Conservative enthusiasm in its middle-class core. It is on the Conservative side that disillusion shows itself most clearly.

Nevertheless, there are some strong hints from our data that New Labour's move to the centre was, albeit in a rather modest way, responsible for muted enthusiasm among the party's traditional supporters. Our analysis thus confirms the story that Curtice and Steed had told from the aggregate data. It also suggests rather strongly that the changes were specific to Labour and were not part of a general trend towards civic disengagement or political cynicism. We do not think these changes should be blamed on wider social processes. We see them as reactions to New Labour's political decisions, its move towards the centre, its distancing from the trade unions, and its active courting of the middle classes.

From a short-term electoral point of view, these political changes and their electoral consequences almost certainly did little damage to Labour's chances. The loss of Labour votes that this muted enthusiasm entailed would have been more than compensated by the extra votes won from the new recruits to Labour in the middle classes (see Heath 2000). The more interesting question concerns the longer-term implications for the political incorporation of the working class—and particularly of the more disadvantaged sections of the working class—into civic society.

Britain has been unusual in the modest scale of the class differences in turnout. They have historically been a great deal smaller, for example, than those in the United States. In an international context Britain has had high levels of class voting but low levels of class non-voting. One plausible explanation for this pattern is that the presence of a party that is seen to represent working-class interests, the presence of a vigorous trade union movement, which helps to institutionalize working-class support for Labour, and the resulting norms and traditions of support for 'the party of the working class' help to counterbalance the other factors (such as lack of a sense of personal efficacy) that lead to working-class abstention.

In the longer term, we would expect that the weakening of these countervailing processes would lead to increased apathy and disengagement among the disadvantaged sectors of society and to a gradual rise in class non-voting.

9

Party Policies and Voter Choices

Margaret Thatcher claimed that the three general election victories won by the Conservatives under her leadership proved that her policies were popular. The evidence we have reviewed suggests that she may well have been correct about her victory in 1979, when Labour policies had failed and the electorate was disenchanted with Jim Callaghan's Labour government. But for much of the eighteen years of Conservative rule the policies that she and her successor espoused were considerably at odds with the preferences of the average elector. This was true of her policies of privatization, of tax cuts and squeezes on public expenditure, and of her emphasis on the evil of inflation rather than unemployment. On all of these the Conservative Party under her leadership (and under that of her successor) was considerably to the right of the average elector. Nor were Conservative policies on the non-economic issues such as defence and devolution all that much more popular. Only on Europe were the Conservatives closely in touch with public opinion, and even here they lost much of the benefit by giving out conflicting messages.

So how did the Margaret Thatcher manage to win three general elections? First and foremost, she had the good fortune to be opposed by a Labour Party that, on a number of the key issues, was even more out of touch with public opinion than she was. The discrediting of Jim Callaghan's moderate left government by the winter of discontent not only gave Margaret Thatcher the chance to put into practice her experiment in radical right-wing policies but also gave Labour activists a chance to experiment with a radical socialist manifesto. Britain's political system is not a perfect market with a large number of parties competing for the electorate's votes. It is a rather imperfect market with just a few dominant sellers, or 'oligopolists', sharing most of the market between them. In this kind of oligopolistic competition, the success or failure of a particular party depends as much on the choices and mistakes made by its rivals as it does on the preferences of the electorate themselves. If British politics operated within a completely free market with no barriers to entry, then parties might be forced to take up the policies preferred by the average elector and we could say that electoral victory proved the popularity of the winning party's policies. Our evidence, however, shows clearly enough that, for much of the Conservatives' eighteen years of government, many of their major policies were distinctly unpopular, although not quite as unpopular as some of Labour's key policies.

We might also note that another aspect of oligopoly—collusion between the dominant sellers—is also present in British electoral politics. Thus there is agreement between the main parties that moral issues such as the death penalty and abortion reform are taken out of conventional party politics and made the subject of free votes in the House of Commons. It is for this reason that British politics generally revolves around the classic issues associated with the left–right dimension rather than the moral issues associated with the libertarian–authoritarian dimension.

At any rate Labour made some serious mistakes in 1983, especially on nationalization and nuclear disarmament, where they chose to pursue policies that were even less appealing to the electorate than the Conservatives' right-wing policies. Still, as we showed earlier, the Labour left's policies were not uniformly unpopular: the electorate did prefer Labour's policies on unemployment and government spending to those of the Conservatives, and the electorate did regard these as some of the most important issues facing the country. Unfortunately for Labour in 1983, the conventional wisdom among politicians, commentators, and opinion pollsters that voters base their decisions on the most important issues is simply wrong. Voters are much more rational than that: our evidence (reviewed in Chapter 3) suggests that they base their decisions on those issues where there is seen to be the biggest difference between the parties and where there is the greatest likelihood that the parties will actually be able to implement their policies. These issues are the ones where the outcome of the election is likely to make a bigger difference to what actually happens in the real world after the election. For example, in 1983 there were big differences between the parties in their policies on privatization and nationalization, and experience showed that governments really could implement these policies through legislation. It was entirely rational for the electorate to give more weight to this type of issue than to one like unemployment where there appeared to be less difference between the parties and where actual unemployment rates were likely to be affected by external forces over which the government had little control. Even though voters agreed that unemployment was the most important issue facing the country, it would still have been rational for them to give more weight to nationalization and privatization in deciding how to vote. Our evidence suggests that this was indeed what they did.

But it would have been wrong to blame Labour's defeat in 1983 wholly on the extremism of their policies on nationalization and nuclear disarmament. As we saw in Chapter 5, Labour lost support even among the most left-wing 10 per cent of voters (who would have been relatively favourable towards nationalization and disarmament). Between 1979 and 1983 the proportion of this group voting Labour fell by 9 percentage points—much the same as the amount by which it fell among voters in the centre of the political spectrum. Most of Labour's losses, and most of the SDP–Liberal gains, in 1983 took the form of 'across-the-board' changes in support. We attribute this to the low opinion, shared by voters at all points on the political spectrum, of Labour's competence.

The fortunes of the SDP are rather instructive. In alliance with the Liberals it performed astonishingly well in the opinion polls and did win some spectacular by-election victories between its foundation in 1981 and its demise after the 1987 election. Its centrist policies were highly popular among the electorate. It rivalled Labour at the 1983 election with respect to share of the vote, but performed much less well in terms of seats in Parliament. Its 26 per cent of the vote brought it only twenty-three seats, whereas Labour's 28 per cent brought it 209 seats.

The imbalance in shares of seats in Parliament is of course a clear demonstration of the barriers to entry that hinder new parties from undermining the market position of the established oligopolists unless they happen to have a geographically concentrated basis of support (as Plaid Cymru does in Wales and the unionist parties do in Northern Ireland). The British first-past-the-post system also means that minor parties which have little chance of winning a constituency will tend to lose votes disproportionately to the more established parties through tactical voting. The BES data show that until 1997 the centre parties have consistently lost more votes through tactical voting than they have gained.

However, once Neil Kinnock began to get a grip on the Labour Party, moving it back towards the centre and improving its reputation for competence, the SDP was bound to lose votes. It had been largely the beneficiary of Labour mistakes in 1983 and was therefore vulnerable to a Labour recovery. The fact that throughout most of our period the rises and falls in centre-party support took an across-the-board form suggests rather strongly that their fortunes were largely determined by the changes in the electorate's judgements about the competence of the three main parties, not by the specific policy experiments.

Undeterred by the failure of the SDP experiment, Tony Blair essentially repeated the experiment in 1994, but this time from within the Labour Party. He continued Neil Kinnock's programme of moderation (now termed 'modernization') and brought Labour back to the centre-left ground that the SDP had tried to capture (although making little change to the policies on Europe, devolution, and defence that had emerged from Neil Kinnock's policy review). He narrowed the gap with the other parties on the left–right spectrum, positioning Labour much closer to the Liberal Democrat position than Neil Kinnock had dared.

This time the moderate left-of-centre experiment was remarkably successful at the ballot box, and even more successful in winning seats in the House of Commons. As we saw in Chapter 6, in 1997 Labour successfully squeezed the Liberal Democrat vote on the left of centre. The closeness of Labour to the Liberal Democrats made tactical switching between them much easier, transforming the pattern of tactical gains and losses and giving both parties more seats than would have been expected from their overall shares of the vote.

Moreover, by moving so far towards the centre along the left–right spectrum New Labour was able to squeeze the Conservative vote as well. In 1997 the discrediting of the Conservatives through their failures in office and divisions over Europe meant that there was an across-the-board movement away from the Tories. Tony Blair's major achievement from his rebranding of New Labour was to secure greater advantage from this good fortune than his predecessor, John Smith, would have done. Tony Blair secured a much higher proportion of the Conservative defectors than Labour would normally have expected, and thus deprived the Liberal Democrats of votes that they might normally have expected to win from a discredited Conservative Party. This also meant that the social profile of New Labour voters was much more middle-class than had previously been the case. For once, then, the movements between 1992 and 1997 did not take an across-the-board form: Labour made bigger gains from voters in the salariat and on the right of centre than it did among traditional left-of-centre groups.

For once, then, a policy experiment did lead to a marked deviation from the usual pattern of across-the-board swings. To be sure, even without the policy experiment, Labour would have fared rather well in 1997. Much of Labour's gains in 1997 can probably be attributed to the general decline in the Conservatives' reputation for competence and to the improvement in Labour's reputation, but the policy experiment probably added 3 points to Labour's share of the vote over and above the level that John Smith would have secured for Labour if he had remained leader and had kept Labour policies unchanged.

The 3 per cent of the vote secured by the Referendum Party in 1997, on the other hand, can be attributed almost wholly to its policy experiment with Euroscepticism. As we saw in Chapter 4, the Referendum Party was not a general beneficiary of discontent with the Conservatives.

How are we to make sense of these diverse findings, some policy experiments leading to specific electoral benefits, others having much less impact? The different points that we have made can be put into a more general framework for understanding election outcomes. It has two main components: utility and probability. First, there is what economists call the 'utility' that the individual voter would get if particular policies put forward by the various parties were implemented successfully. Secondly, there is the probability of the party, if elected, actually succeeding in implementing its policies. These two components—the probability of the desired outcome occurring and the utility of that outcome if it does occur—generate the standard 'expected utility maximization' model of the economists. The idea is that the voter weights the utility of a given policy by the probability of its being implemented and sums this across the different policies. He or she then votes for whichever party gives the greatest expected utility. We should note that, in our version, it is the voter's subjective assessment of the probability that is relevant, not the 'objective' probability (which is almost certainly unmeasurable anyway).

The model can be extended by looking at the factors that are likely to influence these subjective utilities and probabilities respectively. Considering the influences on utility first, we assume that the amount of utility that a particular voter would derive from a party's policy (if it were implemented fully) will depend on the difference between the voter's own position on the issue (as measured, for example, by our 11-point scales described in Chapter 3) and the party's position on that issue: the bigger the difference between the voter's position and that of the party, the less utility the voter will derive if that party wins the election and implements its policy. In turn, we have shown in Chapters 3 and 4 that voters' own positions on the various issues are related to their social class, union membership, housing tenure, and so on.

(We also showed that voters' attitudes towards issues belonging to the left–right domain had a different relationship to their social class from attitudes towards issues belonging to the nationalist domain.)

Turning next to the factors that affect the voters' subjective assessment of the probabilities, we have argued that some of these will be issue-specific and some will be party-specific. For example, as we saw in Chapter 3, in general voters think that, whatever their manifesto promises, parties can do relatively little about the crime rate. Hence the probability that either party can implement its policies on crime will be judged to be low. On the other hand, parties themselves will vary in their competence: voters might believe that one party will be likely to mess up on all issues alike (for example, Labour in 1979, which had failed to implement its policies on inflation, unemployment, industrial relations, and even on devolution), while another party might be expected to carry through all its plans relatively successfully (as the Conservatives did for a time under Margaret Thatcher with victory over Argentina in the Falklands, victory over the evil of inflation, and victory over the miners and industrial unrest).

The party-specific probabilities are much more likely to vary over time than the issue-specific probabilities. Successes over Argentina, inflation, and the miners may rapidly be followed by the disaster of the poll tax or the exit of sterling from the ERM. Governments seem to be able to lose their reputations for effectiveness even more quickly than they gain them. We therefore expect these party-specific probabilities to vary from election to election and thus to be the major source of the across-the-board swings in electoral support that we have observed throughout our research.

We can express the model more formally with the following four equations:

(1) $U_{ij} = (U_{ij1} \times P_{ij1}) + (U_{ij2} \times P_{ij2}) + \ldots + (U_{ijk} \times P_{ijk})$,

where U represents utility and P represents the subjective probability of an issue being implemented. The subscript i denotes individual respondents, j denotes parties, and k denotes issues. U_{ijk} thus gives the utility that individual i would gain if party j were able to implement issue k, and P_{ijk} gives the subjective probability that party j will actually implement issue k. We assume that the individual votes for whichever party generates the highest utility, U_{ij}.

We can then write equations for the influences on U_{ijk} and on P_{ijk}.

(2) $U_{ijk} = f(W_{ik} - W_{ijk})$,

where W_{ik} represents the position of the individual voter i on issue k, and W_{ijk} represents the perceived position of party j on that issue.

(3) $W_{ik} = f(A_i, B_i, C_i \ldots)$,

where A_i, B_i, C_i represent the demographic characteristics such as social class, housing tenure, and union membership of the individual respondent i.

(4) $P_{ijk} = f(X_{ij}, Y_{ik})$,

where X_{ij} represents the perceived competence of party j and Y_{ik} represents the extent to which issue k is thought to be influenceable by government action.

This model provides a comprehensive framework within which to place the main findings of this volume. Equation (1) summarizes the basic 'expected utility' concept. We leave open the question of how many issues the individual voter takes into account. It may well be that more sophisticated voters take into account a wider range of issues than do less knowledgeable voters. A parsimonious model would simply distinguish the three main domains that we reviewed in Appendix 4.2, namely the left–right, nationalist–cosmopolitan, and liberal–authoritarian domains.

Equation (2) then expresses one of the key notions in the rational choice theory of voting behaviour, namely that the utility a voter derives from a particular party's victory will depend on the ideological distance between the party and the voter. We leave open the precise nature of the functional relationship between ideological distance and utility since somewhat different formulations, such as the directional theory discussed in Chapter 3, have been advanced. Note that it may well be sensible to think of someone obtaining negative utility from a particular party's policy. For example, a left-winger whose own preferences are for nationalization might obtain negative utility from a free market policy that privatized industry: the left-winger might positively dislike privatization rather than simply giving it zero utility (and therefore no role).

Equation (3) then summarizes the well-known relationships between the voter's ideological position and his or her social characteristics. Since many of the voter's social characteristics (apart from age) are fairly stable over time, we would expect equation (3) to explain continuity rather than change; it explains why different groups of voters typically support different parties but is not going to be able to explain much of the election-to-election changes in party support. However, given the gradual changes over time in the proportions of voters belonging to the various social classes (as described in Chapter 2), equation (3) does provide a potential explanation for long-run processes of electoral change.

Equation (4), on the other hand, contains both constant and variable elements. It is likely that the issue-specific aspects will be fairly stable too over time: our findings that voters attribute greater responsibility to governments for the level of taxes and standards in health and education than they do for crime rates or one's personal standard of living are almost certainly long-standing patterns and are unlikely to be unique to the 1997 election. However, as conditions in the real world change, so voters' assessments of government responsibility may change too. Globalization, for example, may mean that countries have less and less influence over their own rates of unemployment, and as the voters come to realize this, so they may come to attach lower probability to a party's chances of implementing succesfully its policies on unemployment. In contrast, the voters' assessments of a party's competence is the factor that is most likely to vary in the short term and to explain election-to-election change in levels of party support.

The model that we have formulated here has some similarities with the standard distinction in the literature between what are called 'valence' and 'position' issues. This distinction was formulated by Butler and Stokes (1974). They defined position issues as those such as nationalization and privatization where voters (and parties) take up very different positions on the political spectrum (and are thus analogous to the positions given in our equations (2) and (3)); valence issues, on the other hand, were defined as ones, such as economic growth, where there is broad consensus in the electorate that they are 'a good thing', and the crucial question is how effective a party would be in implementing economic growth (and thus is in some ways analogous to the ability of parties to implement their policies, as expressed by X_{ij} in equation (4)).

The crucial difference between our model and that of Butler and Stokes is that ours weights utility by probability rather than simply adding the valence and position scores. In other words, ours is a multiplicative model rather than the additive model proposed by Butler and Stokes. This leads to some very different conclusions. For example, Margaret Thatcher was seen to have become a very effective leader, even by her political enemies, after her various successes such as the Falklands and the miners' dispute. According to an additive model, this would lead to a general increase in support for her government. The multiplicative model, on the other hand, predicts that feelings towards Margaret Thatcher would become more polarized as she became more effective but that this would not necessarily increase her overall support. In practice the Conservatives' share of the vote actually fell after 1979, and views about the Conservatives did appear to be highly polarized. While we cannot be sure that the multiplicative model is correct, it does seem rather plausible.

The multiplicative model also explains why policy changes often fail to bring much benefit. For example, if a party changes policy on an issue like crime, the electoral impact of this will be heavily muted by the electorate's belief that governments have relatively little impact on crime rates. Furthermore, if a party is believed to be relatively incompetent, this is likely to mute the electoral response to a policy change even more. Hence, a party that is believed to be incompetent will get rather little benefit from policy changes.

This could explain why Neil Kinnock's policy review produced such modest benefits overall and why his move towards the centre, unlike Tony Blair's, did not seem to win extra bonuses from voters on the right of the political spectrum. To be sure, Neil Kinnock did improve his party's reputation for competence somewhat, but his reputation still remained substantially lower than that of his opponents or successor. The overall electoral benefits of the policy review would therefore be muted, and their distribution would be relatively even. An identical policy change by a party that was believed to be highly competent would produce much greater overall benefits and would also see greater unevenness in the distribution of benefits.

Our model also explains why, on the Conservative side, nearly all the electoral changes took an across-the-board form and why there did not seem to be any distinct groups of 'swing voters'. There was little change in Conservative policy (relative to the average voter) over our period, and hence there is no particular reason to expect the social or ideological distribution of their support to vary from election to election. We only really expect to find differential swings in different social groups if a competent party changes its position (or an incompetent one becomes competent and changes position). Since the Conservative Party was scarcely seen to change position (but only competence) over the whole period, that is the main source of differential swing removed immediately.

A few methodological points may also be in order. First, we do not claim that any one individual voter actually follows this model exactly or goes through these calculations explicitly. All we claim is that, on aggregate, voters behave as though they were following this model. No individual voter needs to follow all the details of the model; they simply need to be followed by some voters.

Secondly, it is worth noting that a single cross-section survey like the BES is much better at accounting for the stable features of this model than for the time-varying ones. Time-series models are necessary to account for the time-varying processes such as those that lead to the changes in the electorate's assessments of the parties' competence. What we need are the kinds of time-series model developed by Sanders and his colleagues. However, we would want to argue that there are additional factors, over and above the economic ones that Sanders includes, that can have an effect on the electorate's assessments of party competence (that is, on the party-specific probabilities). However, with only five elections in our period, it is not sensible for us to try and develop formal models of our respondents' subjective estimates of party competence.

Finally, we must consider whether the model needs to be expanded to include some of the other 'non-rational' processes that we have observed in our research. What we have proposed so far is a rational choice model that treats voter preferences as essentially independent factors. This rational choice model is the kind of model of the elector that New Labour strategy was based on: New Labour strategists believed that voters' preferences were affected by external forces such as social change (following equation (3)). They believed that parties must adapt to the electorate and that parties have no scope for converting the electorate to their own views. This is the general model underlying the pragmatic politics of catchall parties. It is fundamentally different from the kind of model that underlies the conviction politics of Old Labour and of Margaret Thatcher.

Old Labour ideas, and the even older Marxist ideas that parties have a role to play in fostering awareness of common interests and shaping group consciousness, have no place in this model. Old Labour believed, to use Kirkheimer's terminology, in the possibility of 'the intellectual and moral encadrement of the masses' (Kirkheimer 1966: 184–5). That is, they believed that the electorate's preferences and values could themselves be shaped by the actions of political parties and were not simply to be regarded as shaped by external social processes. As we noted in the Introduction, Margaret Thatcher also shared rather similar ideas, although she expressed them in rather different language, talking of converting 'disillusion into understanding'. It was perhaps this belief in her ability to convert the electorate that allowed her to press forward with policies substantially at odds with the electorate's own preferences.

There is some evidence that Margaret Thatcher's view was not wholly incorrect. She may not have succeeded in her crusade to shape people's values and to convert them to the virtues of self-help, individual responsibility, and entrepreneurial vigour. But there is some evidence that she did take the public with her on nationalization and on trade union reform. As we showed in Chapter 3, at the beginning of our period a majority of the electorate favoured the status quo. By the end of the period the status quo had changed dramatically, with huge amounts of British industry privatized, volumes of trade union legislation, and many fewer working days lost through strikes; but there was no great desire on the part of the electorate to put the clock back to the *status quo ante*. In this sense Margaret Thatcher had converted them, probably more through the practical economic success of privatization and her trade union reforms rather than through her lectures and moral fervour, to the value of the new economic order. In this respect, then, it seems that the electorate's attitudes may have been affected by their changing experience under different governments, and were not solely determined by the sociological factors captured in equation (3).

Old Labour did not of course have the chance to show the electorate that massive extension of the public sector would have brought economic benefits. They had to rely on lectures and moral fervour. But again there is some evidence that they succeeded, although not entirely in the way they might have wished. In Chapter 4 we showed that the structure of the electorate's attitudes was markedly different in 1983 from the structures before and afterwards. The Labour Party put forward a package in 1983 that combined socialist principles of public ownership and government intervention with policies of nuclear disarmament and Euroscepticism. This was intellectually quite a distinctive package, and we find that in 1983, but not in other years, it was reflected in the structure of the electorate's attitudes as well, left-wing views on economic issues being associated with pacifist views on defence and opposition to Europe. However, once Labour, under Neil Kinnock's gradual modernization of the party, had moved away from this distinctive package, the structure of the electorate's attitudes changed too. By 1992 left-wing views on economic issues like nationalization were unrelated to views on Europe and only weakly related to views on defence.

We cannot be sure of the causal direction, but the 'top down' theory whereby parties help to shape attitudes is consistent with these findings. On the other hand, the theory should not perhaps be accepted over-enthusiastically either. It is noticeable from our evidence that the general structure of the left–right and liberal–authoritarian attitudes remained largely unchanged throughout our period (and even earlier). It was the attitudes towards Europe that seemed to be influenced by party policy. Attitudes towards Europe are not so strongly rooted in social structure or in people's direct experience as are the left–right or libertarian–authoritarian and hence may be more susceptible to political influence. This is directly in line with the original article by Belknap and Cambell (1952) that defined the theory of party identification. They argued that, if voters knew relatively little about an issue, they were likely to turn to their party for a lead.

Our basic model, then, needs to be expanded to include a wider range of influences, especially political influences, on the electorate's attitudes. The sociological determinism of equation (3) needs to be broadened to include political and economic variables.

The basic rational choice model should also be modified to take account of other sorts of social processes. We saw in Chapter 5 how Old Labour failed to win as many votes from left-of-centre electors in the salariat as they did in the working class. The parties' shares of the votes in different social groups cannot be read off simply from the ideological preferences of the various groups. A model that emphasizes policy preferences and subjective assessments of competence to the exclusion of all else is at best a partial one. The rational choice model is also an individualistic model that has no room for processes of social interaction and communication. However, as Akerlof has suggested (Akerlof 1997: 1006),

The key difference between social decisions and conventional economic decisions is that the social decisions have social consequences whereas economic decisions do not. While my network of friends and relatives are not affected in the least by my choice between apples and oranges, they will be affected by my educational aspirations, my attitudes and practices towards racial discrimination,

and, we might add, by my political attitudes and behaviour as well. The technical solution is to include other variables into equation (1), notably the party preferences of one's associates: we do not need to abandon rational choice theory but simply to amend its more simplistic assumptions.

It is possible, therefore, that processes of social interaction within social classes lead people to vote in accordance with the norms and practices of their social class and that this could account for some of the unexplained class differences in voting behaviour and also for the patterns of abstention that we have found. For example, we found in Chapter 7 that members of the salariat who had exactly the same left-wing policy preferences as members of the working class were nevertheless less likely to vote Labour. One possible explanation for this is that individuals in the salariat tend to conform to the voting behaviour of those around them. Similarly, we found that supporters of a particular party tended to have lower rates of abstention, and stronger partisanship, when they belonged to that party's core social groups than when they belonged to groups associated with the opposing party. Processes of conformity to the dominant norms of one's social group provide a parsimonious explanation for both these findings.

Processes of social conformity, or rather their absence in the case of the Liberal Democrats, may also serve to explain why the centre parties consistently seem to poll fewer votes than would be expected from the popularity of their policies. As we have shown in previous work, if voters had based their choices solely on policy preferences, the centre parties in 1983 and 1987 would have increased their share of the vote and would have eaten substantially into the Conservative share. However, unlike the Conservatives, the centre parties do not have any core social groups where social pressures towards conformity with Liberal Democrat values are likely to be strong. The Liberal Democrats tend to be stronger in the salariat, but here they are outnumbered by Conservative-inclined voters and this is likely to strengthen Conservative support at the expense of the Liberal Democrats.

Whether such social processes do operate has become quite a contentious area of research. Some recent research has suggested that the way people vote is influenced by the social class of their neighbourhood or constituency as well as by their own individual characteristics (Harrop *et al.* 1992; Pattie and Johnston 1999; Fisher 2000; Andersen and Heath 2000), although critics have suggested that these alleged neighbourhood effects appear to be present only because various individual characteristics of the voters have been ignored (Kelley and McAllister 1985).

It has also been suggested that modern society is becoming more individualistic over time and that there has been a weakening of social groups and of communities based on social class. If this argument is correct, the real world is changing so as to bring it more into line with the individualistic premises of the rational choice model. And it is almost certainly correct that the cohesive communities based on mining or steel towns have largely disappeared. If the growth of individualism is correct, then the modern catchall party like New Labour may be the party of the future, based on a model of man that fits the nature of the modern elector of the twenty-first century.

However, our theory of social interaction does not depend solely on the existence of cohesive communities. Looser social networks may also be a basis for social persuasion. Moreover, there is a danger for the catchall party if its individualistic assumptions prove to be incorrect. If our theory of social processes is correct, then concentrations of a party's supporters in distinctive social milieux is likely to boost its support in those areas, strengthen their partisanship, and reduce abstention levels. The catchall strategy, appealing to a broader but more thinly distributed range of individuals, may lose the electoral bonus that social interaction can bring.

Finally, the catchall party needs to beware of what we have termed the 'forked tail' effect. We noticed that, even when Labour had adopted Thatcherite policies (for example on taxes and spending), the electorate appeared to be much happier with Labour's version than with the Conservatives' version of the same policies. Possibly this was because disillusionment with Conservative competence in managing the economy had generalized into a general disillusion with all things Conservative. (This can be seen as an example of the standard psychological theory of cognitive dissonance; it also implies that perceptions of party policy are not independent of perceptions of party competence.) Popular policies, therefore, may not be sufficient for electoral success. Margaret Thatcher showed that unpopular policies can come to be accepted if they are implemented successfully. Conversely, popular policies may become discredited if implementation is unsuccessful. Situating oneself close to the policy preferences of the median elector is neither a necessary nor a sufficient condition for electoral success.

Appendix. The British Election Surveys, 1979–1997

Katarina Thomson

The British Election Surveys (BES) constitute the longest academic series of nationally representative probability sample surveys in this country. They have taken place immediately after every general election since 1964, giving a total of ten so far. There have also been two non-election-year surveys (in 1963 and 1969), a postal referendum study in 1975, additional or booster Scottish studies in 1974, 1979, 1992 and 1997, an additional Welsh study in 1979, Northern Ireland Election Studies in 1992, and 1998, Campaign Studies in 1987, 1992, and 1996–7, Scottish and Welsh Referendum Studies in 1997, and Scottish Parliament and Welsh Assembly Election Studies in 1999. All electoral periods have been covered by at least a two-wave panel except the period 1979–83. The 1997 study included an ethnic minority boost and a qualitative study of electoral volatility. There has also been a frequent-interval British Election Panel Study (BEPS) in the period 1992–7 and since 1997. In addition, the 1997 British Social Attitudes survey carried an election module.

The BES series was originated by David Butler (Nuffield College, Oxford) and Donald Stokes (University of Michigan), who continued to direct the studies until 1970. The series then passed to Ivor Crewe, Bo Särlvik, and James Alt at the University of Essex (later joined by David Robertson), who organized the two 1974 studies and the 1979 study. The 1983, 1987, 1992, and 1997 studies were directed by Anthony Heath (Jesus College,then Nuffield College, Oxford), Roger Jowell (National Centre for Social Research, known as Social and Community Planning Research until May 1999), and John Curtice (University of Liverpool, then University of Strathclyde). Since 1994 this collaboration has taken the form of the Centre for Research into Elections and Social Trends (CREST), an Economic and Social Research Council (ESRC)-funded research centre, linking the National Centre for Social Research, and Nuffield College, Oxford. (Since November 1999 CREST has moved from Nuffield College to the Department of Sociology, University of Oxford.) For publications based on these studies see, for example, Butler and Stokes (1974); Särlvik and Crewe (1983); Heath, *et al.* (1985, 1991, 1994*b*); and Evans and Norris (1999).

The data from all the BESs are available from the Data Archive at the University of Essex.

The sample sizes and interrelationship of the studies are shown in Figure A1.

Most of the analyses in this book are based on the 1979, 1983, 1987, 1992 and 1997 general election studies and the 1992–1997 British Election Panel Study, which are described in more detail below.

1979 British Election Study

The 1979 BES was funded by the Social Science Research Council. The principal investigators were Ivor Crewe, Bo Särlvik, and David Robertson (University of Essex).

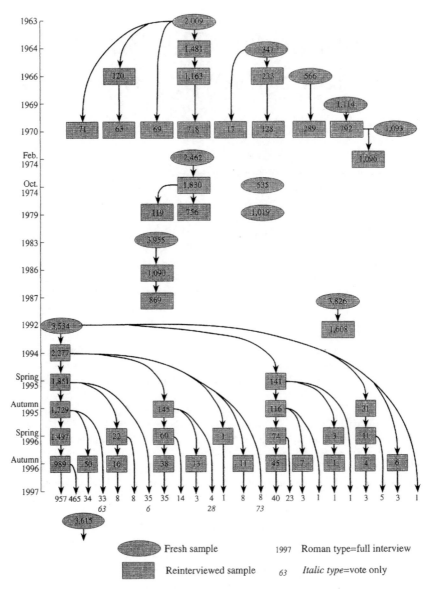

Fig. A1. British Election Surveys, 1963–1997. 1997: roman type = full interview; italic = vote only

The sample was drawn from the electoral registers and was designed to be representative of eligible voters living in private households in Britain south of the Caledonian Canal. It consisted partly of a follow-up to respondents to the 1974 studies and partly of a fresh sample. The fieldwork was conducted by Research Services Ltd following the May 1979 general election. The response rate was 61 per cent.

1983 British Study

The 1983 BES was funded by the ESRC, Pergamon Press, and Jesus College, Oxford. It was the first survey to be undertaken by the team of Anthony Heath, Roger Jowell, and John Curtice.

The sample was drawn from the electoral registers and was designed to be representative of eligible voters living in private households in Britain south of the Caledonian Canal. The fieldwork was carried out by Social and Community Planning Research in July to October 1983. The issued sample was 6,000, of which 5,463 were eligible addresses. There were 3,955 interviews, giving a response rate of 72 per cent.

A subsample of respondents were selected for a panel: 1,090 respondents reinterviewed in November–December 1986, and 869 after the 1987 general election.

1987 British Election Study

The 1987 British General Election Study was funded by the Sainsbury Family Charitable Trust, the ESRC and Pergamon Press. The principal investigators were again Anthony Heath, Roger Jowell, and John Curtice.

The sample was drawn from the electoral registers and was designed to be representative of eligible voters living in private households in Britain south of the Caledonian Canal. The fieldwork was carried out by Social and Community Planning Research in June to August 1987. The issued sample was 6,000, of which 5,463 were eligible addresses. There were 3,826 interviews, giving a response rate of 70 per cent.

1,608 respondents from the 1987 survey were followed up in 1992.

Further details of the survey are given in appendix II of Heath *et al.* (1991).

1992 British Election Study

The 1992 BES was funded by the ESRC and the Sainsbury Family Trusts. The principal investigators were again Anthony Heath, Roger Jowell, and John Curtice. They were joined by Jack Brand and James Mitchell (University of Strathclyde) for the Scottish study.

The sample was drawn from the electoral registers and was designed to be representative of eligible voters living in private households in Britain. The main sample was accompanied by a Scottish boost sample. An extra module of questions was also asked in Scotland.

The fieldwork was carried out by Social and Community Planning Research in April to July 1992. The issued sample was 5,232, of which 4,869 were eligible addresses. There were 3,534 interviews giving a response rate of 73 per cent. Of these, 957 were in Scotland.

Further details of the survey are given in Taylor *et al.* (1994).

1992–1997 British Election Panel Study

The 1992–7 British Election Panel Study (BEPS-1) was funded by the ESRC and carried out by CREST. The principal investigators were Anthony Heath, Roger Jowell, and John Curtice.

The first wave of the panel was the 1992 BES. Further waves were undertaken as follows:

- postal or telephone interview in summer 1993
- face-to-face interview in spring–summer 1994
- face-to-face interview in spring–summer 1995
- telephone or postal interview in autumn 1995
- face-to-face interview in spring–summer1996
- telephone or postal interview in autumn 1996 (part of the sample only)
- face-to-face interview in spring–summer 1997

The face-to-face interviews were about 30–40 minutes in length and repeated many of the questions from the 1992 BES, updating them with information on voting at mid-term elections. The 1995 and 1996 telephone–postal waves had shorter questionnaires, tapping attitudes in the wake of the party conference season.

The fieldwork was carried out by the Social and Community Planning Research. The sample at the final wave was 1,694 giving a panel lifetime response rate of 35 per cent (48 per cent of those interviewed in 1992). A further 170 respondents refused a full interview, but completed a very short interview, mainly recording vote at the 1997 election.

Further details of the panel are given in Brook and Taylor (forthcoming).

1997 British Election Study

The 1997 British General Election Study was funded by the ESRC and the Gatsby Charitable Foundation, and the Commission for Racial Equality. The study was carried out by CREST. The principal investigators, Anthony Heath, Roger Jowell, and John Curtice, were joined by Pippa Norris (Harvard University) for the main cross-section study. They were also joined by David McCrone and Alice Brown (University of Edinburgh) and Paula Surridge (University of Salford) for the Scottish Election Study and Shamit Saggar (Queen Mary and Westfield College, London) for the Ethnic Minority Election Study.

In a departure from earlier election studies, the sample was drawn from the Postcode Address File instead of the electoral registers. It was designed to be representative of the adult population of Britain living in private households and therefore included respondents who were neither on the electoral register, nor, in some cases, entitled to be on the electoral register. For comparability with earlier surveys, the sample can be restricted to eligible voters only. (Respondents were checked against the electoral registers to make this information as accurate as possible.) The main sample was accompanied by a Scottish boost sample and an ethnic minority boost sample. Extra modules of questions were also asked of Scottish and ethnic minority respondents.

The fieldwork was carried out by Social and Community Planning Research in May to July 1997. The issued sample (main cross-section and Scottish boost) was 6,540, of which 5,814 were eligible addresses. There were 3,615 interviews giving a response rate of 63 per cent. Of these, 882 were in Scotland. The 1997 BES also forms the first wave of the 1997–2002 British Election Panel Study (BEPS-2), which is funded by the ESRC via CREST.

Further details of the survey as given in Taylor and Thomson (1999) and Thomson *et al.* (1999).

REFERENCES

ABRAMS, M., ROSE, R., and HINDEN, R. (1960), *Must Labour Lose?* (Harmondsworth: Penguin).

AKERLOF, G. A. (1997), 'Social Distance and Social Decisions', *Economica*, 65: 1005–27.

ALDRICH, J. H. (1993), 'Rational Choice and Turnout', *American Journal of Political Science*, 37: 246–78.

ANDERSEN, R., and HEATH, A. F. (2000), 'Social Class and Voting: A Multilevel Analysis of Individual and Constituency Differences', paper presented at the Fifth International Conference on Social Science Methodology, Cologne, Oct. 2000.

AUSTIN, T. (ed.) (1997), *The Times Guide to the House of Commons, May 1997* (London: Times Books).

BAKER, D., GAMBLE, A., and LUDLAM, S. (1993a), 'Whips or Scorpions? The Maastricht Vote and the Conservative Party', *Parliamentary Affairs,* 46: 151–66.

—— —— —— (1993b), 'Conservative Splits and European Integration', *Political Quarterly,* 62: 420–35.

BALE, TIM (1996), 'The Death of the Past: Symbolic Politics and the Changing of Clause IV', in David Farrell, David Broughton, David Denver and Justin Fisher (eds.), *British Elections and Parties Yearbook 1996* (London: Frank Cass), 158–77.

BELKNAP, G., and CAMPBELL, A. (1952) 'Political Party Identification and Attitudes toward Foreign Policy', *Public Opinion Quarterly*, 15: 601–23.

BLAIR, TONY (1992), *Renewal* (Oct.), no. 4.

—— (1994), *Socialism*, Fabian Pamphlet 565 (London: Fabian Society).

—— (1995), *Let us Face the Future—the 1945 Anniversary Lecture*, Fabian Pamphlet 571 (London: Fabian Society).

BROOK, L., and TAYLOR, B. (forthcoming), *The British Election Panel Study 1992–1997: Technical Report* (London: National Centre for Social Research).

BROWN, A., MCCRONE, D., PATERSON, L., and SURRIDGE, P. (1998), *The Scottish Electorate* (London: Macmillan).

BUDGE, I. (1999), 'Party policy and Ideology: Reversing the 1950s?', in Evans and Norris (1999: 1–22)

BUTLER, G. (2000), *Twentieth-Century British Political Facts 1900–2000* (Basingstoke: Macmillan).

BUTLER, D., and KAVANAGH, D. (1974), *The British General Election of October 1974* (London: Macmillan).

—— —— (1979), *The British General Election of 1979* (Basingstoke: Macmillan).

—— —— (1983), *The British General Election of 1983* (Basingstoke: Macmillan).

—— —— (1987), *The British General Election of 1987* (Basingstoke: Macmillan).

—— —— (1992), *The British General Election of 1992* (Basingstoke: Macmillan).

—— —— (1997), *The British General Election of 1997* (Basingstoke: Macmillan).

—— and STOKES, D. (1974), *Political Change in Britain: The Electoral Choice*, 2nd edn. (Basingstoke: Macmillan).

BUTLER, T., and SAVAGE, M. (1995) (eds.), *Social Change and the Middle Classes* (London: UCL Press).

CAMPBELL, J. (2000), *Margaret Thatcher* (London: Jonathan Cape).

CAUTRES, B., and HEATH, A. (1997), 'Declin du "vote de classe"? Une analyse comparative en France et en Grande Bretagne', *Revue Internationale de Politique Comparée*, 32: 541–68.

CLARKE, T. N., and LIPSET, S. M. (1991), 'Are Social Classes Dying?', *International Sociology*, 6: 397–410.

CREWE, I. (1973), 'The Politics of "Affluent" and "Traditional" Workers in Britain: An Aggregate Data Analysis', *British Journal of Political Science*, 3: 29–52.

—— (1988), 'Has the Electorate become Thatcherite?', in Robert Skidelsky (ed.), *Thatcherism* (London: Chatto & Windus), 25–49.

—— and KING, A., (1995), *SDP: The Birth, Life and Death of the Social Democratic Party* (Oxford: Oxford University Press).

CRITCHLEY, J., and MORRISON, HALCROW, M. (1997) *Collapse of Stout Party: The Decline and Fall of the Tories* (London: Gollancz).

CROSLAND, C. A. R. (1956), *The Future of Socialism* (London: Cape).

CURTICE, J., and PARK, A. (1999) 'Region: New Labour, New Geography?', in Evans and Norris (1999: 124–47).

CURTICE, J., and STEED, M. (1997), 'Appendix 2: The Results Analysed', in Butler and Kavanagh (1997: 295–325).

DENVER, D., and HANDS, G. (1974) 'Marginality and Turnout in British General Elections', *British Journal of Political Science*, 4: 17–35.

—— —— (1985), 'Marginality and Turnout in British General Elections in the 1970s', *British Journal of Political Science*, 15: 381–8.

—— —— (1997), 'Turnout', in Pippa Norris and Neil Gavin (eds.), *Britain Votes* (Oxford: Oxford University Press).

DEPARTMENT OF THE ENVIRONMENT (1978), *Housing and Construction Statistics* (London: Government Statistical Service).

—— (1998), *Housing and Construction Statistics* (London: Stationery Office).

—— (1999), *Housing and Construction Statistics* (London: Stationery Office).

DONOGHUE, B. (1987), *Prime Minister: The Conduct of Policy under Harold Wilson and James Callaghan* (London: Cape).

DOWNS, A. (1957), *An Economic Theory of Democracy* (New York: Harper and Row).

EAGLES, M., and ERFLE, S. (1989), 'Community Cohesion and Voter Turnout in English Parliamentary Constituencies', *British Journal of Political Science*, 19: 115–25.

EVANS, G. (1998), 'Euroscepticism and Conservative Electoral Support: How an Asset Became a Liability', *British Journal of Political Science*, 28: 573–90.

—— (1999), 'Europe: A New Electoral Cleavage?' in Evans and Norris (1999: 207–22).

—— CURTICE, J., and NORRIS, P. (1998), 'New Labour, New Tactical Voting?', in David Denver, Justin Fisher, Phillip Cowley, and Charles Pattie (eds.), *British Elections and Parties Review*, Vol. 8 (London: Frank Cass).

—— HEATH, A., and PAYNE, C. (1999), 'Class: Labour as a Catch-All Party?', Evans and Norris (1999: 87–101).

—— and NORRIS, P. (1999) (eds.), *Critical Elections: Voters and Parties in Long-Term Perspective* (London: Sage).

—— and TRYSTAN, D. (1999), 'Why was 1997 Different?', in Bridget Taylor and Katarina Thomson (eds.), *Scotland and Wales: Nations Again?* (Cardiff: University of Wales Press), 95–117.

FIELDING, S. (1997), 'Labour's Path to Power', in Andrew Geddes and Jonathan Tonge (eds.), *Labour's Landslide* (Manchester: Manchester University Press), 23–35.

FISHER, S. (2000), 'Class Contextual Effects on the Conservative Vote in 1983', *British Journal of Political Science*, 30: 347–82.

FLICKINGER, R. S. (1995), 'British Political Parties and Public Attitudes towards the European Community: Leading, Following or Getting out of the Way?', in David Broughton, David M. Farrell, David Denver, and Colin Rallings, *British Elections and Parties Yearbook 1994* (London: Frank Cass), 197–214.

FORREST, R., and MURIE, A. (1984), 'Residualisation and Council Housing: Aspects of Changing Social Relations of Housing Tenure', *Journal of Social Policy*, 12: 453–68.

FRANKLIN, M., MACKIE, T., and VALEN, H. (1992) *Electoral Change: Responses to Evolving Social and Attitudinal Structures in Western Countries* (Cambridge: Cambridge University Press).

FRANKLIN, M., Marsh, M., and McLAREN, L. (1994), 'Uncorking the Bottle: Popular Opposition to European Unification in the Wake of Maastricht', *Journal of Common Market Studies*, 32: 455–72.

GALBRAITH, J. K. (1993), *The Culture of Contentment* (London: Penguin).

GALLIE, D. (1998), 'Trade Union Allegiance and Decline in British Urban Labour Markets', in Duncan Gallie, Michael White, Yuan Cheng, and Mark Tomlinson (eds.), *Restructuring the Employment Relationship* (Oxford: Clarendon Press), 140–74.

—— (1999), 'The Labour Force', in A. H. Halsey (ed.), *British Social Trends* (Basingstoke: Macmillan).

GALLUP (1992–6), *Political and Economic Index* (London: Dod's Publishing and Research).

GAMBLE, A. (1996), 'The Legacy of Thatcherism', in M. Perryman (ed.), *The Blair Agenda* (London: Lawrence & Wishart).

GARRETT, G. (1992), 'The Political Consequences of Thatcherism', *Political Behaviour*, 14: 361–82.

—— (1994), 'Popular Capitalism: The Electoral Legacy of Thatcherism', in Heath *et al.* (1994c: 107–23).

GAVIN, N. T., and SANDERS, D. (1997), 'The Economy and Voting', *Parliamentary Affairs*, 50: 631–40.

GELLNER, E. (1983), *Nations and Nationalism* (Oxford: Blackwell).

GIBSON, J. (1990), *The Politics and Economics of the Poll Tax: Mrs Thatcher's Downfall* (Cradley Heath: EMAS).

GOLDTHORPE, J. H. (1987), *Social Mobility and Class Structure in Modern Britain* (Oxford: Clarendon Press).

—— LOCKWOOD, D., BECHHOFER, F., and PLATT, J. (1968), *The Affluent Worker: Political Attitudes and Behaviour* (Cambridge: Cambridge University Press).

GOULD, P. (1998), 'Why Labour Won', in Ivor Crewe, Brian Gosschalk, and John Bartle (eds.), *Political Communications: Why Labour Won the General Election of 1997* (London: Frank Cass), 3–11.

GRAAF, N. D. DE, NIEUWBEERTA, P., and HEATH, A. (1994), 'Class Mobility and Political Preferences: Individual and Contextual Effects', *American Journal of Sociology*, 100: 997–1027.

HAHN, F. (1988), 'On Market Economics', in Robert Skidelsky (ed.), *Thatcherism* (London: Chatto & Windus), 107–24.

HALL, S. (1979), 'The Great Moving Right Show', *Marxism Today*, 23 Jan. 1979: 14–20.

HARROP, M., HEATH, A., and OPENSHAW, S. (1992), 'Does Neighbourhood Influence Voting Behaviour—and Why?', in Ivor Crewe, Pippa Norris, David Denver, and David Broughton (eds.), *British Elections and Parties Yearbook 1991* (London: Harvester Wheatsheaf), 103–20.

HEATH, A. F. (1990), 'Class and Political Partisanship', in J. Clark, C. Modgil, and S. Modgil (eds.), *John H. Goldthorpe: Consensus and Controversy* (London: Falmer Press), 161–70.

—— (1998), 'The Need of Data Analysis of Rational Action Theory: Pros and Cons', in H.-P. Blossfeld and G. Prein (eds.), *Rational Choice Theory and Large-Scale Data Analysis* (Boulder, Colo.: Westview Press), 71–187.

—— (2000), 'Were Traditional Labour Voters Disillusioned with New Labour? Abstention at the 1997 General Election', in Philip Cowley, David Denver, Andrew Russell, and Lisa Harrison (eds.), *British Elections and Parties Review*, Vol. 10 (London: Frank Cass), 32–46.

HEATH, A. F., and CLIFFORD, P. (1994), 'The Election Campaign', in Heath *et al.* (1994c: 7–24).

—— and KELLAS, J. (1998), 'Nationalisms and Constitutional Questions', *Scottish Affairs*, Special issue, *Understanding Constitutional Change*, 110–27.

—— and McDONALD, S.-K. (1987), 'Social Change and the Future of the Left', *Political Quarterly*, 58: 364–77.

—— and PARK, A. (1997), 'Thatcher's Children?' in Roger Jowell *et al.* (eds.), *British Social Attitudes: The 14th Report* (Aldershot: Dartmouth), 1–22.

—— and SAVAGE, M. (1995), 'Political Alignments within the Middle Classes, 1972–89', in T. Butler and M. Savage (1995: 275–92).

—— and TAYLOR, B. (1999), 'Turnout: New Sources of Abstention?', in Evans and Norris (1999: 207–22).

—— JOWELL, R., and CURTICE, J. (1985), *How Britain Votes* (Oxford: Pergamon Press).

—— —— —— and EVANS, G. (1990), 'The Rise of a New Political Agenda?', *European Sociological Review*, 6: 31–49.

—— —— —— —— FIELD, J., and WITHERSPOON, S. (1991), *Understanding Political Change: The British Voter 1964–1987* (Oxford: Pergamon Press).

—— EVANS, G., and MARTIN, J. (1994a) 'The Measurement of Core Beliefs and Values: The Development of Balanced Socialist/*Laissez Faire* and Libertarian/Authoritarian Scales', *British Journal of Political Science*, 24: 115–32.

—— JOWELL, R., CURTICE, J. (1994b), 'Can Labour Win?', in Heath *et al.* (1994c: 275–99).

—— —— —— with TAYLOR, B. (eds.) (1994c), *Labour's Last Chance? The 1992 Election and Beyond* (Aldershot: Dartmouth).

—— —— TAYLOR, B., and THOMSON, K. (1998), 'Euroscepticism and the Referendum Party', in David Denver, Justin Fisher, Philip Cowley, and Charles Pattie (eds.), *British Elections and Parties Review*, Vol. 8 (London: Frank Cass), 95–110.

—— McLEAN, I., TAYLOR, B., and CURTICE, J. (1999a), 'Between First and Second Order: A Comparison of Voting Behaviour in European and Local Elections in Britain', *European Journal of Political Research*, 35: 389–414.

—— TAYLOR, B., BROOK, L., and PARK, A. (1999b), 'British National Sentiment', *British Journal of Political Science*, 29: 155–75.

HEFFERNAN, R. (1998), 'Labour's transformation: A Staged Process with no Single Point of Origin', *Politics*, 18: 101–6.

HER MAJESTY'S TREASURY (1998), *Information on Privatization in the UK* (London: HM Treasury).

HEWITT, P., and GOULD, P. (1993), 'Lessons from America: Learning from Success— Labour and Clinton's New Democrats', *Renewal*, 1: 45–51.

HICKS, S. (2000), 'Trade Union Membership 1998–99: An Analysis of Data from the Certification Officer and Labour Force Survey', *Labour Market Trends*, 108: 330–2.

HILLS, J. (1998), *Income and Wealth: The Latest Evidence* (York: Joseph Rowntree Foundation).

HOLLIDAY, I. (1997), 'The Provision of Services: Trouble in Store for Labour?', in Andrew Geddes and Jonathan Tonge (eds.), *Labour's Landslide* (Manchester: Manchester University Press), 120–33.

HOPE, K. (1975) 'Crewe's Test of the Embourgeoisement Thesis', *British Journal of Political Science*, 5: 256–8.

HOTELLING, H. (1929), 'Stability in Competition', *Economic Journal*, 39: 41–57.

HOUT, M., BROOKS, C., and MANZA, J. (1993), 'The Persistence of Classes in Postindustrial Societies', *International Sociology*, 8: 259–77.

—— —— —— (1995), 'The Democratic Class Struggle in the United States', *American Sociological Review*, 60: 805–28.

HUTTON, W. (1995), *The State We're In* (London: Cape).

INGLEHART, R. (1977), *The Silent Revolution: Changing Values and Political Styles among Western Publics* (Princeton: Princeton University Press).

JENKINS, P. (1987), *Mrs Thatcher's Revolution* (London: Cape).

JOHNSTON, R. J., and PATTIE, C. J. (1992), 'Class Dealignment and the Regional Polarization of Voting Patterns in Great Britain 1964–87', *Political Geography*, 11: 73–86.

—— —— and ALLSOPP, J. G. (1988), *A Nation Dividing? The Electoral Map of Great Britain 1979–87* (Harlow: Longman).

JONES, T. (1996), *Remaking the Labour Party: From Gaitskell to Blair* (London: Routledge).

KAVANAGH, D. (1997), 'The Labour Campaign', *Parliamentary Affairs*, 50: 533–41.

KEEGAN, W. (1984), *Mrs Thatcher's Economic Experiment* (London: Penguin).

KELLAS, J. (1991), *The Politics of Nationalism and Ethnicity* (London: Macmillan).

KELLEY, J., and MCALLISTER, I. (1985), 'Social Context and Electoral Behaviour in Britain', *American Journal of Political Science*, 29: 564–86.

KING, A. (1977), *Britain Says Yes: The 1975 Referendum on the Common Market* (Washington, DC: American Enterprise Institute).

—— (1998), 'Why Labour Won—At Last', in Anthony King, David Denver, Iain McLean, Pippa Norris, Philip Norton, David Sanders, and Patrick Seyd, *New Labour Triumphs: Britain at the Polls* (Chatham, NJ: Chatham House), 177–207.

KINNOCK, N. (1985), *The Future of Socialism*, Fabian Tract 509 (London: Fabian Society).

—— (1989), Introduction, in *Meet the Challenge, Make the Change*, Final Report of Labour's Policy Review for the 1990s (London: Labour Party).

KIRKHEIMER, O. (1966), 'The Transformation of the Western European Party Systems', in Joseph LaPalombara and Myron Weiner (eds.), *Political Parties and Political Development* (Princeton: Princeton University Press), 177–200.

KITZINGER, U. (1973), *Diplomacy and Persuasion: How Britain Joined the Common Market* (London: Thames & Hudson).

KRIESI, H. (1989), 'New Social Movements and the New Class in the Netherlands', *American Journal of Sociology*, 94: 1078–116.

LIPSEY, D. (1992), *The Name of the Rose*, Fabian Pamphlet 554 (London: Fabian Society).

LYNN, P. (1990), *Public Perceptions of Local Government: Its Finance and Services* (London: HMSO for the Department of the Environment).

McLEAN, I., HEATH, A., and TAYLOR, B. (1996), 'Were the 1994 Euro- and Local Elections in Britain Really Second-Order?', in David M. Farrell, David Broughton, David Denver, and Justin Fisher (eds.), *British Elections and Parties Yearbook 1996* (London: Frank Cass), 1–20.

MARQUAND, D. (1991), *The Progressive Dilemma: From Lloyd George to Kinnock* (London: Heinemann).

MINFORD, P. (1988), 'Mrs Thatcher's Economic Reform Programme', in Robert Skidelsky (ed.), *Thatcherism* (London: Chatto & Windus), 93–106.

MINKIN, L. (1991), *The Contentious Alliance: Trade Unions and the Labour Party* (Edinburgh: Edinburgh University Press).

MUELLER, W. (1999), 'Class Cleavages in Party Preferences in Germany—Old and New', in Geoffrey Evans (ed.), *The End of Class Politics? Class Voting in Comparative Context* (Oxford: Oxford University Press), 137–80.

MURIE, A. (1997), 'The Housing Divide', in Roger Jowell *et al.* (eds.), *British Social Attitudes: The 14th Report* (Aldershot: Dartmouth), 137–50.

NIEMI, R., WHITTEN, G., and FRANKLIN, M. (1992), 'Constituency Characteristics, Individual Characteristics and Tactical Voting in the 1987 British General Election', *British Journal of Political Science*, 22: 229–40.

NORRIS, P. (1990), 'Thatcher's Enterprise Society and Electoral Change', *West European Politics*, 13: 63–78.

NORTON, P. (1992), 'The Conservative Party from Thatcher to Major', in Anthony King (ed.), *Britain at the Polls 1992* (Chatham, NJ: Chatham House), 59–65.

—— (1998), 'The Conservative Party: "In office but not in power" ', in Anthony King (ed.), *New Labour Triumphs: Britain at the Polls* (Chatham, NJ: Chatham House), 75–112.

PANEBIANCO, A. (1988), *Political Parties: Organization and Power* (Cambridge: Cambridge University Press).

PATTIE, C. J., and JOHNSTON, R. J. (1990), 'One Nation or Two? The Changing Geography of Unemployment in Great Britain 1983–1988', *Professional Geographer*, 42: 288–98.

—— —— (1998), 'Voter Turnout at the British General Election of 1992: Rational Choice, Social Standing or Political Efficacy?', *European Journal of Political Research*, 33: 263–83.

—— —— (1999), 'Context, Conversation and Conviction: Social Networks and Voting at the 1992 British General Election', *Political Studies*, 47: 877–89.

PRZEWORSKI, A., and SPRAGUE, J. (1986), *Paper Stones: A History of Electoral Socialism* (Chicago: University of Chicago Press).

RABINOWITZ, G., and McDONALD, S. E. (1989), 'A Directional Theory of Issue Voting', *American Political Science Review*, 83: 93–122.

RADICE, G. (1992), *Southern Discomfort*, Fabian Pamphlet 555 (London: Fabian Society).

—— and POLLARD, S. (1993), *More Southern Discomfort: A Year On—Taxing and Spending*, Fabian Pamphlet 560 (London: Fabian Society).

SANDERS, D. (1999), 'The Impact of Left–Right Ideology', in Evans and Norris (1999: 181–206).

SÄRLVIK, B., and CREWE, I. (1983), *Decade of Dealignment: The Conservative Victory of 1979 and Electoral Trends in the 1970s* (Cambridge: Cambridge University Press).

SEYD, P. (1992), 'Labour: The Great Transformation', in Anthony King (ed.) *Britain at the Polls 1992* (Chatham, NJ: Chatham House).

—— (1998), 'Tony Blair and New Labour', in Anthony King, David Denver, Iain McLean, Pippa Norris, Philip Norton, David Sanders, and Patrick Seyd, *New Labour Triumphs: Britain at the Polls* (Chatham, NJ: Chatham House), 49–73.

SHAW, E. (1996), *The Labour Party since 1945* (Oxford: Blackwell).

SKIDELSKY, R. (ed.) (1988), 'Introduction', in Skidelsky (ed.), *Thatcherism* (London: Chatto & Windus), 1–23.

SMITH, J. and McLEAN, I. (1994), 'The Poll Tax and the Electoral Register', in Heath *et al.* (1994c: 229–53).

SMITH, M. J., and SPEAR, J. (eds.) (1992), *The Changing Labour Party* (London: Routledge).

SMITHIES, A. (1941), 'Optimum Location in Spatial Competition', *Journal of Political Economy*, 49: 423–39.

SNELSON, G. (1999), *The Milton Keynes Council Budget Referendum: A Case Study* (Milton Keynes: Milton Keynes Council).

SOPEL, J. (1995), *Tony Blair: The Moderniser* (London: Michael Joseph).

SOWEMIMO, M. (1996), 'The Conservative Party and European Integration 1989–95', *Party Politics*, 2: 77–97.

STUDLAR, D., and McALLISTER, I. (1992), 'A Changing Political Agenda? The Structure of Political Attitudes in Britain 1974–87', *International Journal of Public Opinion Research*, 4: 148–76.

SURRIDGE, P., BROWN, A., McCRONE, D., and PATERSON, L. (1999), 'Scotland: Constitutional Preferences and Voting Behaviour', in Evans and Norris (1999: 223–39).

SWADDLE, K., and HEATH, A. (1989), 'Official and Reported Turnout in the British General Election of 1987', *British Journal of Political Science*, 19: 537–70.

TAYLOR, B., and THOMSON, K. (1999), 'Technical Appendix', in Evans and Norris (1999: 272–83).

—— BROOK, L., and PRIOR, G. (1994), 'Appendix: The 1992 Cross-Section and Panel Surveys', in Heath *et al.* (1994c: 301–8).

TAYLOR-GOOBY, P. (1995), 'Comfortable, Marginal and Excluded: Who should Pay Higher Taxes for a Better Welfare State?', in Roger Jowell, John Curtice, A. Park, L. Brook, and D. Arendt with K. Thomson (eds.), *British Social Attitudes: The 12th Report* (Aldershot: Dartmouth), 1–17.

THATCHER, M. (1993), *The Downing Street Years* (London: HarperCollins).

THOMSON, K., PARK, A., BROOK, L. (1999), *British General Election Study 1997: Cross-Section Survey, Scottish Election Study and Ethnic Minority Election Study—Technical Report* (London: National Centre for Social Research).

WEAKLIEM, D. L., and HEATH, A. F. (1994), 'Rational Choice and Class Voting', *Rationality and Society*, 6: 243–70.

—— —— (1995), 'Regional Differences in Class Dealignment', *Political Geography*, 14: 643–51.

—— (1999), 'The Secret Life of Class Voting: Britain, France and the United States since the 1930s', in Geoffrey Evans (ed.), *The End of Class Politics? Class Voting in Comparative Context* (Oxford: Oxford University Press), 97–136.

WICKHAM-JONES, M. (1997), 'How the Conservatives Lost the Economic Argument', in Andrew Geddes and Jonathan Tonge (eds.) (1997), *Labour's Landslide* (Manchester: Manchester University Press), 100–18.

WOOD, Alan H., and WOOD, Roger (eds.) (1992), *The Times Guide to the House of Commons*, April 1992 (London: Times Books).

ZWEIG, F. (1961), *The Worker in an Affluent Society: Family Life and Industry* (London: Heinemann).

INDEX